JUDAICA REFERENCE SOURCES

A SELECTIVE, ANNOTATED BIBLIOGRAPHIC GUIDE

SECOND EDITION

Judaica Reference Sources

A Selective, Annotated Bibliographic Guide

Second Edition

Charles Cutter
Micha Falk Oppenheim

The Denali Press

Denali, derived from the Koyukon name *Deenaalee*, is the native name for Mount McKinley. Mount McKinley, the highest mountain on the North American continent, is located in Denali National Park and Preserve. The lowlands surrounding this majestic mountain provide a diverse wildlife habitat for a variety of animals, including grizzly bears, wolves, caribou and moose.

Copyright © 1993 by The Denali Press
Published by The Denali Press
Post Office Box 021535
Juneau, Alaska USA 99802-1535
Phone: (907) 586-6014   Fax: (907) 463-6780

Ref
Z
6366
.C87
1993

LIBRARY OF CONGRESS CATALOGING-IN-PUBLICATION DATA

Cutter, Charles
     Judaica reference sources : a selective, annotated bibliographic guide / Charles Cutter, Micha Falk Oppenheim. -- 2nd ed.
          p.   cm.
     ISBN 0-938737-31-7 (alk. paper) : $35.00
     1. Jews—Bibliography. 2. Reference books—Jews—Bibliography. I. Oppenheim, Micha Falk. II. Cutter, Charles. Jewish reference sources. III. Title
Z6366.C87   1993
016.909'04924—dc20   92-31392
                                                                          CIP

∞ The paper used in this publication meets the minimum requirements of the American National Standard for Information Sciences—Permanence of Paper for Printed Library Materials, ANSI Z39.48-1984. This book is printed on recycled paper, using soy based ink.

Dedicated in memory of

Mr. Berl Kagan
Dr. Nathan M. Kaganoff
Mr. Amnon Zipin

May their distinguished service and
publications in the field of
Jewish Studies
serve as a living memorial to their memory.

Yehey Zikhram Barukh

TABLE OF CONTENTS

Preface   15

SECTION ONE: GENERAL REFERENCE

Chapter 1. Biographical Dictionaries   19
    A. General   19
    B. Bible   20
    C. Rabbis   20
    D. Indexes   22

Chapter 2. Bibliographies   23
    A. Personal   23
    B. General   26

Chapter 3. Calendars   30

Chapter 4. Children's Literature   31

Chapter 5. Computer Software Programs   33

Chapter 6. Directories, Almanacs, Yearbooks   34
    A. General   34
    B. The Press   35

Chapter 7. Dissertations   36

Chapter 8. Educational Material   37
    A. General Bibliographies   37
    B. Jewish Studies / Courses and Syllabi   38
    C. Educational Media   40

Chapter 9. Encyclopedias   41
    A. Introductory Works   41
    B. Judaica Encyclopedias   41
    C. Judaica Encyclopedias For Youth   44
    D. General Encyclopedias   44

Chapter 10. Filmography   45

Chapter 11. Indexes   **47**
    A. Festschriften 47
    B. Periodicals 47

Chapter 12. Quotations   **49**

Chapter 13. Travel Guides   **50**
    A. General 50
    B. Europe 50
    C. Israel 51
    D. The United States 52

SECTION TWO: SUBJECT REFERENCE

Chapter 14. The Hebrew Book, Judaica Libraries,
and Librarianship   **55**
    A. The Hebrew Manuscript 55
        Surveys And Introductory Works 55
        Catalogs Of Hebrew Manuscript Collections 55
    B. The Hebrew Book 57
        Surveys and Introductory Works 57
        Hebrew Typography 58
        Incunabula 59
        Rare Book and Exhibition Catalogs 60
    C. The Cairo Genizah 61
        Catalogs 61
    D. Judaica Libraries 63
        Cataloging 63
        Catalog of Hebrew Books 64
        Collection Development 65
        Directories 65
        Library Catalogs 65
    E. Archives 67
        Directories 67

Chapter 15. The Jewish Communities Of The Diaspora   **68**
    A. General Material 68
        Atlases and Gazetteers 68
        Introductory Works and Surveys 69
        Bibliography 70
        Chronologies 71
        Oral History Catalogs 72
    B. Individual Countries 72
        Africa and Arab Lands 72
            Sourcebooks 72
            Bibliography 73

Ethiopia 73
Yemen 74
North America 74
    Directories 74
        Educational Institutions 74
        Jewish Organizations 75
        Media 76
        Museums 76
    Overviews 76
Canada 76
    Archival Resources 76
    Bibliography 77
    Biographical Dictionaries 77
    Canadian Jewish Literature 78
    Historical Overviews 78
United States 79
    Directories 79
        Educational Institutions 79
        Foundations 79
        General 79
        Jewish Organizations 80
    Yearbooks 80
    Historical Overviews 80
    Archival Resources 81
    Oral History Catalogs 82
    Bibliography 83
        General 83
        Anti-Semitism 87
        Cults 87
        Demography 87
        Ethnic Relations 88
        Holocaust 88
        Jewish Christians 88
        Philanthropy 89
        Publications 89
        Regional History 90
        Women 90
    Biographical Directories 90
    Chronology 92
    Encyclopedias 92
    Indexes (Periodical Literature) 93
    American Jewish Literature 93
Latin America 95
    Bibliography 95
Argentina 96
Brazil 96
Asia 96
China 96
India 97
Australia / New Zealand 97

Europe 98
        Bibliography 98
        Encyclopedias 98
        Readers 99
France 99
        Archival Resources 99
        Bibliography 100
        Biographical Dictionaries 100
Germany (Including Central Europe) 101
        Archival Resources 101
        Bibliography 101
        Biographical Dictionaries 103
        Library Catalogs 104
Greece 104
Great Britain 105
        Bibliography 105
        Biographical Dictionaries 106
        Yearbooks 106
Hungary 107
Italy 107
        Bibliography 107
The Netherlands 108
Poland / Russia 109
        Archival Resources 109
        Bibliography 109
        Biographical Dictionaries 112
        Gazetteers 112
Romania 112
Spain / Portugal 113

Chapter 16. Israel / Palestine   **114**
    A. Archival Resources 114
    B. Atlases and Gazetteers 115
    C. Biographical Dictionaries 117
    D. Bibliography / Handbooks / Filmography 118
    E. Book Reviews 123
    F. Chronologies 124
    G. Demography 124
    H. Directories 124
    I. Dictionaries / Encyclopedias 126
    J. Indexes 127
    K. Yearbooks 127

Chapter 17. Zionism   **129**
    A. Bibliography 129
    B. Encyclopedias 129

Chapter 18. Holocaust   **131**

    A. Archival Resources 131
    B. Atlases and Gazetteers 132
    C. Bibliography 132
    D. Directories 137
    E. Encyclopedias 137
    F. Filmography 138

**Chapter 19. Biblical Studies, Apocrypha and Pseudepigrapha
    and Dead Sea Scrolls**   **139**

    A. Biblical Studies 139
        History Of Biblical Times 139
        Introductory Works 140
        Atlases 140
        Bibliography 141
        Dictionaries 143
        Concordances 143
        Encyclopedias 144
        Grammar (Hebrew) 145
        Grammar (Aramaic) 146
        Periodical Literature Indexes 146
        Library Catalogs 147
        Texts (Critical Editions) 147
        Texts (English Translations) 148
        Texts (Critical Commentaries) 148
        Commentaries (Rabbinic) 149
    B. Apocrypha and Pseudepigrapha 150
        Introductory Works 150
        Bibliography 150
        Texts, Commentaries 151
    C. Dead Sea Scrolls 151
        Bibliography 151
        Concordances 152
        Inventories 152
    D. Ancillary Materials 152
        Biblical Archeology 152
        Ancient Near Eastern Texts and Pictures 153
        Computer Software Programs (Biblical Studies) 154

Chapter 20. Rabbinic Literature, Jewish Law and Judaism   **155**

    A. Rabbinic Literature 155
        Introductions 155
        Gazetteers 156
        Bibliography 157
        Manuscript Catalogs 158
        Concordances 158
        Dictionaries 159
        Text Indexes 161
        Handbooks and Manuals 162

Quotations 163
B. Jewish Law 163
 Introductions 163
 Encyclopedias 163
 Bibliography 164
 Responsa Literature (Indexes) 165
 Codes (Indexes) 166
C. Computer Software (Rabbinic Literature and Jewish Law) 168
D. Judaism 169
 Bibliography 169
 Encyclopedias / Dictionaries / Handbooks 169
 Laws / Customs / Ceremonies 172

Chapter 21. Jewish Thought   **173**
A. Philosophy 173
 Overviews 173
 Bibliography 174
 Dictionaries 174
B. Mysticism 175
 Overviews 175
 Bibliography 175
 Anthologies 176
 Concordances / Dictionaries / Indexes 176
C. Hasidism 176
 Bibliography 176
 Biography 177
 Dictionaries 177

Chapter 22. Language And Literature (General Materials) **178**
History 178
Bibliography 178
A. Hebrew Language 178
 Bibliography 178
 Dictionaries 179
 Abbreviations / Acronyms 181
 Grammars 181
B. Hebrew Literature 182
 Bibliography 182
 Indexes 183
 Biographical Dictionaries 184
C. Aramaic 184
 Bibliography 184
D. Sephardic Languages And Literature 185
 Bibliography 185
E. Yiddish Language 186
 History 186
 Dialectologies 187
 Bibliography 187
 Dictionaries 187
 Grammars (Text Books) 188

F. Yiddish Literature 189
    History 189
    Bibliography 189
    Bio-Bibliography 190
G. Yiddish Theatre 191
    Biographical Dictionaries 191

Chapter 23. Miscellaneous Subjects   **192**
A. Aging 192
B. Anti-Semitism 192
    Bibliography 192
    Surveys 193
C. Art And Ceremonial Objects 193
    Bibliography 193
D. Cookery 194
    Bibliography 194
E. Ethics 194
    Bibliography 194
F. Family 195
    Bibliography 195
G. Folklore and Legends 196
    Bibliography 196
    Anthologies 196
H. Genealogy and Onomasticons 198
    Manuals And Sourcebooks 198
    Bibliography 199
    Compiled Genealogies 200
    Onomasticons 200
I. Jewish Political Studies 202
    Bibliography 202
J. Jewish Women's Studies 203
    Bibliography 203
    Directories 204
    Libraries 204
K. Jewish-Christian Relations 204
    Bibliography 204
L. Musi c and Dance 205
    Bibliography 205
    Encyclopedias 206
    Resource Guide 206
    Biography 206
M. The Press 207
    Encyclopedias 207
    Bibliography 207

Author Index   **211**

Title Index   **216**

PREFACE

In the decade since the publication of the first edition of *Jewish Reference Sources: A Selective Annotated Bibliographic Guide,* there has been a continued growth in the number of courses being offered in Judaic studies at colleges and universities throughout the United States. We are also witnessing a continued interest on the part of the general public in learning about the history of the Jewish people, their religion and culture. Many new studies, as well as reference works, in the basic areas of Jewish Studies, e. g., Bible, History and Politics, Jewish Thought, Rabbinic literature and Halakha (Jewish Law), the Holocaust, Israel and Zionism, Language and Literature, and Women's Studies, have been published in the past decade.

The previous edition of our book included both reference works and basic monographs. Recent publications such as *The Book of Jewish Books: A Reader's Guide to Judaism* (see entry 49) and *The Schocken Guide to Jewish Books: Where to Start Reading About Jewish History, Literature, Culture and Religion* (see entry 55) provide guidance in locating current basic monographs in English in all areas of Jewish Studies. However, an updated tool to guide individuals to reference works in the various disciplines of Jewish Studies, as well to topics of contemporary interest, continues to be a desideratum. We therefore offer this reference guide in the hope that it will meet this need.

Judaica Reference Sources includes a selection of general reference works, reference works related to specific topics and a small selection of "basic works", i.e. Biblical texts, introductory works, readers, etc., in Judaic Studies. Some of the material was published in the first edition of this work. Other materials were included in our feature column "Recommended Judaica Reference Works" published in *Judaica Librarianship*. The "basic works" that have been included in this book are represented in core Jewish Studies Collections and in Jewish Studies Reference Collections. A number of bibliographic essays published in books and journals have also been included. The guide is intended to assist scholars, students, librarians and laymen in their search for information. Librarians in synagogue, Jewish center, public, college and university libraries, will also find this bibliography useful in developing collections in Judaica-related subject areas.

The *terminus a quo* for this second edition is 1975. Earlier works which have not been superseded, or which are still basic to the discipline, have been included. Although Sholomo Shunami's *Bibliography of Jewish Bibliographies* (second edition) and its *Supplement* (see entries 56-57) remain the major resource for Judaica bibliographies published prior to 1975, our intent is to supplement and bring up-to-date a portion of the materials in this classic work which pertain to the core areas of Judaic Studies, the Hebrew Book and topics of current interest not included in Shunami's work.

Terminus ad quem is 1992. However, a few major works that were published in 1993 were included. The latter, for the most part, supplement earlier works listed in our bibliography. We took into consideration language, availability and permanent value. Greater representation has been given to materials written in English because the intended users of this work may be more fluent in this language. Materials in other European languages, as well as Hebrew and Yiddish are also included. The annotations are descriptive. They focus on the scope and use of each work.

Judaica Reference Sources is divided into two sections: General Reference and Subject Reference. In the first section the chapters are arranged alphabetically with the exception of Chapter One, Biographical Dictionaries, which precedes Bibliography. The second section is arranged thematically. There are selected cross-references throughout the volume. Author and Title indexes are included to facilitate access to the material.

As noted, this is a selective bibliography. The materials included represent those items that we deemed to be most useful to the intended users. Subject areas considered by us to be of peripheral interest were not included. We would, therefore, welcome suggestions regarding materials and/or subjects which users feel should be included or deleted from future editions of *Judaica Reference Sources.*

ACKNOWLEDGEMENTS

It remains our pleasant task to express thanks to Dr. Bella Hass Weinberg for permission to reprint materials that were included in *Judaica Librarianship*'s feature column "Recommended Judaica Reference Works"; to Dr. Aaron Katchen whose immeasurably helpful technical assistance made this work in its present format possible ; and last, but certainly not least, to Mr. James Rosenbloom for reading the typescript and for his valuable suggestions.

Section One

General Reference

CHAPTER 1

BIOGRAPHICAL DICTIONARIES

See also listings of biographical dictionaries within Chapters 15, 16 and 22.

A. GENERAL

1   Comay, Joan. *Who's Who in Jewish History: After the Period of the Old Testament.* New York: McKay, 1974. 448p.
> An illustrated biographical dictionary listing Jews "who have made significant contributions to the history and thought of the Jewish people," Jews who have been "eminent in the general life and culture of their times," as well as, "non-Jews who have had a special impact on Jewish history." The dictionary covers the period from 135 B.C.E. to the present. Living persons at the time of the writing were excluded. It includes a chronology and a thematic index.

2   Greenberg, Martin H. *The Jewish Lists: Physicists and Generals, Actors and Writers, and Hundreds of Other Lists of Accomplished Jews.* New York: Schocken, 1974. 327p.
> This classified dictionary is divided into nine sections, e. g., public life, the professions, arts and entertainment, sports, prize winners. Brief biographical sketches of Jews are listed under each section. The dictionary includes an index of birthplaces and an index of names.

3   Halperin, Raphael. *Atlas 'Ets Hayim.* Tel-Aviv: Hotsa'at Hekdesh Ruah Ya'akov, 1980- .
> A bio-bibliographic dictionary which sketches the lives of rabbis, communal leaders, scholars, and authors throughout the ages. The accompanying maps, tables, diagrams, and family trees enable the reader to visually conceptualize the relationship of the major personalities in each generation to earlier generations. The fourteen volumes published to date cover the period from creation to 1945. An index to the entire set appears in part one of the introductory volume.

4   Landau, Ron. *The Book of Jewish Lists.* New York: Stein & Day, 1982. 227p.
> A listing of Jews in such fields as sports, religion, show business, the military, business, etc.

5   Wigoder, Geoffrey. *Dictionary of Jewish Biography.* New York: Simon & Schuster, 1991. 567p.
> A biographical dictionary which includes sketches of the lives of approximately 1,000 Jews from biblical to modern times. Persons alive at time of publication are not included. The dictionary is well illustrated, and the entries for creative artists are illustrated with examples of their work. Most entries have one or two bibliographic citations for further reading.

6   *Who's Who in World Jewry: A Biographical Dictionary of Outstanding Jews.*
     New York: Who's Who in World Jewry, Inc., 1955- .

> Brief biographical sketches of noteworthy Jews in all fields of endeavor.
> Latest edition, 1987. Previous editions appeared in 1955, 1965, 1972, 1978,
> and 1981.

7   Zubatsky, David S. *Jewish Autobiographies and Biographies: An Interna-
     tional Bibliography of Books and Dissertations in English.* New York:
     Garland, 1989. 370p.

> A comprehensive list of biographies and autobiographies in English. The
> bibliography is arranged alphabetically by the name of the biographee.
> There is a subject index.

B. BIBLE

8   Comay, Joan. *Who's Who in the Old Testament, Together with the Apocry-
     pha.* New York: Holt, Rinehart & Winston, 1971. 448p.

> An illustrated biographical dictionary covering the period to 135 B.C.E.
> This work is continued by the author's *Who's Who in Jewish History.* It
> includes a valuable chronology.

9   Hasidah, Yisrael Yitshak. *Otsar Ishe ha-TaNaKH be-Aspeklarya shel
     HaZaL.* Jerusalem: R. Mass, 1991. 399p.

> A new expanded edition of a lexicon which depicts the lives of over 700
> Biblical personalities as reflected in Rabbinical literature.

C. RABBIS

10   Bader, Gershom. *Encyclopedia of Talmudic Sages.* Northvale, NJ: Jason
     Aronson, 1988. 876p.

> This comprehensive biographical dictionary is a translation of *Unzere
> Gaystige Riezen* (New York, 1934-1937). An earlier English translation was
> published under the title: *Jewish Spiritual Heroes* (New York: Pardes, 1940.
> 3v.) It is divided into three sections: A. Mishnah B. Jerusalem Talmud C.
> Babylonian Talmud. The introduction to each section describes the history
> of the period. The biographical sketches of the sages offer the reader an
> understanding of their lives and teachings.

11   *Early Acharonim: Biographical Sketches of the Prominent Early Rabbinic
     Sages and Leaders from the Fifteenth-Seventeenth Centuries.* Compiled and
     edited by Hersh Goldwurm, Brooklyn: Mesorah Publications, 1989.
     252p.

> This is a chronologically arranged biographical dictionary containing
> sketches of 300 sages and leaders who lived in Turkey, Greece, Palestine,
> Italy, Poland, Lithuania, Austria, Germany, Bohemia, and Moravia. It
> includes a Hebrew title index, and a name index arranged by first name.
> This work continues *The Rishonim* (see below).

12   Finkel, Avraham Yaakov. *The Great Chasidic Masters.* Northvale, NJ: J.
     Aronson, 1992, 245p.

This work includes brief sketches of the lives of 50 prominent Hasidic "Rebbes," and selections from their books. The selections provide the reader with insight into their teachings. In addition the author outlines the Hasidic dynasties and lists the Hasidic "Rebbes" and their disciples. The work includes a glossary, bibliographic notes, an index of biblical verses, an index of "Rebbes" according to cities, and a name index.

13   —. *The Great Torah Commentators*. Northvale, NJ: J. Aronson, 1990. 256p.

A biographical dictionary of more than 100 Torah sages grouped in one of the following areas: A. Torah B. Mishnah C. Talmud D.Midrash E. Halacha (Jewish law) F. Mussar (Jewish ethics) G. Hasidism I. Philosophy and J. Kabbalah (Jewish mysticism). The excerpts from the writings of the sages provide the reader with insight into the process of interpreting the Torah. The work includes portraits and photographs of the sages, facsimiles of pages from their commentaries, a list of additional commentators whose works were not included for lack of space, and an index of biblical verses.

14   Friedman, Nathan Zvi. *Otsar ha-Rabanim*. Bnei Brak, Israel: Agudat Otsar ha-Rabanim, 1975. 461p.

This is a concise bio-bibliographic dictionary listing 20,000 rabbinical personalities, who lived in the period from 970-1970. The dictionary is arranged alphabetically by first name. It includes family name, community, and title indexes.

15   Hyman, Aaron. *Toldot Tana'im ve-Amoraim*. Jerusalem: Boys Town Publishers, 1964. 3v.

This is an alphabetically arranged biographical dictionary compiled from Talmudic and Midrashic sources of personages mentioned in Talmudic literature.

16   Kohn, Naftali Jacob. *Sefer Otsar ha-Gedolim Alufe Ya'akov*. Haifa: The author, 1966-1970. 9v.

This is a detailed bio-bibliographical dictionary of Rabbinic scholars who lived in the period from 590 to 1590. It includes a name index.

17   *The Rishonim: Biographical Sketches of the Prominent Early Rabbinic Sages and Leaders from the Tenth-Fifteenth Centuries*. This is based on research by Shmuel Teich and edited by Hersh Goldwurm. Brooklyn, NY: Mesorah Publications, 1982. 224p.

This work contains biographical sketches of some 300 tenth to fifteenth century rabbinic sages and leaders from the Mediterranean countries and Western Europe. The book includes a historical introduction, maps and charts, a Hebrew title index, an index of Hebrew-English geographical names, and an index of personal names arranged alphabetically by first name. The name index aids the reader to find a biographical sketch because the entries are arranged chronologically. This work is continued by *Early Acharonim*.

D. Indexes

The following general indices may be useful in locating biographies of individuals:

18 *Author Biographies Master Index.* Edited by Barbara McNeil and Miranda C. Herbert. 2nd Edition. Detroit, MI: Gale Research Company, 1984. 2v.
> This work is "a consolidated index to more than 658,000 biographical sketches concerning authors living and dead as they appear in a selection of the principal biographical dictionaries devoted to authors, poets, journalists, and other literary figures."

19 *Biography and Genealogy Master Index.* Edited by Miranda C. Herbert and Barbara McNeil. 2nd Edition. Detroit, MI: Gale Research Company, 1980. 8v.

20 —. *1981-1985 Cumulation.* Edited by Barbara McNeil. Detroit, MI: Gale Research Company, 1985. 5v.

21 —. *1986-1990 Cumulation.* Edited by Barbara McNeil. Detroit, MI: Gale Research Company, 1990. 3v.
> This work is "a consolidated index to more than 3,200,000 biographical sketches in over 350 current and retrospective biographical dictionaries." Although the emphasis remains on the United States, works on foreign countries are also included.

22 *Historical Biographical Dictionaries Master Index.* Edited by Barbara McNeil and Miranda C. Herbert. Detroit, MI: Gale Research Company, 1990. 1,003 p.
> This work is "a consolidated index to biographical information concerning historical personages in over 35 of the principal retrospective dictionaries. ... The emphasis of the works indexed ... is on deceased persons who were prominent in the United States. However, some general sources have been included, so not all persons cited are deceased nor are they all from the United States.

CHAPTER 2

BIBLIOGRAPHIES

A. PERSONAL

Personal bibliographies are published as separate monographs. They are also included in Festschriften, collected works, or other serial publications. A comprehensive listing of personal bibliographies published to 1975 may be found in Shlomo Shunami's *Bibliography of Jewish Bibliographies* (entries 56-57.) See *Kiryat Sefer* (entry 51) and the *Index of Articles in Jewish Studies [RAMBI]* (entry 141) for later publications not included in Shunami's work. The following is a select list of personal bibliographies.

23   Abramowitz, Molly. *Elie Wiesel: A Bibliography.* Metuchen, NJ: Scarecrow Press, 1974. 194p.
        A bibliography of works by and about Elie Wiesel.

24   Anckaert, Luc and Bernhard Casper. *Franz Rosenzweig: A Primary and Secondary Bibliography.* Leuven: Bibliotheek van de Faculteit der Godgeleerheid, 1990. 106 p.
        A revision and expansion of "Bibliographie der Werke Franz Rosenzweig's" in *Arbeitspapiere zur Verdeutschung der Schrift,* by Franz Rosenzweig, 309-324. Dodrecht: M. Nijhoff, 1984. The bibliography is divided into two parts. Part 1, the Primary Bibliography, covering the years 1917-1989, lists the published editions and translations of Rosenzweig's texts. Part 2, the Secondary Bibliography, covering the years 1921-1990, lists studies about Rosenzweig and his work. It includes an index of titles to the Primary Bibliography and Secondary Bibliography and an index of authors and editors to the Secondary Bibliography.

25   Arnon, Yohanan. *Uri Tsevi Grinberg: Bibliyografyah shel Mif'alo ha-Sifruti ....* Jerusalem: Edi Mozes, 1980. 368p.
        This bibliography covers the period from 1912 to 1980. It is divided into two parts: A. A chronological listing Uri Zvi Greenberg's literary works. This section also includes separate listings of Greenberg's translations, works he edited, sketches, and published letters. B. A topically arranged listing of books and essays about the poet. The bibliography includes a title index of Hebrew poems, a title index of Yiddish poems, an index of Hebrew prose, and an index of Yiddish prose.

26   Attal, Robert. *Bibliyografyah shel Kitve Prof. Shelomoh Dov Goitain: Hashlamot.* Jerusalem: Makhon Ben-Zvi. 1987. 22p.
        A supplement to the author's previous bibliography of the late Prof. Goitein's works (Jerusalem: Israel Oriental Society, 1975). The present bibliography lists chronologically 118 works written from 1975 to 1985. It also includes earlier publications that were omitted from the initial listing. Indexed.

27 Catane, Moche. *Bibliyografyah Shel Kitve Gershom Sholem.* Jerusalem: Magnes Press, 1977. 78p.

This chronologically arranged bibliography of Gershom Scholem's writings, compiled in honor of his 80th Birthday, is a revision of a bibliography compiled by Fania Scholem and Baruch Yaron, published in *Studies in Mysticism and Religion* (Jerusalem: Magnes Press, 1967). Within each year, beginning with 1915, the 579 items are listed in the following order: A. Books in Hebrew B. Articles in Hebrew C. Books in other languages D. Articles in other languages. The Bibliography includes title indices for the materials in Hebrew and other languages.

28 Coppenhagen, Jacob H. *Menasseh ben Israel: Manuel Dias Soeiro, 1604-1657: A Bibliography.* Jerusalem: Misgav Yerushalayim, 1990. 407p.

This is a topically arranged bibliography that lists works in English, Dutch, French, German, and Hebrew relating directly or indirectly to Menasseh ben Israel and his activities. It includes bibliographical references and indexes.

29 Feldman, Louis H. *Josephus: A Supplementary Bibliography.* New York: Garland, 1986. 696p.

This bibliography serves as an annotated supplement to Heinz Schreckenberg's *Bibliographie zu Flavius Josephus* (Leiden: Brill, 1968). It also includes corrigenda to the aforementioned work and its supplementary volume (Leiden: Brill, 1979). The author also provides indices to citations of Josephus, and Greek words in Schrekenberg's *Bibliographie* and, corrigenda to his *Josephus and Modern Scholarship* (1937-1980) (Berlin: Walter de Gruyter, 1984).

30 Golan, Zivah and Havivah Yonai. *Sha'ul Tshernihovski: Bibliyografyah.* Tel-Aviv: Makhon Kats le-Heker ha-Sifrut, 1981. 191p.

This bibliography includes only Saul Tchernichovski's writings in Hebrew. All entries are arranged chronologically within the following categories: original works; translations; and works edited by Tchernichovski. Indexed.

31 Goldschmidt-Lehmann, Ruth P. *Moshe Montefyori, 1784-1885: Bibliyografyah.* Jerusalem: Misgav Yerushalayim, 1984. 166p.

This is a topically arranged bibliography of printed Montefioriana, in the form of books, pamphlets, periodicals and broadsheets, mainly in Hebrew, English and German. Listed are: a representative selection of his official correspondence with communal bodies, reports of communal organizations, and references to journal articles. The work is accompanied by a name index.

32 Jerushalmi, Joseph. *'Amos 'Oz: Bibliyografyah.* Tel-Aviv: Am Oved, 1984. 143, 120p.

This is a bibliography of Amos Oz's publications and works about them that were published between 1953 and 1981. It is divided into two parts: A. Literary works by Amos Oz which appeared in book form or in periodicals as well as interviews with him, literary and political essays, and plays and films based on his works B. Works pertaining to the above. The work is accompanied by several indexes: authors (Latin alphabet/ Hebrew alphabet); periodicals, newspapers, and books cited in the bibliography (Latin alphabet/Hebrew alphabet); translators (Latin alphabet); and an index of works (Hebrew alphabet).

33 Klein, Zanvil E. *Joseph B. Soloveitchik: A Bibliography (1931-1984)*. Chicago: The Author, 1985. 43p.

This is a preliminary edition of a partially annotated bibliography of the works of Rabbi Joseph Soloveitchik, with a selection of studies pertaining to his writings. The 486 citations represent materials which were published in books, journals, newspapers and organizational bulletins between 1931 and 1984.

34 Kressel, Getzel. *Kitve Dov Sadan: Bibliyografyah*. Tel-Aviv: Am 'Oved, 1981. 129p.

This bibliography lists the works published by Dov Sadan in the following order: A. Books written from 1921 -1981 B. Articles in newspapers and periodicals to 1936. Kressel includes a name and subject index to facilitate access to the items listed in the bibliography.

35 ——. *Kitve G. Kressel: Bibliyografyah*. Lod: Makhon Haberman le-Mehkere Sifrut, 1986. 389p.

This is a partially annotated comprehensive bibliography of the writings of Getzel Kressel covering the years 1929-1985. The bibliography is divided into two major sections: books and pamphlets; and articles in newspapers, periodicals, anthologies, etc. Each section is arranged chronologically. The work is prefaced by an autobiographical essay. It includes an author/subject index.

36 Miller, David Neal. *Bibliography of Isaac Bashevis Singer, 1924-1949*. New York: Peter Lang, 1983. 315p.

The more than 900 entries in this bibliography document I. B. Singer's publications for the years 1924 to 1949. The bibliography is divided into three sections: A. Books B. Contributions to newspapers, periodicals and anthologies C. Translations from other languages. The materials are listed in chronological order. The Yiddish titles are romanized. An alphabetical index of titles is included to direct the user to the chronologically arranged entries, which are grouped under bold faced section headings for the year.

37 ——. *A Bibliography of Isaac Bashevis Singer, January 1950-June 1952*. New York, Yivo, 1979. 57p.

In this supplement, Miller lists additional books and contributions to newspapers, periodicals and anthologies that were published between January 1950 and June 1952. In addition, he lists translations of Singer's works into English.

38 Moonan, Willard. *Martin Buber and his Critics: An Annotated Bibliography of Writings in English through 1978*. New York: Garland, 1981. 240p.

This bibliography, consisting of 667 items, is divided into the following sections: A. Writings by Buber B. Writings about Buber. It includes only materials in English published through 1978. The critical material is annotated. The following indexes are included: A. Title Index: Writings by

Buber B. Translator Index: Writings by Buber C. Author Index: Writings about Buber D. Subject Index: Writings by and about Buber.

39 *Pirsume Moshe Devis: Reshimah Bibliyografit.* Edited: Orah Zimer. Jerusalem: [n. p.], 1992. 23p.

This is a chronologically arranged list of the publications of the noted educator and historian Moshe Davis covering the years, 1935/36-1991/92.

40 Radice, Roberto and David T. Runia. *Philo of Alexandria: An Annotated Bibliography, 1937-1986.* Leiden: E.J. Brill, 1988. 469p.

This is an annotated bibliography of the scholarly literature pertaining to the life, writings, and thought of Philo of Alexandria. The present edition is an English translation and revision of Radice's earlier work entitled *Filone de Alessandria: Bibliografia Generale, 1937-1982.* The bibliography is divided into the following three parts: A. Bibliographies, editions, fragments, translations, anthologies, commentaries, indices and lexica, etc. B. Critical studies pertaining to Philo and related studies C. Indexes of authors, reviewers, Biblical passages, Philonic passages, subjects, and Greek terms.

41 Teitelbaum, Gene. *Justice Louis D. Brandeis: A Bibliography of Writings and Other Materials on the Justice.* Littleton, CO: Fred B. Rothman, 1988. 128 p.

This annotated bibliography is a continuation of *Louis Dembitz Brandeis, 1856-1941: A Bibliography,* by Roy M. Mersky (New Haven: Yale Law School, 1958). It lists books and articles written about Justice Brandeis since 1957, correspondence to and from Brandeis in manuscript collections, as well as speeches by and about Brandeis. The entries which chronicle Brandeis's Jewish and Zionist activities will be of special interest to the student of American Jewish history and Zionism. There are no author and subject indexes.

42 Weiser, R. *Bibliyografyah Mu'eret shel Kitve Hayim Hazaz.* Jerusalem: Hebrew University, 1992. 102p.

This annotated bibliography of the writings of Hayyim Hazaz is divided into five sections: A. Books B. Publications in collections, periodicals and newspapers C. Published letters D. Interviews E. Translations. It includes a title index and an index of languages.

B. General

On the tenth anniversary of its publication, the editors of *Modern Judaism* 10: 3 (October 1990): 221-395; 11: 1 (February 1991): 1-172 published a series of articles in which scholars review recent developments in their fields. These articles contain extensive bibliographies. They are listed in this bibliography under the related subject. What follows is a select list of bibliographies that pertain to more than one discipline.

See *Kiryat Sefer* (entry 51) for a listing of more current bibliographies published as monographs and the *Index of Articles in Jewish Studies [RAMBI]* (entry 141) for related materials published in collective works or in serial publications. Additional bibliographies may also be found listed in *Bibliographical Index: A Cumulative Bibliography of Bibliographies* (New York: H. W. Wilson, 1938-)

43 *The Atid Bibliography: A Resource for the Questioning Jew.* Edited by Bertie Schwartz. New York: United Synagogue of America, Dept. of Youth Activities, 1977. 153p.

> This comprehensive annotated bibliography cites over 550 books. The bibliography is divided into 24 subject areas. It offers guidance for finding resources for further reading and study in all areas of Jewish knowledge. There are author and title indexes.

44 *Back to the Sources: Reading the Classic Jewish Texts.* Edited by Barry W. Holtz. New York: Summit Books, 1984. 448p.

> This is a comprehensive introduction to the study of classical Jewish literature: the Bible, the Talmud, the Midrash, medieval Bible commentaries, medieval Jewish philosophy, Cabalistic texts, teachings of the Hasidic masters, prayer and the prayer book. Each chapter is written by a leading scholar who discusses a particular genre of literature in terms of its history, perspective and significance. Instruction is provided for the study of texts through literary analysis of sample texts. Excellent bibliographies at the end of each chapter provide the reader with guidance for further study. This text is exceptionally suitable for adult education and introductory university courses.

45 *Bibliographical Essays in Medieval Jewish Studies.* New York: Anti-Defamation League of B'nai Brith, 1976. 393p.

> This is the second volume of the series entitled *The Study of Judaism*. It contains scholarly and definitive bibliographical essays by specialists on the following topics: The Jews in Western Europe, Fourth to sixteenth century; The Church and the Jews, From St. Paul to Paul IV; The Jews under Islam, From the Rise of Islam to Sabbatai Zevi; Medieval Jewish religious philosophy; Medieval Jewish mysticism; Minor Midrashim.

46 Brisman, Shimeon. *A History and Guide to Judaic Bibliography.* Cincinnati: Hebrew Union College, 1977.

> This guide is the first volume in the series *Jewish Research Literature*. It traces the history and development of Jewish bibliography from the time of Johannes Buxtorf to 1975. The author discusses the following topics: general Hebraica bibliographies; catalogs of Hebraica book collections; bio-bibliographical works; subject bibliographies of Hebraica literature; Judaica bibliographies; bibliographical periodicals; indexes to Jewish periodicals and monographs; miscellaneous Jewish bibliographical works. The work includes chronological lists of bibliographies, extensive bibliographical references, and an index.

47 Cutter, Charles. *Syllabus and Bibliography ... for Introduction to Jewish Bibliography.* Waltham, MA: Brandeis University, 1978. 55p.

> This textbook is designed to enable the student to become familiar with the major bibliographic tools and research materials related to Jewish studies.

48 Faber, Salamon. "Judaica Libraries and Literature." In *Encyclopedia of Library and Information Science*, Vol. 13, 325-91. NY: Dekker, 1975.

In this essay the author describes "existing Judaica libraries and major collections of Judaica library materials ... in Israel, Western Hemisphere and Europe." He also discusses the major works within such categories of Jewish literature as Bible, Rabbinics, Jewish thought, Liturgy, Jewish historiography, and belles lettres. A supplementary bibliography is included at the end of the discussion of each genre of literature.

49   Frank, Ruth S. and William Wolheim. *The Book of Jewish Books: A Reader's Guide to Judaism.* San Francisco: Harper and Row, 1986. 320p.
    The authors describe and evaluate more than 500 books of interest to the general reader who wishes to learn about Judaism, Jewish thought, history, and culture. The guide is divided into 12 subject areas: the Bible, children's books, Jewish history, the Holocaust, Israel and Zionism, Jewish living, Jewish thought, literature and the arts, periodicals, prayer books, reference and resources, books on women and Judaism. Each subject area is introduced by an essay written by a noted expert in the field. A glossary and an index of authors and titles are included.

50   Griffiths, David B. *A Critical Bibliography of Writings on Judaism.* Lewiston, PA: Edwin Mellen Press, 1988. 2v.
    This is a comprehensive, critically annotated bibliography of books and articles. Included are works in English, Hebrew, Yiddish, French and German. The bibliography includes a listing of resource materials, e.g., bibliographies, surveys, guides to literature, as well as citations on such topics as Jewish history, Zionist thought and history, the Holocaust, and Jewish thought. The bibliography is not indexed.

51   *Kiryat Sefer; Bibliographical Quarterly of the Jewish National and University Library.* Jerusalem: Hebrew University, 1924/25- .
    This is a comprehensive bibliographical quarterly arranged by subject, providing international coverage for all Judaica publications regardless of language, as well as general publications that include Judaica, and all materials published in Israel. The citations are often annotated and may include lengthy scholarly reviews. There are annual cumulative author and title indexes.

52   Miller, Philip E. "A Bibliography of Festschriften Relating to Jewish Studies, 1971-1986." *Jewish Book Annual* 46 (1988): 118-142.
    Miller lists Festschriften not included in the aforementioned works.

53   *The Reader's Adviser: A Layman's Guide to Literature.* 13th ed. New York: R. R. Bowker, 1986-1988. 4v.
    This reference work, designed as an introduction to literature for the non-specialist, includes the following valuable annotated bibliographies of interest to Judaica scholars: v.2 "Yiddish Literature," by Zachary M. Baker; "Hebrew Literature," by Linda P. Lerman v. 3 includes bibliographies on Jewish history and Israeli history v. 4 includes a section on "Judaism" by Richard E. Cohen and Jacob Neusner. The items cited are in English and "currently" available. The Bibliographies by Zachary Baker and Linda Lerman include literary works in English translation. Biographies of authors "worthy of mention" are included. The six volume 14th edition is available Fall 1993.

54 Rothenberg, Joshua. *Judaica Reference Materials: A Selective Annotated Bibliography.* Waltham, MA: Brandeis University Library, 1971. 87p.

> An annotated listing of reference materials in ten basic fields of Jewish studies. Although dated, this preliminary edition based on the holdings of the Brandeis Library Judaica Department's reference collection, provides the librarian with guidance in establishing a core Judaica reference collection. It directs the student to reference works in the major areas of Judaic studies.

55 *The Schocken Guide to Jewish Books: Where to Start Reading About Jewish History, Literature, Culture and Religion.* Edited by Barry W. Holtz. New York: Schocken Books, 1992. 357p.

> Experts list, describe, and discuss, the works in their field and recommend titles that should be read. The chapters include discussions pertaining to such topics as aspects of Jewish life and experience, the Bible, Jewish history, Israel and Zionism, Hebrew and Yiddish literature, Jewish feminism, and the Holocaust. A final chapter is devoted to books that are appropriate for young adults. It includes an author and title index.

56 Shunami, Shlomo. *Bibliography of Jewish Bibliographies.* 2nd ed. Jerusalem: Hebrew University, 1969. 992p.

> This is a largely expanded edition of a work published in Jerusalem in 1936 under the same title. The present edition includes 4,750 bibliographies arranged by broad subject categories. The Dead Sea scrolls, the State of Israel, and the Holocaust are among the new subjects included in this edition. The book includes both name and subject indexes.

57 —. *Supplement to 2nd ed.* Jerusalem: Hebrew University, 1975. 464p.

> This work lists an additional 2,000 bibliographies, and corrects and updates citations in the earlier volume.

58 Strangelove, Michael. *Electric Mystic's Guide to the Internet.* Ottawa: University of Ottawa. Religious Studies Department, 1992-93. 2v.

> The guide is "a complete bibliography of networked electronic documents, online conferences, serials, software and archives relevant to Religious Studies." The Judaica scholar will find much material of interest in this bibliography. Volumes one and two have been published and are available through the Internet. A published edition is forthcoming.

59 *The Study of Judaism: Bibliographical Essays.* New York: Anti-Defamation League of B'nai Brith. 1972. 229p.

> This work contains definitive bibliographical essays by specialists, covering the following topics: Judaism in New Testament Times; Rabbinic Sources; Judaism on Christianity; Christianity on Judaism; Modern Jewish Thought; The Contemporary Jewish Community; The Holocaust, Antisemitism and the Jewish Catastrophe.

CHAPTER 3

CALENDARS

60 Freund, Salomon W. *Corresponding Date Calendar and Family Record.* New York: Hebrew Publishing, 1925. 370p.

> This calendar provides the corresponding date of the Hebrew and civil calendars for the years 1784-2000.

61 Levi, Leo. *Halachic Times for Home and Travel.* Jerusalem: R. Mass, 1992. 301, 49p.

> This work is a revision of the author's *Jewish Chrononomy* (Brooklyn, NY: Gur Aryeh Institute, 1967.) Following a general introduction, the author outlines the Halakhic regulations for the traveller. The main body of the work is divided into three parts: A. The Fixed Jewish Calendar which includes tables for converting between civil and Jewish dates, etc. B. Times-of-Day in Jewish Law which includes laws involving times of day, formulae for computing times-of-day, and numerous tables C. Treatise on Halakhic Aspects of Twilight Determination (in Hebrew).

62 Mahler, Eduard. *Handbuch der Jüdischer Chronologie.* Hildesheim: Olms, 1967. 635p.

> The author establishes the systems of the different Jewish calendars and chronologies in the light of Ancient Near Eastern and medieval reckonings. In this work, first published in 1916, the author provides comparative tables, which make possible the conversion of a date in one system to the corresponding date in another system. This work is especially useful for converting dates to and from the Christian calendar.

63 Segal, Hyman A. *Hebrew English Corresponding Calendar: 1960-2116.* New York: Hebrew Publishing, 1970. 370p.

> This book is designed to show which Hebrew date exactly corresponds to any given English date from 1960-2116. One can also find the English date matching any given Hebrew date.

64 Spier, Arthur. *The Comprehensive Hebrew Calendar: 1900-2100.* 3rd rev. ed. Jerusalem: Feldheim, 1986. ca. 400p.

> In this work, the Civil and Hebrew calendars for the years 1900 to 2100 (5660 to 5860) appear in facing columns. This arrangement enables the user to easily determine which Hebrew date corresponds to any given civil date and vice versa. The weekly and holiday Torah readings are noted in the Hebrew calendar. The handbook includes concise information on all aspects of the Hebrew calendar. It is indispensable for determining Bar/Bat Mitzvah Torah portions and dates, as well as yahrzeit (anniversary of death) dates.

CHAPTER 4

CHILDREN'S LITERATURE

65   Davis, Enid. *A Comprehensive Guide to Children's Literature with a Jewish Theme.* New York: Schocken, 1981. 265p.

This is a guide to books for children from pre-school through junior high school. More than four hundred books are reviewed and appropriate age levels are noted for all the books that are listed. A chapter is devoted to films, film strips, records, cassettes, toys, and visual products. The author provides guidelines for selecting books for children, as well as a directory of book publishers and distributors. It is indexed by author, title, and subject.

66   Fischer, Rita Berman. *Word Weavers: Collections of Stories Old and New.* New York: Jewish Book Council, 1992. 20p.

This work is a selected bibliography of Jewish story collections, including traditional legends, children's stories, midrashic tales and modern works.

67   Grossman, Cheryl S. and Susy Engman. *Jewish Literature for Children: A Teaching Guide.* Denver, CO: Alternatives in Religious Education, 1985. 221p.

The guide, based on an article by Barbara Leff entitled "Creative Use of the Library," In *The Jewish Teachers Handbook, Volume 1.* Denver, CO: Alternatives in Religious Education, 1986), lists 300 library/book activities that can be integrated into the curriculum to enrich it. The *Guide* is divided into ten chapters dealing with such subjects as Bible, Ethics, Holidays, Holocaust, Israel, History, Jewish Identity, etc. Each chapter includes an annotated book list for children and adults and reviews for ten books, accompanied by suggestions for teaching activities geared for three different grade levels. The authors include a useful reference list (arranged by subject) which contains curriculum related library media materials and an index which enables one to find multiple applications for books reviewed.

68   Ofek, Uriel. *Leksikon Ofek le-Sifrut Yeladim.* Tel-Aviv: Zemorah-Bitan, 1985. 2v.

This bio-bibliographic lexicon lists authors of children's literature from around the world. It provides the following information for each entry: a brief biography of the author, an evaluation of his or her literary work, a complete listing of his or her children's books, the dates of their publications and comments pertaining to awards, translations, and plays. The lexicon includes authors of children's literature in Hebrew and Yiddish.

69   Posner, Marcia. *Jewish Children's Books: How to Choose Them, How to Use Them.* New York: Hadassah, 1986. 48p.

This attractive illustrated tool guides teachers, librarians, and parents in selecting Jewish children's books through a discussion of book selection criteria such as age level, quality, and Jewish content. More than 30 books, grouped by age level (4 to 8; 8 to 11; 11 to 14) are described. Each entry includes a bibliographical description of the book, an outline of its major themes and a summary of its contents, a discussion of the issues raised, and questions and activities for adults and children. The last section, entitled, "Further Resources," presents additional annotated readings about Basic Judaism, Holidays, Israel, and American Jewish life. See also the author's "A Celebration of Jewish Children's Books" in *The Book of Jewish Books*, by Ruth S. Frank and William Wolheim (San Francisco: Harper & Row, 1986).

70 —. *Juvenile Judaica: The Jewish Values Book-Finder*. New York: Association of Jewish Libraries, 1985. 97p.

This is a critically annotated listing of books arranged alphabetically by author. The author notes the suitable age level and the subject and themes of each book cited. A title index is included. The heart of this work is the detailed subject index, which lists books in some 350 topics, making it an invaluable selection tool. *Juvenile Judaica* is issued in loose-leaf format for insertion into a binder. It is updated by annual supplements, with accumulations scheduled to be published every five years. It serves as a supplement to Enid Davis' *A Comprehensive Guide to Children's Literature With a Jewish Theme* (New York: Schocken, 1981).

71 *Selected Children's Judaica Collection*. New York: Jewish Book Council, 1990. 77p.

This is an annotated bibliography of over 700 books in 12 categories. The list includes fiction and non-fiction works on such wide ranging subjects as Bible, exploring your Jewish identity, biography and growing up in the Diaspora. It includes author and title indexes.

CHAPTER 5

COMPUTER SOFTWARE PROGRAMS

72 Hughes, John Jay. *Bits, Bytes & Biblical Studies*. Grand Rapids, Michigan: Academic Books, 1987. 643p.

> The author reviews and provides detailed information about products, projects and resources for text oriented computing. He focuses on the use of computers in Biblical and Classical studies. See the author's *Bits & Bytes Review* for detailed reviews of new products and reports of a broad spectrum of computing related activities.

73 *Software Bible: A Guide to Software in Religious Organizations*. Silver Spring, MD: Communal Computing Inc., 1991. 165p.

> This is a listing of 500 micro and mini computer software products arranged in 15 categories, including Hebrew, Bible studies, administration, yahrzeit management, cemetery management, fund raising, library management, religious and educational games, and membership management. It is intended for use in synagogues, schools, associations, social service institutions, and non-profit organizations. The address of the publisher is: P.O. Box 6599, Silver Spring, MD 20916.

74 *Springwells Jewish Computing Catalog: A Guide to Jewish Computing Resources Including Software and Telecommunications*. Boulder, CO., Springwells Company, 1990?- .

> The aim of the catalog is to "present information on the widest possible range of resources for Jewish Computing." It includes information on a large number of varied software packages and computing support services for Jewish computing, as well as ordering and vendor information. The address of the publisher is P. O. Box 18091, Boulder, Co. 80308.

CHAPTER 6

DIRECTORIES, ALMANACS, YEARBOOKS

A. GENERAL

See also Chapters 15 and 16 for additional directories.

75 *The Jewish Almanac*. Edited by Richard Siegel and Carl Rheins. New York: Bantam Books, 1980. 640p.
> This is a compendium of facts on Jewish history, religion, culture and thought, presented in compact handy-to-use form. Topics range from the serious and reflective to the humorous and off-beat. It includes extensive illustrations, maps and charts, as well as indexes.

76 *The 1987-88 Jewish Almanac*. Compiled and edited by Ivan T. Tilem. New York: Pacific Press, 1987. 516, 166p.
> This is the third edition of the Almanac. Part 1 includes over 70 articles divided into such subject categories as demographics, current issues, Holocaust, Israel, history, institutions, Torah, campus, media, and sports. Among the novel features included in this edition are a Hebrew-English linear Pirke Avot, a digest of Israeli laws, and a Jewish calendar to the year 2001. Part 2, the *Yellow Pages*, is a directory listing 17,000 Jewish communal organizations and commercial establishments in the United States and Canada. A helpful alphabetical table of contents to the directory is provided which lists the headings — from Advertising agencies to Zionist organizations. It includes a general index to the articles, and the table of contents of the articles in the previous two editions are reproduced.

77 Lipsitz, Edmond Y. *World Jewish Directory*. Downsview, Ontario: J. E. S. L. Educational Products, 1991. 2v.
> This is "an up-to-date, comprehensive world-wide listing of Jewish resource centers complete with phone numbers and contact names." The focus is on the Diaspora. Israel is included only in the chapters on Holocaust Research and Museums. Volume One contains the listings of Book Fairs in North America; Boards and Central Agencies for Jewish Education; Colleges, Universities, Yeshivoth and Schools of Higher Learning; Holocaust Resource Centers; Museums and Art Galleries; Jewish and Judaica Libraries; Theaters. Volume Two has listings for all Federations, Welfare Funds and Community Councils; Foundations and Trusts, Jewish Organizations in the U.S.S.R.; Small Diaspora Jewish Communities; Major Jewish Organizations; Population Statistics; Jewish Holidays 1990-1999. It includes a geographic index, general index and brief bibliography.

78 *Sefer ha-Shanah li-Kehilot ve-Irgunim Yehudiyim*. Chief Editor: Zvi Porat Noy. Tel-Aviv, 1970- .
> This directory, arranged by country, provides addresses and phone numbers of Jewish communal organizations throughout the world. 1992 is the latest edition published.

79   *Survey of Jewish Affairs.* Rutherford, NJ: Fairleigh Dickinson University
      Press, 1983- .
>   This annual reviews the major events of the previous year that are of
>   relevance to world Jewry. It is divided into four sections: A. Israel B. Middle
>   East C. The United States D. World Jewry. The volumes contain a chronol-
>   ogy, a necrology and a selected classified bibliography.

80   *World Register of University Studies of Jewish Civilization: Inventory of
      Holdings.* Edited by Mervin F. Verbit. New York: Markus Wiener, 1985.
      140p.

B. THE PRESS

81   *Directory of World Jewish Press and Publications.* Jerusalem: D.W.J.P.P.,
      1984. 133p.
>   This is a comprehensive and current worldwide listing of Jewish periodi-
>   cals. Approximately 900 publications are listed, including bulletins, news-
>   letters, newspapers, and journals. The titles are arranged alphabetically by
>   continent, and further subdivided by country. Information for each entry
>   is organized in 15 data fields; the bottom of each page features a key to the
>   field codes, which represent address, telephone numbers, editor, pub-
>   lisher, language, frequency, and circulation. The address of the publisher
>   is: P.O. Box 7699, Jerusalem 91076.

CHAPTER 7

DISSERTATIONS

Dissertations completed at participating American and Canadian universities are listed in *Dissertations Abstracts International*. *Kiryat Sefer* provides international coverage for published academic doctoral dissertations and master's theses in all areas of Judaic studies. *Jewish Studies: Forum of the World Union of Jewish Studies* lists in the section entitled "Doctoral Dissertations" dissertations in progress, as well as dissertations completed at selected universities. The following are recently published bibliographies of completed dissertations:

82   Fichier Central des Thèses (France). *Catalogue des Doctorats Hebraica-Judaica*. Nanterre: Fichier Central des Thèses, Université de Paris, 1983-
       This is a classified list of doctoral dissertations completed at French universities. The bibliography is divided into three major areas: A. Judaism and Its Environment B. Diaspora C. Israel and the Arab States in the Middle East, 19-20 Centuries. Each entry includes the author and title, the University at which it was completed, the date it was accepted, the name of the supervisor of the dissertation, and subjects. To-date, four volumes, covering the years 1979-1992, have been published.

83   Ilsar Mednitzky, Nira. *Bibliyografyah shel 'Avodot Doktor be-Mada'e ha-Ruah veha-Hevrah she-Niktevu be-Universita'ot Yisra'el*. Jerusalem: Jewish National and University Library, 1992. 284p.
       This is a list of 1,975 doctoral dissertations in the humanities and social sciences completed at universities in Israel between 1936 and 1990. "The dissertations are arranged by subject, according to the university department of the chief doctoral advisor. Within the subject divisions, the arrangement is alphabetical, by Hebrew author. The information given in each entry includes author, title, year and university." The following sections are of particular interest to the Judaica scholar: 01. Bible 02. Talmud 03. Hebrew Literature 05. History of the Jewish People 06. Jewish thought 07. Contemporary Jewry 08. Hebrew Language 09.Yiddish Language and Literature 53A. Law-Jewish Law. This book includes author indexes in Latin and Hebrew alphabets.

CHAPTER 8

EDUCATIONAL MATERIAL

A. GENERAL BIBLIOGRAPHIES

84 Hessell, Carolyn Starman. *The Jewish Materials Resource Guide for Families and Havurot.* New York: Jewish Education Service of North America / Council of Jewish Federations, 1986. 253p.

> This annotated guide of available resource materials was prepared, under the sponsorship of the World Zionist Organization, to help strengthen Jewish educational programming for individual families and Havurot in the Diaspora. The materials listed in the catalog are diverse, and reflect the pluralistic nature of Jewish society. The catalog is organized by subject, and includes materials for all age levels. It complements *Materials Resource Guide for Jewish Education* (below), which was designed for the formal Jewish school setting. It includes a Directory of Publishers and Resources, and is indexed.

85 —. *NER Catalog.* New York: Jewish Education Service of North America, 1986. 96p.

> The catalog is a guide to the extensive collection of book and non-book educational material housed at the National Educational Resource Center (NERC). The materials in this collection are designed to aid the educator make educational programs more exciting and effective. The titles are listed in forty-seven subject areas —from Adult Education to Zionism. The catalog also includes a list of Jewish education and media centers in North America. Personalized packets of educational materials can be ordered from the Center.

86 —. *The Whole Sephardic Catalog.* New York: CAJE, 1992. 100p.

> This is a guide for educators and laymen to resources about the history and culture of Sephardic Jewry. It includes over 740 entries divided as follows: Part 1. The Sephardic experience divided by geographic origin. Part 2. Annotated bibliography, consisting of articles, books, classroom materials, literature. Part 3. Media selections. Part 4. Resources of people, places, experiences. Part 5. Author index.

87 *The Jewish Teachers Handbook, Volume 1.* Edited by Audrey Friedman Marcus. Rev. ed. Denver, CO: Alternatives in Religious Education, 1986. 204p.

> This new edition, with updated bibliographies, includes: "Research Tools for Jewish Education," by Micha F. Oppenheim, a list of indexes, periodicals, bibliographies, directories, dissertations, organizations, and institutions, and *"Resource Guide for Jewish Education,"* by Audrey F. Marcus, which enumerates twenty five sources for purchasing everything a teacher might need — from Hebrew letters to posters.

88 *Materials Resource Guide for Jewish Education.* New York: Jewish Education Service of North America, 1980- .

> This is a comprehensive annotated bibliography of books, audio-visual materials, and periodicals, covering the full spectrum of Judaica. The guide is divided into eleven broad subject categories, each of which is subdivided by age level and user type. Updates were published in 1982, 1984, and 1986-87.

B. JEWISH STUDIES / COURSES AND SYLLABI

89 *Agnon: Texts and Contexts in English Translation.* Edited by Leon I. Yudkin. New York: Markus Wiener, 1988. 308p.

> This handbook is designed to provide teachers offering courses on Shmuel Yosef Agnon with background information about Agnon. It includes essays on Agnon's writing, on specific works (e. g., *Sipur Pashut*), teaching aids and references.

90 *Contemporary Jewish Civilization: Selected Syllabi.* Edited by Gideon Shimoni. New York: Markus Wiener, 1985. 254p.

> This work contains a collection of syllabi of courses dealing with contemporary Jewish civilization, offered at universities outside Israel or in the special foreign language (i.e., non-Hebrew) programs offered by some Israeli universities to students from abroad. The collection is divided into the following sections: survey courses in contemporary Jewry; courses in modern Jewish history; and thematic courses in contemporary Jewry, e.g., Holocaust, Zionism, and American Jewry. Each syllabus is introduced with a short description of the conceptual framework of the course.

91 *The Holocaust in University Teaching.* Edited by Gideon Shimoni. Pergamon Press, 1991. 279p.

> This book is divided into two sections: A. Essays in which the authors examine various issues relevant to teaching the Holocaust, e. g., the place of theological and philosophical reflection, the use of art and film. B.Sample syllabi. Each syllabus includes a course outline, readings and an explanation of the conceptual framework and objectives of the course. A bibliography is included in the book.

92 *Jewish Political Studies: Selected Syllabi.* Edited by Daniel J. Elazar and Tzipora D. Stein. New York: Markus Wiener, 1985. 173p.

> This collection of syllabi is divided into the following sections: A. General courses in Jewish political studies B. Specialized courses in Jewish political studies C. The governance and politics of historic Jewish polities D. Comparative courses in contemporary diaspora governance E. Governance of specific diaspora communities.

93 *The Jewish Women's Studies Guide.* Compiled by Sue Ellen Levi Elwell. 2nd ed. Lanham, MD: University of America; Fresh Meadows, NY: Biblio Press, 1987. 142p.

> First published in 1982, this edition contains an updated collection of course syllabi on the Jewish woman. It includes 18 syllabi classified under the following headings: A. University courses in Jewish Women's Studies

B. Integrating Jewish Women's Studies into the university curriculum C. Adult and continuing education courses.

94 *Medieval Jewish Civilization: A Multi-Disciplinary Curriculum, Bibliographies, and Selected Syllabi.* Editor, Ivan G. Marcus. New York: Markus Wiener, 1988. 279p.

This multi-disciplinary resource curriculum is intended for the use of college teachers who offer survey courses in Medieval Jewish history and Jewish philosophy, courses in cross-cultural fertilization, and thematic courses in medieval Jewish civilization. It includes bibliographies on Medieval Jewish Philosophy and Jewish Literature in the Islamic World.

95 *Modern Hebrew Literature in English Translation.* Edited by Leon I. Yudkin. New York: Markus Wiener, 1987. 264p.

This handbook is designed to aid teachers who offer courses in modern Hebrew Literature in English translation. It is divided into three sections: A. Essays on such subjects as Hebrew poetry in translation, the specific character of modern Hebrew literature, cross-cultural aspects of teaching Hebrew literature in translation, teaching the literature of the Holocaust in translation B. Syllabi, including Modern Hebrew Literature in translation, modern Jewish fiction, modern Hebrew literature in the context of modern Jewish literature C. Bibliographies on such subjects as Hebrew literature in translation, modern Hebrew literature, and Holocaust literature.

96 *Modern Jewish Experience: A Readers Guide.* Edited by Jack Wertheimer. New York: New York University Press, 1993. 392p.

This *Guide* is divided into two sections: Part 1: A Guide to Fields of Study (Area Studies; Social and Political Issues; Religious and Theological Movements) Part 2: Teaching Resources. "The first section offers twenty-nine essays by leading scholars who seek to orient their colleagues to the major interpretive and methodological issues in the fields of modern Jewish studies. Each essay identifies the most helpful books and articles for the college professor who wishes to learn more about a topic for teaching, as opposed to research purposes. Most of these essays also recommend a means of structuring three class sessions to highlight key aspects of a topic. They also identify helpful reading assignments for students. Part 2. offers practical resources to expand the teaching repertoire for undergraduate courses on the modern Jewish experience. It opens with an annotated listing of bibliographies on specialized topics, catalogs to films, music, the arts, periodicals, and guides to collections and databases pertaining to modern Jewry. A concluding section provides sample syllabi for survey courses taught in diverse linguistic settings." The *Guide* includes an index of authors.

97 *State of Jewish Studies.* Edited by Shaye J. D. Cohen. Detroit, MI: Wayne State University Press, 1990. 277p.

In this work "contributors describe the key points of controversy and concern that currently engage scholars in most areas of Judaic research. Respondents discuss the contributor's views, marking out areas of disagreement and delineating avenues for further research and debate." The work includes bibliographical references.

98 *World Register of University Studies of Jewish Civilization: Inventory of Holdings.* Edited by Mervin F. Verbit. New York: Markus Wiener, 1985. 140p.

> The *World Register*, sponsored by the International Center for University Teaching of Jewish Civilization (ICUTJC), is designed to enhance the teaching of Jewish studies in institutions of higher learning. The handbook is divided into two sections: A. A list of institutions offering courses in Jewish civilization, arranged alphabetically by country. B. A list of syllabi in Jewish civilization divided into two parts. Part 1 - syllabi listed alphabetically by author (faculty); Part 2 - subject index, subdivided by author. The following fifteen subjects are included: Archaeology, Art, Bible, Contemporary Jewry, History, Holocaust Studies, Judaism and Jewish Thought, Languages, Literature, Near and Middle Eastern studies, Sephardic studies, Social Sciences, State of Israel and Zionism. The collection of syllabi can be examined in Jerusalem. Photocopies of syllabi can be obtained at cost from I.C.U.T.J.C., P.O. Box 4234, Jerusalem 91042.

C. Educational Media

99 *Filmstrip and Slide Catalog.* Rev. ed. Omaha, NE: Jewish Federation Library 1982. 144p.

> This catalog is arranged by subject and includes a title index. The address of the Federation Library is: 333 South 132nd Street., Omaha, NE 68154.

100 Schultz, Hadassah. *Non-Print Catalog.* New York: Board of Jewish Education, 1978. 57p.

> This catalog of audio-visual materials is arranged by subjects. Each entry is annotated, and the intended age level is noted.

101 Shoham, Joseph. *Annotated Catalogue of Audio-Visual Materials.* Toronto: Board of Jewish Education, 1979. 418p.

> This comprehensive guide to audio-visual resources is arranged topically.

102 *Video Catalog and Addendum.* New York: Board of Jewish Education Media Center, 1992. 122p.

> This annotated catalog lists 600 videos of Jewish content that are available for rent. The videos are suitable for classroom use.

CHAPTER 9

ENCYCLOPEDIAS

A. INTRODUCTORY WORKS

103 Brisman, Shimeon. *A History and Guide to Judaic Encyclopedias and Lexicons.* Cincinnati, OH: Hebrew Union College Press, 1987. 502p.

This work, the second in the series *Jewish Research Literature*, continues the author's pioneering work, *A History and Guide to Judaic Bibliography* (see entry 46). The author describes in detail over 360 general and specialized encyclopedias and lexicons dating from the mid-eighteenth century to the present. The specialized works relate to such topics as Bible, Talmudic/Rabbinic literature, Biography, Israel and Zionism, and Diaspora Communities. Enhanced by the chronological lists and summaries that follow the narrative in each chapter, as well as by the extensive notes which serve as a guide to further reading. It is indexed.

B. JUDAICA ENCYCLOPEDIAS

104 *Algemeyne Entsiklopedye: Yidn.* Paris: Dubnov Fund; New York: Cyco Publishing House, 1939-1966. 7v.

This is a series of complementary volumes to the *Algemeyne Entsiklopedye,* (Paris, New York, 1935-1944), a general encyclopedia in Yiddish. Each volume in the *Yidn* series contains monographic essays thematically related to each other and pertaining to aspects of Jewish history and culture. Volume 5 of the series, for example, contains essays which discuss various aspects of Jewish life in the Americas. Volumes 6-7 are devoted to the Holocaust. Bibliographies are included at the end of each article.

105 *The Blackwell Companion to Jewish Culture from the Eighteenth Century to the Present.* Edited by Glenda Abramson. New York: Blackwell Reference, 1989. 853p.

Through the many biographies of notable Jews, essays and survey articles, the *Companion* seeks to provide the reader with an understanding of "Ashkenazi" Jewish culture in the twentieth century and its contribution to Western civilization. Detailed bibliographies are included to enable the reader to probe "more deeply into the topics and figures treated" in the *Companion.* It includes an index of names and topics.

106 *The Blackwell Dictionary of Judaica.* Edited by Dan Cohn-Sherbok. Oxford: Blackwell Publishers, 1992. 597p.

This comprehensive ready reference dictionary provides, in concise format, information pertaining to all aspects of Jewish civilization.

107 *Encyclopaedia Judaica.* Jerusalem: Keter, 1971/72. 16v.

This is an up-to-date illustrated work containing signed scholarly articles of varying degrees of comprehensiveness pertaining to all aspects of Jewish history and culture. Most articles are accompanied by bibliographies. Volume one includes the index, general, rabbinical, and bibliographical abbreviations, a Jewish calendar for the years 1920-2020, a list of Hebrew newspapers and periodicals, a chart of Hasidic dynasties, and other special features. Supplementary articles, e. g., "Hebrew Language," "Masorah," etc. and a corrigenda section, are included in volume 16.

108 *Encyclopaedia Judaica: Das Judentum in Geschichte und Gegenwart.* Berlin: Verlag Eschkol [1928-1934]. 10 v.

This incomplete work in German contains signed scholarly articles covering all aspects of Jewish culture. The bibliographies accompanying the articles remain valuable. The Encyclopedia is especially rich in biographies. Only ten volumes were published, covering Aach-Lyra.

109 *Encyclopaedia Judaica Year Book.* Jerusalem: Keter, 1973- .

The yearbooks update and supplement the *Encyclopaedia Judaica.* They include new comprehensive studies about topics not treated in the original work, as well as additional biographical sketches. Nine volumes have been published as of 1992.

110 *Encyclopedic Dictionary of Judaica.* Edited by Geoffrey Wigoder. New York: L. Amiel/Keter, 1974. 672p.

One volume concise encyclopedia based on the aforementioned *Encyclopaedia Judaica.* It is intended for readers requiring reliable, concise facts at their fingertips. The many illustrations and maps on each page, lists, tables, and charts enhance the value of this work.

111 *The First Jewish Catalog: A Do-It-Yourself Kit.* Edited by Richard Siegel, Michael Strassfeld, and Sharon Strassfeld. Philadelphia: Jewish Publication Society, 1973. 310p.

The first volume in the *Catalog* series covers such topics as kashrut, blessings, the Shabbat and Jewish festivals, the Jewish wedding, creating a Jewish library, a basic Judaica bibliography, children's books, a guide to Jewish women's activities, where to learn, etc. The authors' intent is to provide practical information, presented from different perspectives, to enable the reader to live a creative and meaningful Jewish life.

112 —. *The Second Jewish Catalog: Sources and Resources With the Jewish Yellow Pages.* Edited by Sharon Strassfeld, and Michael Strassfeld. Philadelphia: Jewish Publication Society, 1976. 464p.

The second volume in the *Catalog* series continues the discussion of Jewish observances and customs, offering suggestions on how to go about making them part of modern life. It also provides information about the life cycle, study, the synagogue, and the arts. A supplement, written by the editors and Mark Nulman entitled *The Jewish Yellow Pages,* enumerates services and products available in the United States and includes a directory of American Jewish institutions. It is appended to the end of the volume. See under *The 1987-88 Jewish Almanac* (above) for a later edition of the *Yellow Pages.*

113 —. *The Third Jewish Catalog: Creating Community.* Edited by Sharon Strassfeld, and Michael Strassfeld. Philadelphia: Jewish Publication Society, 1980. 416p.

The third volume in the Catalog series deals with Jewish communal responsibility and discusses such topics as: giving charity, social action, Soviet Jewry, the Jewish poor and elderly, and the ecology, Information is also provided about such topics as Yiddish, Jewish genealogy, and Hasidism. A cumulative index to all three catalogs is included.

114 Frankel, Ellen and Betsy Platkin Teutsch. *The Encyclopedia of Jewish Symbols*. Northvale, NJ: J. Aronson, 1992. 234p.

The compilers have defined symbols loosely. Therefore, they list not only ceremonial objects and images, but also places, concepts, motifs, and events that have come to represent central Jewish ideas. Most entries trace a symbol's history from its "ancient roots to its modern expression." The 226 entries are arranged alphabetically. Cross references direct the user to term that is used. The articles do not contain bibliographic references. A list of symbols by generic categories, a list of symbols by abstract concepts, and a time line of Jewish history are included in appendices. The *Encyclopedia* is illustrated and includes a glossary, a list of sources and an index.

115 *The Jewish Encyclopedia*. New York: Funk & Wagnalls, 1901-1906. 12v. (Photographically reduced edition, New York: Ktav, 1964).

Although dated, this standard scholarly work remains useful for many of its articles, biographies and bibliographies. *The Jewish Encyclopedia: A Guide to Its Contents, An Aid to its Use*, by Louis Jacobs, (New York: Funk & Wagnalls, 1906. (Reprinted, New York: Ktav, 1967?) serves as an index to this work.

116 *The Jewish People: Past and Present*. New York: Jewish Encyclopedic Handbooks, 1946-1955. 4v.

This abundantly illustrated work is based largely on the aforementioned *Algemeyne Entsiklopedye: Yidn* (Paris: Dubnov Fund; New York: Cyco Publishing House, 1939-1966). Each volume contains monographic essays that are thematically related to each other pertaining to aspects of Jewish history and culture. The articles have bibliographies.

117 *Jüdisches Lexikon: Ein Enzyklopädisches Handbuch des Jüdisches Wissens*. Berlin: Jüdischer Verlag, 1927-1930. 4v. bound in 5. (Photographic reproduction, Königstein: Jüdischer Verlag, 1982).

This encyclopedia contains concise articles, written in a popular style, pertaining to all aspects of Jewish history and culture. Particular emphasis is placed on the contemporary period. Many articles include bibliographies.

118 *Kratkaia Evreiskaia Entsiklopediia*. Jerusalem: Keter Publishing, 1976- .

The *Kratkaia* is an abridged and adapted Russian version of the *Encyclopaedia Judaica* (Jerusalem: Keter, 1972). Entries from the *Encyclopaedia Judaica* have been rewritten, and new material has been added in order to meet the specific Jewish needs of Soviet born and educated readers. These materials fall into three categories: A. Definition of terms relating to Judaism and Jewish history. B. Materials relating to all aspects of Russian Jewish culture and the contributions of Jews to Russian culture. C.. Israel. The entries are not signed, and they lack bibliographies for further reading. Six volumes, covering the letters, A-P, have been published to-date.

119 *The New Standard Jewish Encyclopedia*. Edited by Geoffrey Wigoder. 7th ed. New York: Facts On File, 1992. 1,036p.

> A revised and updated one volume encyclopedia, first published in 1959, this work contains concise factual information. It is intended to be consulted for current reference information.

120 *Universal Jewish Encyclopedia and Reference Guide*. New York: The Universal Jewish Encyclopedia, 1939-1943. 10v. (Reprint edition, New York: Ktav, 1969).

> This popularly written illustrated work remains useful for American-Jewish biography and local history. The *Seven-Branched Light*, a reference guide, serves as a classified index.

C. Judaica Encyclopedias For Youth

121 *Junior Jewish Encyclopedia*. Edited by Naomi Ben-Asher, Naomi and Hayim. Leaf. 11th ed. New York: Shengold, 1991. 350p.

> This one-volume illustrated comprehensive up-to-date reference work is suitable for students in elementary and junior high school.

122 *Junior Judaica: Encyclopaedia Judaica for Youth*. Jerusalem: Keter, 1982. 6v.

> This work was published originally in 1975 under the title *My Jewish World*. Its articles are based on materials drawn largely from the *Encyclopaedia Judaica*. The clearly written articles pertaining to all aspects of Jewish history and culture are accompanied by illustrations, charts and maps. This is an excellent reference tool for elementary and junior high school students. It is indexed.

123 *New Jewish Encyclopedia*. Edited by David Bridger, and Samuel Wolk. New York: Behrman House, 1976. 541 p.

> Although dated, this excellent reference work remains useful for junior and high school age students.

D. General Encyclopedias

124 *ha-Entsiklopedyah ha-'Ivrit*. Jerusalem: Massada, 1949-1981. 32v.

125 —. *Supplement* v. 1-16. Jerusalem: Encyclopaedia Publishing Co., 1967.

126 —. *Supplement* v. 1-32. Jerusalem: Encyclopaedia Publishing Co., 1983.

127 —. *Index*. Jerusalem: Encyclopaedia Publishing Co., 1985.

> This is an authoritative work which offers the Hebrew reader scholarly articles about all aspects of culture and civilization, as well as information on all aspects of Judaic culture and the Land of Israel. Bibliographies accompany most articles.

CHAPTER 10

FILMOGRAPHY

See also Chapters 16 and 18.

128 Arkhiv Seratim be-Nosim Yehudiyim ´al Shem Avraham F. Rad. *Filmography: Catalogue of Jewish Films in Israel.* Jerusalem: Abraham F. Rad Jewish Film Archives, Institute of Contemporary Jewry, Hebrew University, 1972. 427p.

> This is a detailed listing of 1,700 films of Jewish content that are in various libraries in Israel. The films are listed in the order in which information about them was received by the Archives. The following information is given about each of the films: A. Classification number B. Film title C. Technical details about the film D. A film summary E. Code number of the institution supplying the information. The following aids have been supplied to facilitate access to the material: A. Index of film titles B. Index of subjects C. Index of Hebrew titles D. List of institutions and their code names.

129 *Guide to Films Featured in the Jewish Film Festival.* Edited by Deborah Kaufman, Janis Plotkin, and Rena Orenstein. Berkeley, CA: Jewish Film Festival, 1991. 96p.

> This guide to the films shown at the Jewish Film Festivals is divided into the following sections: A. Films listed in alphabetical order B. Films listed by subject matter category C. Films listed by print source or distributor D. A check list for film programming E. Film resources.

130 Harvard University Library. *Guide to Judaica Videotapes in the Harvard College Library.* Prepared by Charles Berlin. Cambridge, MA: Harvard University Library, 1989. 80p.

> This *Guide* lists over 1,000 video cassette titles in all areas of Jewish studies which are housed at the Harvard University Library. Of particular interest are the video cassettes which depict the cultural, social and political life in Israel. The filmography includes a title and name and a subject indexes.

131 *Jewish Film Directory.* Trowbridge, England: Flicks Books, 1992. 298p.

> More than 1,200 films of Jewish interest produced in 35 countries over a period of 85 years are listed in this directory. The following genres are included: foreign language dramas; film testimonies; made for television films; Hollywood features; educational films; animation; documentaries; Yiddish cinema. The title, technical details, film summary, and credits are provided for each title. The section of sources provides further information about Jewish film festivals and archives, and includes a brief bibliography. A number of indexes are provided to guide the reader including an alphabetical listing of films by directors, country of production and subject.

132 *Jewish Films in the United States: A Comprehensive Survey and Descriptive Filmography.* Compiled by Stuart Fox. Boston: G. K. Hall, 1976. 359p.

This listing of about 4,000 films, produced and/or released and distributed in the United States through 1970, was prepared under the auspices of the Abraham F. Rad Contemporary Jewish Film Archives and the Division of Cinema at the University of Southern California. The list includes feature films, short subjects, propaganda films, documentaries, educational films, cartoons, and films produced for television showings. The titles are listed by genre. The following information is provided for each title, when available: A. Filmography number and title B. Technical details C. Film summary D. Source of information on the film in abbreviated form. The filmography includes an index of film titles, an index of subjects, and a key to sources.

Chapter 11

Indexes

A. Festschriften

133 Berlin, Charles. *Index to Festschriften in Jewish Studies.* New York: Ktav, 1971. 319p.
> This work contains an index to 243 Festschriften in Jewish studies that were published primarily after the publication of the Marcus/Bilgray index. The articles are indexed alphabetically by author and then topically by subject.

134 Marcus, Jacob Rader and Albert Bilgray. *An Index to Jewish Festschriften.* Cincinnati: Hebrew Union College, 1937. Reprint. New York: Kraus, 1970. 154p.
> This work contains an author-title-subject index to 53 Festschriften published through 1935. Festschriften limited to Biblical and Semitic philological studies are not indexed.

B. Periodicals

See also entry 495.

135 *Index to Jewish Periodicals of General and Scholarly Interest.* Cleveland Heights, OH: College of Jewish Studies Press, 1963- .
> This semiannual publication provides author and subject access to articles in selected American and Anglo-Jewish journals. Book reviews are also indexed.

136 *Leket Divrey Bikoret 'al Sefarim Hadashim.* Jerusalem: Center for Public Libraries in Israel, 1968- .
> This monthly publication reproduces a selection of book reviews that were published in the literary supplements of the Israeli press.

137 *Mafteah le-'Itonut Yomit 'Ivrit.* Tel-Hai: Tel Hai Regional College, 1985- .
> This index, first published under the title *Katalog Analiti Selektivi ...* (1981-1985), provides selective coverage for the Israeli daily press. Little attention is paid to the literary supplements. This index is now available as a CD-ROM product.

138 *Mafteah le-Khitve-'Et be-'Ivrit=Index to Hebrew Periodicals.* Haifa: University of Haifa Library, 1977-
> This annual provides author and subject access to articles and book reviews in Hebrew periodicals published in and outside Israel. The subject index is also published separately in a microfiche edition, and appears six times a year. A cumulation, covering the years 1977-1991, is available.

Note: A CD-ROM version of the *Index*, plus the *Eretz Israel Data Base* and the *Tel-Hai Index to Israeli Hebrew Newspapers* is expected to be available shortly. A version of the *Index* and the *Eretz Israel Data Base* is available for searching on the ALEPH (Israeli library network).

139 *Mafteah le-Maamarim ba-Musafim ha-Sifrutiyim ba-'Itonut ha-Yomit.* Edited: Aryeh Ben-Yosef. Ramat Gan: Universitat Bar-Ilan, ha-Sifriyah ha-Merkazit, 1987- .

This annual publication provides author-subject index access to the articles and features in the literary supplements of the following Israeli newspapers: ha-Arets, Davar, Yedi´ot Aharonot, Ma´ariv, ´Al ha-Mishmar, and ha-Tsofeh. Indexes of reviews of books written in Hebrew and Yiddish and books written in other languages are included in a separate section. To-date three volumes, covering the years 1984/85-1987/88, have been published.

140 *Meir le-Tsiyon.* Edited by Meir Wunder. Jerusalem: Research Institute of Religious Jewry, 1970/72. 2v.

This is a topically arranged index of articles in Hebrew periodicals relating to Jewish law and contemporary halakhic problems, covering the years 1970-1979. It is continued in *Tekhumin,* beginning with volume 3 (1981/82). Wunder's annotated index to responsa and journal articles pertaining to medicine and halakhah is published in Assia.

141 *Reshimat Maamarim be-Mada'e ha-Yahadut [RAMBI]=Index of Articles in Jewish Studies.* Jerusalem: Hebrew University, 1966- .

This annual provides indexing for scholarly articles in journals and collected works that pertain to all aspects of Jewish studies. The index is arranged by broad subject areas, e.g., Bible, Rabbinic literature and Jewish law, Jewish history in the Diaspora, The State of Israel. Each section has its own internal arrangement. Book reviews are also indexed. Separate author and subject indexes for Hebrew (and Yiddish) articles and the articles in European languages are provided.

CHAPTER 12

QUOTATIONS

See also Chapter 20.

142 Alcalay, Reuben. *A Basic Encyclopedia of Jewish Proverbs, Quotations and Folk Wisdom.* New York: Hartmore House, 1973. 586 columns.

> This encyclopedia is arranged alphabetically by English subject. It includes an index of authors and books and glossary of Hebrew words, as well as an index of Hebrew subjects. Each quotation is listed in both Hebrew and English.

143 Larinman, Zevi. *Otsar Imre Avot.* Jerusalem: R. Mass. 1959-1969. 5v.

> This work contains 70,000 quotations, proverbs, etc., from rabbinic and classical Jewish literature. They are arranged alphabetically.

144 Rosten, Leo. *Leo Rosten's Treasury of Jewish Quotations.* Northvale, NJ: J. Aronson, 1988. 715p.

> Rosten's *Treasury* lists 4,300 proverbs, folk sayings, and philosophical quotations arranged in more than 500 categories. It includes the author's preface on the art, joys, and torments of language and translation, biographical vignettes of great writers, a glossary of Jewish customs, and a bibliography.

145 Sever, Moshe. *Mikhlol ha-Maamarim veha-Pitgamim.* Jerusalem: Mosad Harav Kook, 1961/62. 3v.

> This collection of over 100,000 rabbinic proverbs and sayings is arranged alphabetically by incipit.

146 *Treasury of Jewish Quotations.* Edited by Joseph Baron. Northvale, NJ: J. Aronson, 1985. 650p.

> This collection of 18,000 aphorisms, maxims, proverbs, and comments by Jewish authors or on Jewish themes is arranged topically. It includes a glossary, bibliography, and subject and author indexes.

Chapter 13

Travel Guides

A. General

147 *Jewish Travel Guide.* Edited by Sidney Lightman. London: The Jewish Chronicle, 1951- .

> This guide lists the addresses and telephone numbers of hotels, kosher restaurants, synagogues, places of historic interest, and Jewish organizations and businesses around the world. The primary focus of the *Guide*, however, is on Great Britain, Israel and the United States. It is issued annually and is indexed.

148 Seidel, Jefferey. *The Jewish Travelers' Resource Guide, 1992.* Jerusalem: Jewish Student Information Center; Feldheim, 1992. 152p.

> This guide is divided by country and subdivided by city. It includes brief sketches pertaining to the history of the Jews of each region, and descriptions of sights of Jewish interest. In addition, the author lists under each city the names, addresses and phone numbers of local contacts. These contacts service local campuses and are available to host guests for kosher meals and for the Sabbath and holidays.

B. Europe

149 Fiedler, Jiri. *Guide Book: Jewish Sights of Bohemia and Moravia.* Prague: Sefer, 1991. 224p.

> This illustrated guide book includes historical essays. The author notes the location of each town, and provides information about the Jewish quarter, the Jewish cemetery, Jews of note who resided in the town or its environs, etc. Similar information is provided for the city of Bratislava, the capital of Slovakia (at the end of the book). The guide includes bibliographic sources and a place index.

150 Gruber, Ruth Ellen. *Jewish Heritage Travel: A Guide to Central and Eastern Europe.* New York: Wiley, 1992. 305p.

> This guide provides information about the many remaining traces of Jewish culture and civilization in Poland, Czechoslovakia, Hungary, Romania, Bulgaria, and Yugoslavia. It is designed both as a practical guide for tourists and for those seeking information about the Jewish communities in these countries. The guide provides general tourist information, e. g., hotels, visa requirements, etc. It also includes under each country a brief historical survey of Jewish life, addresses of the Jewish communities, kosher restaurants, historical societies,etc.

151 Israelowitz, Oscar. *Guide to Jewish Europe: 7th Western Europe Edition.* Brooklyn, NY: Israelowitz Publishing, 1991. 312p.

> This practical guide-book includes information on kosher restaurants, butchers, bakeries, hotels, Jewish historical landmarks, museums, cem-

eteries and mikvaot. The *Guide* also contains tourist information of general
interest.

152 Postal, Bernard and Samuel H Abramson. *The Traveler's Guide to Jewish
Landmarks in Europe*. New York: Fleet Press, 1971. 342p.
> This ia a guide to everything Jewish in Europe. The authors identify,
> describe and provide the location of landmarks, buildings, monuments,
> etc. of Jewish interest.

153 Sacerdoti, Annie. *Guide to Jewish Italy*. Brooklyn, New York: Israelowitz
Publishing, 1989. 199p.
> The guide is divided into seventeen sections that correspond to the differ-
> ent regions of Italy. Each section is preceded by a map and an overview of
> the history of the Jewish community in the region. The towns and villages
> are listed alphabetically within each region. The landmarks of Jewish
> Italian culture are fully described. The guide includes many photographs
> which illustrate the contents of the guide, an index of towns and villages,
> and an extensive bibliography.

154 Stavroulakis, Nicolas P. and Timoty J. De Vinney. *Jewish Sites and
Synagogues of Greece*. Athens, Talos Press, 1992. 299p.
> This illustrated guide provides information about synagogues and other
> sites of Jewish interest in Greece. It includes historical essays, a glossary, a
> bibliography for further reading and an index.

C. ISRAEL

155 *Bazak Guide to Israel*. New York: Harper & Row, 1965- .
> This annual guide includes numerous maps, including road maps.

156 *Fodor's Israel*. New York: D. McKay, 1969- .
> This illustrated annual guide includes maps and city plans. Hotels, restau-
> rants, etc. are listed by city.

157 *Israel, Including the West Bank and Gaza Strip*. Edited by George Melrod.
Singapore: APA Productions; New York: Prentice-Hall Press, 1986.
380p.
> This work provides the reader with an introduction to Israel, its people and
> landscapes. The 57-page "Guide", contains information on transportation,
> shopping, accommodations, entertainment, restaurants, and embassies.
> The work contains lavish photographs. It is indexed.

158 Vilnay, Zev. *Guide to Israel*. Jerusalem, 1955- .
> This guide provides the traveller with detailed historical information
> about sites in Israel and includes biblical references, illustrations and a
> map. The latest edition is 1985.

D. The United States

159 Israelowitz, Oscar. *The Complete United States Jewish Travel Guide.* Brooklyn, N. Y.: Israelowitz Publishing, 1992. 455p.

The illustrated *Guide* contains up-to-date information about Jewish communities throughout the United States. It lists kosher restaurants, and provides information about social activities in Jewish community centers, and religious services in synagogues. It describes Jewish historic sights and museums as well as tourist sights of general interest. The many photographs and maps enhance its attractiveness and utility. Of related interest is the author's *Canada Jewish Travel Guide.*

160 —. *Guide to Jewish New York.* Rev. ed. Brooklyn, N. Y.: O. Israelowitz, 1984. 199p.

Designed to acquaint the visitor with Jewish life in New York City, the guide includes directions for 12 complete walking and driving tours, with detailed maps showing locations of kosher restaurants, Jewish theaters, museums, landmarks, synagogues, and mikvehs in all five boroughs. It is indexed. The author has also published the following related guides: *Lower East Side Guide* and the *Flatbush Guide.*

161 Levitt, Joy and Nancy Davis. *The Guide to Everything Jewish in New York.* New York: Adama Books, 1986. 334p.

This is a selective guide to Manhattan's Jewish resources. The following topics are covered: Children, College students, Singles, Marriage, Seniors, How we learn, Cultural resources, How we belong, Resources for Jewish holiday celebrations, Where we eat, How we help each other, Israel, and Major Jewish organizations. It is indexed.

162 Postal, Bernard and Lionel Koppman. *American Jewish Landmarks: A Travel Guide and History.* Rev. ed. New York: Fleet Press, 1977-1986. 4v.

This successor to *A Jewish Tourist's Guide to the U.S.* identifies, describes and provides the location of landmarks, sites, memorials, public buildings, and other places whose collective story constitute over three centuries of Jewish life in America. Volume 1—the Northeast; Volume 2—the South and Southwest; Volume 3—the Midwest; Volume 4—the West. Each chapter is divided into two parts: A. An introductory essay B. A travel section. Each volume is indexed.

163 *Traveling Jewish in America: The Complete Guide for Business & Pleasure.* Compiled by Brynna C. Bloomfield and Ellen Chernofsky. 3r ed. rev. and updated. Lodi, NJ: Wandering You Press, 1991. 493p.

The guide, arranged alphabetically by state, provides addresses and phone numbers for kosher restaurants, food shops, synagogues, mikvehs, Jewish student organizations, day schools, bookstores, and accommodations near synagogues. Other related guides by the author include *Catskills Guide* and *Canada Jewish Travel Guide.*

SECTION TWO

SUBJECT REFERENCE

CHAPTER 14

THE HEBREW BOOK, JUDAICA LIBRARIES, AND LIBRARIANSHIP

A. THE HEBREW MANUSCRIPT

SURVEYS AND INTRODUCTORY WORKS

164 *Oriental Manuscripts in Europe and North America: A Survey.* Compiled by J. D. Pearson. Zug: Inter Documentation Co., 1971. 515 p.
This is a survey of oriental manuscripts housed in the libraries of Europe and North America. Of particular interest are the chapters on Hebrew, Syriac, Arabic, Persian and Turkish manuscripts. An index of former owners is included at the end of the work.

165 Richler, Binyamin. *Hebrew Manuscripts: A Treasured Legacy.* Jerusalem: Ofeq Institute/Feldheim, 1990. 165p.
This is a profusely illustrated work "aimed at introducing the general public to the fascinating world of manuscript study" and at providing "... the scholar with basic information to facilitate his use of codices in his studies and research." Included is *A* Chapter on the Cairo Genizah, by Robert Brody. The inclusion of bibliographies, a description of the important collections of Hebrew manuscripts and a listing of their respective printed catalogs, enhance the value of this book.

CATALOGS OF HEBREW MANUSCRIPT COLLECTIONS

166 Makhon le-Tatslume Kitve ha-Yad ha-'Ivriyim. *Collective Catalogue of Hebrew Manuscripts: From the Institute of Microfilmed Hebrew Manuscripts ... of The Jewish National and University Library.* Jerusalem; Paris: Chadwyck-Healey France, 1989. Microfiche.
This is a two part catalog of codices and fragments written in Hebrew characters. Part one is a reproduction of the catalog of approximately 50,000 codices and 200,000 fragments in some 700 collections that the Institute of Microfilmed Hebrew Manuscripts has microfilmed and cataloged. It includes the following files: 1) An alphabetically arranged name file listing, authors, copyists, owners, etc. 2) Subject file 3) Non-Hebrew language file listing manuscripts written in Hebrew characters in languages other than Hebrew 4) Illuminated manuscripts file 5) Geographic index files 6) Title file 7) Library catalogue file consisting of a listing of the holdings of contributing libraries, arranged by library and then call number. Part two is a reproduction of Bet ha-Sefarim ha-Leumi veha-Universitai bi-Yerushalayim, Mahlakah le-Khitve Yad's *Katalog*. It includes the following files: 1) Dictionary file arranged by author, title and subject 2) General catalogue file listing codices by inventory number. A user's guide is provided.

167 —. *Supplement, 1990.* Paris: Chadwyck-Healey France, 1990. Microfiche.

> This contains additions to the title, subject and author files of the Makhon's *Katalog.* Note: The Institute's current catalog is now available for searching on the Net through ALEPH (Israel library network).

168 Freimann, Aron. *Union Catalog of Hebrew Manuscripts and Their Location.* New York: American Academy for Jewish Research, 1973. 2v.

> This is an "incomplete" descriptive catalog of Hebrew manuscripts and their location. The author index volume (v.1), by Menahem Schmelzer, includes a list of frequently used abbreviations; a list of locations, owners of manuscripts, catalogs, and their symbols; and an author-title index in Roman characters. Volume 2, the *Union Catalog* is arranged by title. Its references to secondary literature about the manuscript and or author are valuable to the bibliographer and researcher.

169 *Hebräische Handschriften.* Beschrieben von Ernst Róth und Hans Striedel. Wiesbaden: Steiner, 1965- .

> This is a multi-volume descriptive catalog of Hebrew manuscripts that are housed in German libraries. The following volumes have been published to-date: Part 1a. *Hebräische Handschriften in Frankfurt* Part 1b. *Die Handschriften der Stadt und Universitätsbibliothek Frankfurt a/M* Part 2. *Hebräische Handschriften* (a listing of manuscripts in 59 different German libraries and collections) Part 3. *Die Handschriften H. B. Levy an der Staats und Universitätsbibliothek Hamburg.*

170 *Hebrew and Judaic Manuscripts in Amsterdam Public Collections.* Compiled by Lajb Fuks and R. G. Fuks-Mansfeld. Leiden: E. J. Brill, 1973-75. 2v.

> This is a descriptive catalog of the manuscript collections housed in the Bibliotheca Rosenthaliana, University Library of Amsterdam (v.1) and Ets Haim, Livraria Montezinos (v.2). The manuscripts are arranged within such subject areas as Bible, Polemics, Belles Lettres, etc. Included are a subject index, index of names, Hebrew index of names, and index of titles. The Ets Haim collection is now housed in Jerusalem at the Bet ha-Sefarim ha-Leumi veha-Universitai.

171 Jewish Theological Seminary of America Library. *A Guide to the Hebrew Manuscript Collection of the Jewish Theological Seminary of America.* Edited by Jay Rovner. New York: Jewish Theological Seminary of America Library, 1991. 5v.

> This is a short title bilingual catalog of the more than 10,000 manuscripts housed in the Seminary Library. The following data (where available) is provided about each manuscript: author, title or description of contents, date, script type, place, and foliation. A table of Rabbinic numbers which correspond to the general manuscript numbers has been provided to facilitate reference to the more detailed description of those manuscripts provided in J. Brumer's *Rabbinic Manuscript Catalog* (see below). It includes title index (Volume 4); and author, place, date, and topic indexes (Volume 5). The Jewish Theological Seminary Library's collection of manuscripts may be accessed in RLIN and in the Library's local ALEPH system.

172 —. *Hebrew Manuscript Catalogs From the Jewish Theological Seminary.* New York: Clearwater, 1986. Microfiche.
Part 1. *Rabbinic Manuscript Catalog,* by Judah Brumer.
Part 2. *Bible Manuscript Catalog,* by Morris Lutzki.

173 Netzer, Amnon. *Otsar Kitve ha-Yad shel Yehude Paras bi-Mekhon Ben-Tsevi.* Jerusalem: Ben-Zvi Institute, 1985. 234 p.
This catalog provides a full physical and bibliographical description of the more than 300 Persian Jewish manuscripts housed at the Ben-Zvi Institute in Jerusalem. It includes an introductory essay about Judeo-Persian literature, a bibliography, and a general index.

174 *Ohel Hayim: Katalog Kitve ha-Yad ha-'Ivriyim be-Sifriyat Mispahat Menasheh Refa'el ve-Sarah Lehman.* Prepared by Moshe Halamish with the participation of Elazar Hurvitz. New York: Manfred and Anne Lehmann Foundation, 1988-
These are descriptive catalogs of the Kabbalistic (v. 1) and Biblical manuscripts (v.2) in Manfred Lehmann's private collection. Each item described is accompanied by a facsimile reproduction of a page from the manuscript, to enable the user to gain a better understanding of the text that is described. The work concludes with numerous indexes, including title, author, geographic, and former owner. Forthcoming volumes will describe other segments of this rich collection.

175 Tovi, Yosef. *Kitve ha-Yad ha-Temaniyim bi-Mekhon Ben-Tsevi.* Jerusalem: Ben-Zvi Institute, 1982. 404 p.
This is a full physical and bibliographical description of the Yemenite Jewish manuscripts in the Ben-Zvi Institute. The catalog is arranged by subject. The works are listed in chronological order within each subject. The author has appended many indexes to aid the reader, including a general index, a subject index, a title index and an index of poem incipits. The work is enhanced by the inclusion of many facsimiles.

B. THE HEBREW BOOK

Shlomo Shunami, in his *Bibliography of Bibliographies* (see entries 56-67) refers to numerous bibliographies pertaining to the history of Hebrew printing in various communities throughout the world. He also lists published catalogs of both Hebraica and Judaica book and manuscript collections. What follows is a brief list of older works and a selection of newer works.

SURVEYS AND INTRODUCTORY WORKS

176 *The Hebrew Book: An Historical Survey.* Edited by Raphael Posner, and Israel Ta-Shema. Jerusalem: Keter, 1975. 225 p.
This is a collection of essays based on the *Encyclopaedia Judaica* which provides the reader with an introduction to the writing and printing of the Hebrew book. A listing of the libraries that house major collections of Hebrew manuscripts and their published catalogs is included in Chapter 3, "The Manuscript." A brief bibliography is included.

See also Chapter 15 (subsections: Great Britain and Italy).

177 *Hebrew Typography in the Northern Netherlands, 1585-1815.* Compiled by Lajb Fuks and R. G. Fuks-Mansfeld. Leiden: E. J. Brill, 1984-1987. 2v.
This is an historical essay about Hebrew printing in Leiden, Franeker, and Amsterdam from 1585-1815, and a bibliography of works that were published in these cities. The following indexes are included to aid the reader: Index of names (in Latin and Hebrew characters); Index of Titles (in Latin and Hebrew characters); Subject Index; Index of Financiers; Index of Compositors; Index of Correctors; Index of Approbations; Index of Hebrew Laudatory Poems.

178 Heller, Marvin J. *Printing the Talmud: A History of the Earliest Printed Editions of the Talmud.* Brooklyn, New York: Im Hasefer, 1992. 447p.
This is an overview of, and an introduction to the history of the printing of the Talmud from the 15th century to the mid-17th century. The author discusses the Talmud's printing against the background of prevailing social conditions and contemporary events, as well as in the context of Hebrew bibliography. It includes many facsimiles of pages from the editions discussed in the book, a listing of the printed editions of the Babylonian Talmud that were printed until 1880, a bibliography, and author-title index. For an earlier scholarly discussion of the subject, see Raphael Nathan Rabinowitz's *Maamar Hadpasat ha-Talmud.* (Jerusalem: Mosad ha-Rav Kook, 1951 or 2).

179 Kagan, Berl. *Sefer ha-Prenumerantn.* New York: Jewish Theological Seminary of America Library/Ktav, 1975. 384p.
Berl Kagan, in his preface, sheds light on the prevalent practice among Jewish authors in the 18th-20th century to obtain financial support for their printing expenses from pre-subscribers. These authors were for the most part East and Central European Rabbis. The main body of the work consists of a list of these pre-subscribers. It includes the following indexes: A. Hebrew titles .B. Name index .C. Synagogues .D. Societies. E. Geographic index which lists 8,767 Jewish communities in Europe and North Africa in Hebrew and Roman script.

180 Katsav, Shlomo. *Sefer ha-Hatumim.* Petach Tikva: The Author, 1986. [300 *l.*]
This work follows the arrangement in the above work by Kagan. Katsav lists an additional 152 books.

181 Martsiano, Eliyahu Refael. *Bene Melakhim: ve-Hu Toldot ha-Sefer ha-'Ivri be-Maroko mi-Shenat 277 'ad Shenat 749.* Yerushalayim: Hotsaat Mekhon ha-Rasham, 1989. 210p.
This comprehensive annotated bibliography lists more than 1,000 items printed in Morocco, including responsa, novellae, sermons, amulets and handbills. It covers the years 1517-1989. The bibliography is arranged by printing center. The work includes an introductory essay about the history of Hebrew printing in Morocco. Title, subject, author and publisher and editor indexes complete this important bibliography.

182 Rosenfeld, Moshe. *ha-Defus ha-'Ivri me-Reshito 'ad Shenat 5708 [1948]*. Jerusalem: The Author, 1992. 530p.

> This is a gazetteer of printing centers in which Hebrew books were printed. The author cites the first book printed in each center. Reproductions of the title pages of the majority of the books that are cited are included in a separate section. The author provides a list of "Erroneous places of printing," i. e., a list of titles believed to have been printed in a given city, but in fact were printed elsewhere. The gazetteer includes an index of places in Hebrew characters and Latin character equivalent, and a Latin character listing and Hebrew equivalent.

INCUNABULA

183 Goldstein, David. *Hebrew Incunables in the British Isles: A Preliminary Census*. London: British Library, 1985.

> The author lists 106 incunabula in British institutions.

184 Iakerson, Semen Mordukhovich. *Evreiskie Inkunabuly ...* . Leningrad: Ban, 1988. 337p.

> A full physical and bibliographical description of 43 incunabula and fragments in 111 copies housed in the Lenin State Library, Moscow, the Library of the Leningrad Branch of the Institute of Oriental Studies of the Academy of Sciences of the USSR (formerly the Asiatic Museum), and the M. E. Saltykov-Shchedrin State Public Library, St. Petersburg. These works are from the collections of Moses Friedland, Daniel Chwolson, and David Ginzburg. The entries are arranged in topographical-chronological order. Each bibliographical entry is given in Hebrew and in Latin transcription. The text of the description and the commentary (which includes a brief biography of the author and data on his work, as well as information on the publication), are in Russian. Numerous indexes to aid the reader include the following: authors, commentators, translators; publishers, proofreaders, compositors; donors; owners; censors; titles. Facsimiles of pages from the works described are included.

185 —. *Katalog Ivkunabulov ....* Leningrad: Ban, 1985. 107 p.

> This work contains a full physical and bibliographical description of 38 incunabula in 63 copies from the Moses Friedland and Daniel Chwolson collections housed at the Library of the Leningrad Branch of the Institute of Oriental Studies of the Academy of Sciences of the USSR (formerly The Asiatic Museum). The entries are in Hebrew and in Latin transcription. The text of the description, including a brief biography of each author, is in Russian. Numerous indexes to aid the reader including: authors, commentators and translators; printers, correctors, typesetters donators; and title are appended. Facsimiles of pages from the works described are included.

186 Mendel Gottesman Library of Hebraica-Judaica. *Sifre ha-Defus ha-Rishonim (Inkunabulim)*, me-et Gershon Kohen. New York: Yeshiva University, 1984. 112p.

> This is an alphabetically arranged descriptive catalog of the forty incunabula housed in the Gottesman Library. The author provides full bibliographic information about each item listed and notes the unique features of the Gottesman Library's copy.

187 Offenberg, A. K. *Hebrew Incunabula in Public Collections: A First International Census.* Nieuwkoop: De Graaf, 1990. 74, 214p.

Offenberg lists in this *Census* 139 editions (c. 2,000 copies) of Hebrew books works known to have been printed before 1 January 1501. The books are housed in 155 libraries throughout the world. The census is arranged alphabetically by author (romanized) or title main entry (for anonymous works). Each entry contains: a brief bibliographical citation; references to standard works in incunabular studies by Hain, Goff, etc.; locations of all known copies; and brief citations of relevant literature. To aid the user the author includes: A register of collections by geographic location and the name of the library within each location; lists of abbreviations; concordances of corresponding numbers in works by Hain, Goff, etc.; index of printing places, printers and publications; index of Hebrew titles; list of copies printed on parchment and a general index of names.

188 —. *A Choice of Corals; Facets of Fifteenth-Century Hebrew Printing.* Nieuwwkoop, De Graaf, 1992. 245p.

This work contains studies by the author which have, for the most part, been published during the last twenty-odd years. The first two studies in this collection provide a general introduction to the study of Hebrew incunabula "by surveying the existing literature on Hebrew incunabula since the Second World War and the location of the preserved copies all over the world." Some additions and corrections to the Introduction of the aforementioned work are included in the second chapter. The work also includes a list of c. 200 copies of Hebrew incunabula which have disappeared from seventeen collections since the outbreak of the Second World War (Appendix I).

RARE BOOK AND EXHIBITION CATALOGS

189 Hill, Brad Sabin. *Hebraica (Saec. X ad saec. XVI): Manuscripts and Early Printed Books from the Library of Valmadonna Trust.* London: Valmadonna Trust, 1989. 1v. (unpaged).

This is a richly illustrated descriptive catalog of an exhibit held at the Pierpont Morgan Library in New York. The exhibit traced the history and art of the Hebrew book from the Middle Ages to the end of the 16th century. The catalog is preceded by an introductory essay by Brad Sabin Hill. Appended to the catalog are a series of indexes (authors, titles, printers, censors, formats) and a bibliography of literature in English on the subject of Hebrew manuscripts, Hebrew incunabula, and Hebrew books in the 16th century.

190 Rosenfeld, Moshe. *'Atikim u-Nedirim=Antique and Rare Books.* Jerusalem: The Author, 1987. 2v.

This is an illustrated descriptive catalog of books sold at auctions. The compiler provides a brief bibliographic description of the item, notes its rarity and condition, and supplies details about the sale, including the name of the auction firm, its catalog number and the sale price. The items in the catalog are often accompanied by a facsimile of a page from the text. Volume one lists incunabula, Italian imprints, Hasidic works, and Polish-Russian imprints. Volume two lists books published in Constantinople, Salonika, Smyrna (Ismir), Holland, London, Paris, and Central Europe (Part 1). Volume three (forthcoming), will list additional Central European imprints, as well as books published in New York, Argentina, and Brazil. In addition it will list Siddurim, Mahzorim, Selihot, Kinot, and Haggadot. It includes an index of title page facsimiles.

191 *Sefarim 'Ivriyim 'Atikim: Reshimat Sefarim she-Nimkeru bi-Mekhirot Pumbiyot ba-Tekufah 1976-1987.* Edited by Yeshayahu Vinograd and Valia Trionyo. Jerusalem: Society of Judaica Collectors, 1987. 220, 50p.
This descriptive catalog lists by title over 3,000 books sold at auctions held between 1976 and 1987. The compiler provides a brief bibliographic description of each book, notes its condition and supplies details about the sale, including the name of the auction firm, the sale date, and the closing price. The list includes indexes of authors, titles, places in Hebrew and Latin characters, and dates of publication. See also *Yudaikah Yerushalayim*, a series of descriptive auction sale catalogs of rare books, manuscripts, documents and Jewish art that the Society of Judaica Collectors conducts in Jerusalem.

192 *A Sign and a Witness: 2,000 Years of Hebrew Books and Illuminated Manuscripts.* Edited with Introduction by Leonard Singer Gold. New York: New York Public Library, 1988. 223p.
This collection of twelve scholarly essays was published in conjunction with an exhibit of Hebrew manuscripts and books at the New York Public Library. The essays deal with such topics as the making of Hebrew manuscripts and their decoration, Hebrew manuscripts as a resource of scholarship, the history of Hebrew book printing, issues relating to Hebrew book publishing, Christian involvement with the Hebrew book in the transmission of culture. "A Selected Bibliography of the Hebrew Book" by Sharon Lieberman Mintz, a checklist of the exhibition, and many facsimile reproductions (in both color and black-and-white) of the items on display, enhance the value of this important work.

193 *A Visual Testimony: Judaica from the Vatican Library.* Edited by Philip Hiat. New York: Union of American Hebrew Congregations, 1987. 104p.
This is a richly illustrated checklist of an exhibit of Judaica books and manuscripts from the Vatican Library. The checklist includes the following introductory essays: "The Hebrew Collections of the Vatican Library," by Leonard E. Boyle; "Texts in Context: Hebraica in the Vatican Library as a Resource for Jewish-Christian Relations," by Michael A. Singer; "Hebrew Illuminated Manuscripts in the Vatican Library," by Joseph Gutmann.

C. THE CAIRO GENIZAH
See also entry 165.
CATALOGS

194 Bet ha-Sefarim ha-Leumi veha-Universitai. *Katalog shel Osef Z'ak Motseri.* Yerushalayim: Bet ha-Sefarim ha-Leumi veha-Universitai, 1990. 407 p.
The catalog fully describes the approximately 5,600 bibliographical units in the the Jack Mosseri Genizah Collection. The items vary in extent, and cover most of medieval Judaica. Many indexes are provided to aid the reader, including an index of titles and subjects; an index of authors;

incipits of the piyutim and the poems; and an index of the melody indicators.

195 Cambridge University Library. *Hebrew Bible Manuscripts in the Cambridge Genizah Collections,* by Malcom C. Davis incorporating material compiled by H. Knopf. Cambridge; Cambridge University Library, 1978-1980. 2v.

> This is a bibliographical record of the Hebrew Bible manuscript fragments in the Cambridge Genizah Collections. Volume 1 lists the fragments in the Taylor-Schechter Old Series and other Genizah collections.

> Volume 2 lists the fragments in the Taylor-Schechter New Series and the Westminster College Cambridge Collection. Both volumes include a scriptural index to chapters and an alphabetical subject index. Volume one also includes an "Or. 1080 Relative Index which relates the original classmarks of Bible items selected by Dr. Knopf from the Or. 1080 Genizah Collection to form a separate 'A' section ... to their present numbers."

196 —. *Karaite Bible Manuscripts From the Cairo Genizah Collection,* by Geoffrey Khan. Cambridge: Published for the Cambridge University Library by the Cambridge University Press, 1990. 186p.

> This work is an edition and description of Karaite Hebrew Bible fragments in Arabic script from the Cairo Genizah collection. Most fragments described in this work are housed in the Cambridge University Library. Facsimiles and indexes are included.

197 —. *A Miscellany of Literary Pieces from the Cambridge Genizah Collections,* by Simon Hopkins. Cambridge: Cambridge University Library, 1978. 110p.

> This is an edition and description of a selection of "loosely classed" Apocrypha and Pseudepigrapha texts from Box A45 of the Taylor-Schechter Old Series Genizah Collection. The facsimile of each fragment is accompanied by a transcription of the text and a description of the manuscript.

198 —. *Published Material from the Cambridge Genizah Collections: A Bibliography, 1896-1980.* Edited by Stefan C. Reif. Cambridge: Published for Cambridge University Library by Cambridge University Press, 1988. 608p.

> This bibliography covers the years 1896-1980. It lists texts and fragments in the Cambridge Genizah Collection that have been published and research publications about texts in the collection. The volume is divided into three sections: A. Material arranged in order of classmark. B. Material arranged alphabetically by author . C. A list of Genizah works cited.

199 —. *Targumic Manuscripts in the Cambridge Genizah Collection,* by Michael L. Klein. Cambridge: Published for the Cambridge University Library by the Cambridge University Press, 1992. 136p.

> This is an indexed descriptive catalog of about 1,600 fragments of Targum of every known oeuvre and form. Twenty four fragments have been reproduced in facsimile and are included at the end of the volume. In addition, the decorations in the manuscripts have also been reproduced in facsimile and have been included with a reference note which identifies the

manuscript in which the decoration is found. Scriptural references are provided for each text. The catalog includes a short title index and a general index.

200 —. *Vocalized Talmudic Manuscripts in the Cambridge Genizah Collections*, by Shelomo Morag. Published for the Cambridge University Library by the Cambridge University Press, 1988. 56p.

This publication provides a complete as possible description of the vocalization appearing in the Talmudic fragments in the Taylor-Schechter Old Series Genizah Collection. It includes facsimiles and an index.

201 Fenton, Paul. *Reshimat Kitve Yad be-'Aravit-Yehudit be-Leningrad.* Yerushalayim: Mekhon Ben-Tsevi, 1991. 152p.

This work contains a handlist of Judeo-Arabic manuscripts from the second Abraham Firkovich collection housed in the Saltykov-Shchedrin State Public Library in Leningrad. The compiler identifies these manuscripts as being from the Cairo Genizah. Appended to the list are: a selective list of the philosophical, ethical and medical manuscripts to be found in the second Firkovich collection; a list of Judeo-Arabic items in the first Firkovich collection; an index of authors; an index of works.

202 Halper, Benzion. *Descriptive Catalogue of Genizah Fragments in Philadelphia.* Philadelphia: Dropsie College for Hebrew and Cognate Learning, 1924. 235p.

This is a catalog of the Genizah fragments housed at the College's Library. The catalog is arranged by genre of literature, e. g., Bible, Talmud, Documents and Letters, etc. This collection is now housed at the Annenberg Institute in Philadelphia.

203 Shaked, Shaul. *Tentative Bibliography of Geniza Documents.* Paris: Mouton, 1964. 355p.

This is a listing of Genizah texts ordered by cities, and within each city, by the library in which the manuscripts are found. For each text listed, Shaked notes which fragments have been published and to what extent and where they have been discussed.

D. JUDAICA LIBRARIES

CATALOGING

204 Galron-Goldschläger, Joseph. *Library of Congress Subject Headings in Jewish Studies.* 4th edition. New York: Association of Jewish Libraries, 1993. 2v. (553p.)

This is a comprehensive list of LC subject headings for Judaica libraries. It includes a new supplement entitled: "Free Floating Subdivisions."

205 Stuhlman, Daniel D. *Library of Congress Subject Headings for Judaica.* 3rd ed. Chicago: BYLS Press (6617 N. Mozart, Chicago, IL 60645), 1988. 62p.

This is a useful tool for Judaica catalogers and reference librarians. The compilation is based on the 9th edition of Library of Congress. *Subject Headings*, The list includes see and see also references. It is available in either paper or MS-DOS disk formats.

CATALOGS OF HEBREW BOOKS.

See Shimeon Brisman, *History and Guide to Judaic Bibliography* (entry 46), chapters 1 and 5 , for discussion and description of works published to 1975. What follows is a brief list of older works and a selection of newer works.

206 Ben-Jacob, Isaac. *Otsar ha-Sefarim.* New York: Hotsa'at Yerushalayim [1944/45 or 1945/46] 678p.

This is a comprehensive bibliography arranged by title of approximately 15,000 Hebrew and Yiddish works published until the year 1863. Approximately 3,000 manuscripts are also listed. Full bibliographic citations are given. In addition, the author notes the content of each work cited.

207 Friedberg, Bernhard. *Bet Eked Sefarim.* 2 ed., rev. Tel-Aviv: Bar-Juda, 1951-1956. 4v.

This is a revised and expanded edition of a bibliography published originally in Antwerp, 1928-1931 under the same title. This inclusive annotated bibliography lists books written in Hebrew, Yiddish, and other Jewish dialects in Hebrew characters, printed up to 1950. The bibliography is arranged by title and includes subject and author indexes. Reprint editions were published in Jerusalem? 1969 or 1970 and Tel Aviv, 1971.

208 Moria, M. *Bet Eked Sefarim he-Hadash.* Kiryat Shemonah: Hotsa'at Makhon Tsiyon, 1974-1976. 5v.

Moria updates Friedberg's work to 1975 (volumes 1-2, alef-tet, includes titles published to 1973). The bibliography is arranged by title and is not annotated. Full bibliographic citations are given.

209 —. *Otsar ha-Mehabrim.* Tsefat: Makhon Tsiyon, 1977. 2v.

This is an author index to the aforementioned work.

210 Slatkine, Menahem Mendel. *Otsar ha-Sefarim Helek Sheni.* Jerusalem: Kiryat Sefer, 1965. 481p.

The author corrects and revises more than 4,000 entries in Isaac Ben-Jacob's *Otsar.* Slatkine has also compiled an index of authors, translators, commentators, and editors to the *Otsar* and included it in his book.

COLLECTION DEVELOPMENT

211 Lubetski, Edith and Meir Lubetski. *Building a Judaica Library Collection:*

A Resource Guide. Littleton, CO: Libraries Unlimited, 1983. 185p.

> The handbook is arranged in two parts: A. A bibliographic guide to selection aids for all types of Judaic material in various formats. B. A directory of booksellers, publishers, and distributors.

Directories

212 Hoogewood, F. J. *A Guide to Libraries of Judaica and Hebraica in Europe.* Copenhagen: Det Koneglige Bibliotek, 1985. 122p.

> This is a geographically arranged provisional guide to libraries in Europe that house Judaica and Hebraica books and/or manuscripts. It provides the following information for each entry: the institution's address, the name of the librarian, hours, the size and nature of the collection, and the library's policy regarding use, loan, etc. The guide is accompanied by the following three appendices: A. A list of the European libraries and collections containing Hebrew manuscripts microfilmed for the Institute of Microfilmed Hebrew Manuscripts in Jerusalem B. Hebrew incunabula in European libraries: a provisional list of bibliographical tools C. Names and addresses for information concerning national associations of Jewish studies in Europe. Additional information about European collections of Judaica may be found in *Hebrew Studies; Papers Presented at a Colloquium on Resources for Hebraica in Europe Held at the School of Oriental and African Studies University of London 11-13 September 1989/11-13 Elul 5749* (London: The British Library, 1991).

Library Catalogs

Many libraries throughout the world have begun to automate their catalogs and to convert their bibliographic records to machine readable format. Many of these institutions are now contributing bibliographic data to national databases such as ALEPH, OCLC, and RLIN. The automated catalogs of many institutions can be accessed through the NET (International Academic Computer Networks). See "Catalogs of Hebraica Book Collections" in *A History and Guide to Judaica Bibliography*, 36-73 (entry 46) for a detailed discussion of this subject and a listing of relevant publications. The following is a list of recently published book catalogs of institutions in Israel, Germany and the United States.

213 Bet ha-Sefarim ha-Leumi veha-Universitai. *Judaica Collection Card Catalogue.* Zug: Inter Documentation Company, 1980. Microfiche.

> This microfiche reproduction of the Library's Judaica classified catalog provides access to its more than 300,000 titles. The Library's Scholem Classification Scheme is contained in an appended paper index and is also reproduced on the fiche.

214 *Bibliographie zum Antisemitismus=A Bibliography on Antisemitism.* Edited by Herbert A. Strauss. Munich; New York: K. G. Saur, 1989- .

> This multi-volume work lists the holdings of the special collection housed at the Library of the Zentrum für Antisemitismusforschung, Technische Universität, Berlin. See under anti-Semitism for a description.

215 Harvard University Library. *Catalogue of Hebrew Books.* Cambridge, MA: distributed by Harvard University Press, 1968. 6v.

216 —. *Supplement I.* Cambridge: Harvard University Press, 1972. 3v.
The catalog and its supplement provide author, subject (in Latin characters) and title access to the Hebraica collection at Harvard's Weidener Library. Materials owned by the Library to 1972 are listed. Yiddish materials are not listed. The supplement includes a listing of Harvard's rare Judaica in the Houghton Library.

217 —. *Judaica.* Cambridge: Harvard University Press, 1971. 302p.

218 —. *Judaica in the Houghton Library.* Cambridge, MA: Harvard University Press, 1972. 193p.
This is a listing of Harvard's rare Judaica previously listed in its *Catalogue of Hebrew Books: Supplement I,* volume 1. The catalog includes indexes to the collection by date of publication, place of publication and title.

219 Hebrew Union College. Jewish Institute of Religion, Library. *Dictionary Catalog of the Klau Library,* Cincinnati. Boston: G.K. Hall, 1964. 32v.
The catalog provides author and subject (in Roman characters) access to the library's extensive holdings of Judaica, Hebraica and Ancient Near East materials. Hebrew title access is also provided in a separate title catalog (volumes 27-32). Hebrew and Yiddish titles are interfiled in this catalog.

220 —. *Supplement [Hebrew Titles],* 1966-1972. (on microfilm)

221 —. *Supplement [Hebrew Titles],* 1972-1982. (on microfiche)

222 New York Public Library. Reference Department. *Dictionary Catalog of the Jewish Collection.* Boston: G.K. Hall, 1960. 14v.

223 —. *First Supplement.* Boston: G.K. Hall, 1975. 8v.
The original catalog and its supplement list the Hebraica and Judaica holdings of the Jewish Division to 1971. The catalog is arranged by author and subject (in Latin characters). The title catalog lists the Hebrew, Yiddish, and Ladino titles in separate alphabets.

224 —. *The Hebrew-Character Title Catalog of the Jewish Division.* Boston: G.K. Hall, 1981. 4v.
The set published in 1981 combines all titles in Hebrew characters that were listed in the earlier set and its supplement.

225 YIVO Institute for Jewish Research. *Yiddish Catalog and Authority File of the YIVO Library.* Edited, with Introductions by Zachary M. Baker and Bella Hass Weinberg. Boston: G. K. Hall, 1990. 5v.
This author-title catalog lists approximately 40,000 Yiddish books and periodicals housed at the YIVO Institute for Jewish Research, New York. The catalog also lists Yiddish periodicals conserved on microfilm. Of

particular interest and importance is the published authority file which lists Yiddish headings and cross references for author, co-author, editor, translator and series.

E. ARCHIVES

See Chapters 15, 16 and 18 for additional archival resources.

DIRECTORIES

226 *Guide to Jewish Archives: Preliminary Edition.* Edited by Aryeh Segall. Jerusalem: World Council on Jewish Archives, 1981. 90p.

> This is a guide to 58 institutions in Israel, the United States, Canada, Europe, and Australia which "preserve and maintain specific collections of Jewish archival materials." Included in the guide is information about each institution, its services, and a brief description of selected record groups of special importance. This work supersedes the *Directory of Jewish Archival Institutions*, edited by Philip P. Mason (Detroit: published for the National Foundation for Jewish Culture by Wayne State University, 1975. 76p.). See also under entries such as Jews, Judaism, etc. in National Historical Publications and Records Commission. *Directory of Archives and Manuscript Repositories in the United States.* 2nd ed. (Phoenix: Oryx Press, 1988. 853p.) and U. S. Library of Congress. *National Union Catalog of Manuscript Collections.* Hamden, Conn.: Shoe String Press, 1959/61- .

CHAPTER 15

THE JEWISH COMMUNITIES OF THE DIASPORA

See also Chapters 8 (subscection: Jewish Studies/Courses and Syllabi) and 23 (subsection: Jewish Political Studies).

A. GENERAL MATERIALS

ATLASES AND GAZETTEERS
See also entry 507.

227 Beinart, Haim. *Atlas of Medieval Jewish History*. New York: Simon & Schuster, 1992. 144p.

This atlas, intended for use by both the scholar and layman, is a translation of *Atlas Karta le-Toldot 'Am Yisrael bi-Yeme ha-Benayim* (Jerusalem: Karta, 1981). The author portrays, through the use of maps, the changes that befell the Jewish people during the period beginning with the Barbarian Invasions in the fifth century and continuing to the period after the Chmielnicki Massacres of 1648-1649 and the collapse of the Sabbatean movement. The texts that accompany the more than 100 maps " provide a supplementary evaluation and give a geographical-historical expression to the relevant period in the history of the Jews."

228 De Lange, Nicholas. *Atlas of the Jewish World*. New York: Facts on File, 1984. 240p.

This atlas is divided into three parts: Part I presents the historical background Part II focuses on their cultural background Part III presents a guided tour through the Jewish communities of today's world. The atlas contains more than 300 maps and 400 illustrations, half of which are in full color. A glossary, bibliography, gazetteer and index are included.

229 Friesel, Evyatar. *Atlas of Modern Jewish History*. Revised from the Hebrew Edition. New York: Oxford University Press, 1990. 159p.

This historical atlas, covering the period of the seventeenth century through the 1980's, is a revised and updated version of the Hebrew *Atlas Karta le-Toldot 'Am Yisrael ba-Zeman he-Hadash* (Jerusalem: Karta, 1983). It contains more than 500 maps, diagrams, charts, illustrations, and accompanying text. The atlas is divided into seven sections: I. Jewish Demography II. European Countries: Seventeenth Century to World War I III. Major Themes in Modern Jewish History, e. g., professions of the Jews, legal situation of the Jews, the Haskalah (Jewish Enlightenment) Sabbateanism, Frankism, Hasidism, Jewish Nationalism, Jewish Socialism, anti-Semitism, etc. IV. Muslim Countries V.European Jewry in the Interwar Years VI. European Jewry, 1940-1980's VII. The New Centers of Jewry, e. g., Palestine / Israel, Canada, the United States, Latin America, South Africa, Australia and New Zealand. It includes a bibliography, general index, and index of geographical names.

230 Gilbert, Martin. *The Illustrated Atlas of Jewish Civilization: 4,000 Years of Jewish History.* New York: Macmillan,1990. 224p.

> The Atlas includes 100 colored annotated maps from Gilbert's *Jewish History Atlas*, illustrations of archaeological sites, individuals through the centuries, paintings and other artistic reproductions, and photographs of the past century. This rich illustrated material accompanies a most readable text by Josephine Baker, who provides a capsulized version of Jewish history from the time of Abraham to the present. The *Atlas* includes a general index .

231 —. *Jewish History Atlas.* 4th ed. London: Weidenfeld & Nicolson, 1992. 123p.

> Through the use of maps Gilbert "traces world-wide Jewish migrations, from ancient Mesopotamia to modern Israel." It sheds light on the role of the Jews in their national settings, their complex history, their reaction to persecution, and their contribution to world civilization. The new edition includes up-dated maps and new maps which portray the events in Jewish history during the past twenty years, e. g., emigration of Jews from the Soviet Union between 1970 and 1990 and the emigration of Jews from Ethiopia to Israel.

INTRODUCTORY WORKS AND SURVEYS

232 Baron, Salo Wittmayer. *A Social and Religious History of the Jews.* 2nd ed., rev. and enl. Philadelphia: Jewish Publication Society of America, 1952-1983. 18 v.

> This is a scholarly discussion of Jewish history from ancient times to 1650. Baron pays particular attention to the social, political and intellectual developments which impacted on Jewish life through the ages. Each volume includes " Notes" containing references to sources for further study. Index: volumes 1-8; 9-18.

233 Ben-Sasson, H. H. *A History of the Jewish People.* Cambridge, MA: Harvard University Press, 1976. 1,170p.

> This is a scholarly comprehensive one-volume history, written by various scholars, which examines Jewish history from political, economic, social and religious perspectives. Includes a selected bibliography.

234 *The Jew in the Modern World: A Documentary History.* Edited by Paul R. Mendes-Flohr and Jehuda Reinharz. New York: Oxford University Press, 1980. 556p.

> The editors have collected and translated into English more than 200 primary documents. These documents "illustrate the processes at work in modern Jewish history". The documents are arranged in eleven chapters: I. Harbingers of political and economic change II. Harbingers of cultural and ideological change III. Process of political emancipation in western Europe, 1789-1871 IV.Emerging patterns of religious adjustment: Reform, Conservative, and neo-orthodox Judaism V. Science of Judaism VI. Jewish identity challenged and redefined VI. Political and racial anti-Semitism VIII. Russian experience IX.American experience X. Zionism XI. The Holocaust. The introductory essay to each chapter places the documents into context. Explanatory notes are included in the documents when

necessary, and the source of each document is noted. The reader includes an appendix: "The Demography of modern Jewish History," which includes numerous demographic tables. Indexed.

235 *Jewish Communities of the World: A Contemporary Guide.* 4th ed. Edited by Antony Lerman. New York: Facts On File, 1989. 206p.
This guide is arranged alphabetically by country. It provides a brief historical sketch of the Jewish community in each country and information on its current state. It also notes the general population of each country and that of the Jewish community.

236 *Modern Jewish History: A Source Reader.* Edited by Robert Chazan and Marc Lee Raphael. New York: Schocken Books, 1979. 381p.
The documents that have been selected for inclusion in this anthology focus on "Western European Jewry, its emancipation, its internal crises and the development of a post emancipation anti-Semitism by the close of the nineteenth century. . . . ." Coverage of the twentieth century is divided into the periods 1914-1939, the World War II years and the Holocaust, and the dramatic decades from 1945 to the present." The prefatory material to each document deals with authorship and places the document into context. The compilers have included a bibliography at the end of the volume which lists additional primary sources, secondary literature, fictional works and movies that relate to modern Jewish history. Includes a general index.

BIBLIOGRAPHY
See also entries 244 and 455.

237 Edelheit, Abraham J. and Hershel Edelheit. *The Jewish World in Modern Times: A Selected Annotated Bibliography.* Boulder, CO: Westview Press, 1988. 569p.
This is a selective annotated bibliography of books, pamphlets and articles in English, covering modern Jewish history. Part I, which treats the Jewish world as whole, is divided into 9 chapters: Surveys; Social history; Emancipation; Religious trends; Cultural trends; Antisemitism; Public affairs; Holocaust; and Zionism. Part II deals with individual Jewish communities, arranged geographically in nine chapters: Central Europe; Eastern Europe; USSR; Western Europe; The Americas; USA and Canada; Middle East; Israel; Africa and Asia. The volume includes an introduction, "An Outline of Modern Jewish History," which briefly describes key events, personalities, and movements. The book concludes with a bibliography of bibliographies, a glossary, and author, title and subject indexes.

238 Kaplan, Jonathan. *International Bibliography of Jewish History and Thought.* Munchen: K.G. Saur; Jerusalem: Magnes Press, 1984. 483p.
This multilingual annotated and selected bibliography of Jewish history and thought is designed to assist the educator, student and librarian. Some 2000 books were chosen in Hebrew, English, German, Spanish, Portuguese and French. There are chapters on General works; Biblical works; Period of the Second Temple; Medieval period; Modern period, and Jewish communities. A name index is included. This work was originally published under the title: *2000 Books and More* (Jerusalem: Magnes Press, 1983).

239 Rakover, Nahum. *ha-Kehilah.* Jerusalem: Merkaz Zalman Shazar, 1977. 160p.

This bibliography lists the published ordinances and community registers (takkanot and pinkasim) of various Jewish communities. This material is invaluable for the study of the organization and government of these communities. There is an index of places and authors. The material was originally published in the author's *Otsar ha-Mishpat* (Jerusalem, 1975) in the section entitled "Communities—Organization and Administration."

CHRONOLOGIES

240 Bloch, Abraham P. *Day by Day in Jewish History.* New York: Ktav, 1983. 336p.

This is a day-by-day chronology of events arranged by the Hebrew calendar. A cross reference to civil dates is provided. The time span covered is from Biblical times to the present. It includes a brief bibliography and index of personalities and events.

241 Edelheit, Abraham J. and Hershel Edelheit. *World in Turmoil: An Integrated Chronology of the Holocaust and World War II.* New York: Greenwood Press, 1991. 450p.

The authors provide the readers with a chronology of " political and diplomatic events affecting the world and Jewish history" from January 30, 1933 (Nazi Machtergreifung) until May 14, 1948 (the establishment of the State of Israel). The book includes an essay-"The world since 1948", a glossary, and a bibliography. Name, place, and subject indexes provide access to the data in the chronology.

242 Gribetz, Judah, Edward L. Greenstein and Regina Stein. *The Timetables of Jewish History: A Chronology of the Most Important People and Events in Jewish History.* New York: Simon & Schuster, 1993. 808p.

The Timetables of Jewish History offers a concise record of the figures of the most important events in the history of the Jewish people from the earliest times to the present. Its format displays entries chronologically, when read vertically and geographically, when read horizontally, thus allowing the reader to see important people, significant events ... in their three dimensional historical context." The chronology includes a glossary and an index.

243 Kantor, Mattis. *The Jewish Time Line Encyclopedia.* Northvale, NJ: J. Aronson, 1989. 362p.

This is a chronological digest of over 5700 years of Jewish history from the Biblical age to the present. Three different time lines are given: the first presents a broad, skeletal overview; the second indicates the major names and places; and the third, which makes up the body of the book, is more detailed. The encyclopedia includes charts, as well as an index of names and places.

244 Universitah ha-'Ivrit bi-Yerushalayim. Makhon le-Yahadut Zemanenu. Bibliographical Center. *Oral History of Contemporary Jewry: An Annotated Catalogue.* New York: Garland Publishing, 1990. 245p.

This catalog contains a descriptive listing of the interviews recorded from 1979 through 1987 by the Oral History Division. The entries are arranged in the following five categories: A. Jewish communities, e. g., the Latin American Jewish communities, England, Germany, Tunisia. B. World War II—The Holocaust, resistance and rescue. C. The Yishuv and the State of Israel. D. Youth Movements. E. Culture and Education. The interviews are arranged by project number within each chapter. A brief description of the project and the list of interviewers are given at the beginning of each project. Interviews are arranged numerically within each project. The following elements are contained in each interview description: item no., project no., interview no., interviewee, abstract, language, length of transcription, year interview was held. The inclusion of interviewer, interviewee and subject indices facilitates the use of this catalog. Interviews recorded by the Oral History Division from 1963 to 1979 are listed in its *Catalogue*. no. 1-5 (Jerusalem: 1963-79). Current materials may be accessed through ALEPH (Israel library network).

B. INDIVIDUAL COUNTRIES (ARRANGED WITHIN CONTINENTS)

AFRICA AND ARAB LANDS

For materials pertaining to Jews in South Africa and Rhodesia see this chapter, under Great Britain. See also entries 852 and 855.

SOURCEBOOKS

245 Stillman, Norman A. *The Jews of Arab Lands: A History and Source Book.* Philadelphia: Jewish Publication Society, 1979. 473p.

This work is divided into two parts: Part I surveys Jewish social history in the traditional Arab world from the rise of Islam to the last quarter of the nineteenth century Part II contains a collection of documents (in English translation) that relate to the chapters in Part I. The source book includes a bibliography and an index.

246 —. *The Jews of Arab Lands in Modern Times.* Philadelphia: Jewish Publication Society, 1991. 604p.

This work is divided into two parts: Part I surveys Jewish social history in the arab world from the beginning of the nineteenth century until 1967. Part II. contains a collection of documents (mostly in English translation) that relate to the chapters in Part I. The source book includes a bibliography and an index.

247 Attal, Robert. *Yadahut Tsefon Afrikah.* Jerusalem: Ben-Zvi Institute, 1973. 248p.

This work is a bibliography of books, articles and chapters from books pertaining to all aspects of the history and culture of the Jewish communities in North Africa. The 5,741 items are alphabetical by author within the following sections: A. North Africa B. Libya C. Tunisia D. Algeria E. Morocco. The bibliography is not annotated. It includes place, name, and subject indexes in Hebrew and French.

248 —. "Yehude ha-Mizrah u-Tsefon Afrikah: Bibliografyah Mu'eret, 1974-1976" *Sefunot* 1 (16) (1979): 401-495.

This annotated bibliography lists scholarly and popular materials published from 1974-1976 pertaining to the history of Oriental and North African Jewry from the 15th century to the present. The more than 450 items are listed in two categories: A. Topical (General Materials) B. Geographic. The author includes in this category materials pertaining to Jewish communities in Europe, e. g., Spain, Portugal, the Balkan States, Turkey, North Africa, and Asia. Materials pertaining to the Karaite community are also included.

249 —. *Yehude ha-Mizrah u-Tsefon Afrikah: Bibliografyah Mu'eret (1977-1979).* Jerusalem: Ben-Zvi Institute, 1986. 161p.

This volume continues and supplements the author's "Yehude ha-Mizrah u-Tsefon Afrikah: Bibliografyah Mu'eret (1974-1976)." It lists materials published from 1977 to 1979. The author has added to the geographic section the Sephardic Jewish communities in England, Holland and Romania. Indexes of authors, places and subjects in both Hebrew and Latin characters simplify the use of the bibliography.

250 Stillman, Norman A. "Jews of the Islamic World." *Modern Judaism* 10 (1990): 367-378.

Stillman reviews the scholarly literature that has been written about the Jews of "Islamicate" Jewish communities in North Africa and elsewhere. He notes major desiderata for future research. The essay includes bibliographic notes.

251 *Yehude Asyah ve-Afrikah ba-Mizrah ha-Tikhon, 1860-1971.* Edited by Hayyim J. Cohen and Zvi Yehuda. Jerusalem: Division for the Study of Asian and African Jewry, Institute of Contemporary Jewry, Hebrew University of Jerusalem and Ben-Zvi Institute, 1971. 431 p.

This is an annotated bibliography of books, pamphlets and articles in periodicals and newspapers, covering the years 1860-1971. The bibliography is arranged by subject in two main divisions: A. Jewish Communities of the Muslim Middle East and B. Jews of Asia and Africa in Palestine / Israel. Author and place name indexes are included.

ETHIOPIA

252 Kaplan, Steven and Shoshanah Ben-Dor. *Yehude Etyopiyah:*

Bibliyografyah Mu'eret. Jerusalem: Ben-Zvi Institute, 1988. 163 p.
The authors of this comprehensive bibliography list and describe 1,461
books and articles pertaining to Ethiopian Jewry. The bibliography incorporates the material listed in Aaron Zeev Aescoly's *ha-Falashim; Bibliografyah*
(Jerusalem, 1937) and Wolf Leslau's "A Supplementary Falasha Bibliography" *Studies in Bibliography and Booklore* 3 (1957): 9-27. Four indices have
been provided to facilitate access to the bibliography: A. Authors. B. Co-
Authors. C. Subjects. D. Travellers References.

YEMEN

253 Ratzaby, Yehuda. *Heker Yahadut Teman*. Jerusalem: Jewish Nationl and
University Library Press, 1976- .
This is a series of classified annotated bibliographies pertaining to all
aspects of the history and culture of Yemenite Jewry. Each cumulation
includes an index of authors and titles in Hebrew characters and of authors
and titles in Latin characters. Volume one was issued as a supplement to
Kiryat Sefer 50 (1974/75), and includes publications for the years 1935-1975.
Volume 2 is in *Kiryat Sefer* 56 (1981): 497-528, and includes publications for
the years 1976-1981, as well as supplementary material for the years 1935-
1975. Volume 3 was reprinted by the Jewish National University Library in
1988/89 from *Kiryat Sefer* 62(1988/89). It includes publications for the years
1982-1987, as well as supplementary materials for the years 1935-1981.

254 Tovi, Yosef. *Yahadut Teman*. Jerusalem: Merkaz Zalman Shazar, 1975.
130p.

This selective bibliography lists c. 825 articles, chapters from books, and
monographs about Yemenite Jewry. The material is arranged in the following four broad categories and further subdivided: A. General works B. The
Jews of Yemen C. The Jews of Yemen in Erets Yisrael D. Spiritual and
cultural creativity. The bibliography includes an index of authors in
Hebrew characters and an index of authors in Latin characters.

NORTH AMERICA

DIRECTORIES

See also this chapter, under United States for related materials.

EDUCATIONAL INSTITUTIONS

255 *Directory of Day Schools in the United States and Canada*. Brooklyn, NY:
Torah Umesorah Publications, 1992. 45p.
This directory contains an extensive listing by state of yeshiva day schools
and high schools in the United States and Canada. Each entry includes the
name of the school, address, phone number, administrative personnel,
grades, language of instruction and date of founding. A list of schools for
Special Education is included.

256 Goldberg, Lee and Lana Goldberg. *The Jewish Student's Guide to American Colleges.* New York: Shapolsky Publishers, 1989. 221p.

This alphabetically arranged directory is designed to provide guidance to college-bound Jewish students and their parents in choosing an appropriate school. It provides detailed information about 93 public and private colleges and universities in the United States and Canada, including the religious, social and cultural activities at each of the institutions listed. The guide also provides information about colleges in Israel.

257 *Jewish Education Directory: Schools and Agencies in the United States and Canada.* 7th ed. New York: Jewish Educational Service of North America, 1984. 50p.

This directory provides the names, addresses, and telephone numbers of national Jewish educational agencies, local central educational agencies, accredited teacher-training schools, and Jewish schools. It also includes a list of public high schools in the United States that offer Hebrew language courses. JESNA is no longer publishing this directory, but is maintaining current data in a database.

258 *Jewish Studies Courses at American and Canadian Universities: A Catalog.* Prepared by Elizabeth Vernon. Edited by Charles Berlin. Cambridge, MA: Association for Jewish Studies, 1992. 210p.

This catalog lists courses in Jewish studies offered at 410 institutions of higher learning in the United States and Canada. Courses at Jewish institutions of higher learning are not listed. However, the reader is referred to the catalogs of these institutions. The arrangement is geographic by state, and within each state institutions are listed alphabetically. This directory includes a list of 104 endowed academic positions in Jewish Studies in non-Jewish colleges and universities in the United States and Canada.

JEWISH ORGANIZATIONS

259 *The Encyclopedia of Jewish Institutions: United States and Canada.* Oded Rosen, editor. Tel Aviv: Masadot Publications, 1983. 501p.

This is a reference guide to synagogues, community centers, service agencies, libraries and museums, fraternal organizations, hospitals and nursing homes, and other Jewish organizations throughout the United States and Canada. The entries contain information on the institution's affiliation, accreditation, goals, services, activities, programs, names of current officers and staff, history, and full address and telephone number. The entries are alphabetized by state or province, then by local community and by name of institution. An alphabetical index to institutions is included at the end of the book.

260 *The 1987-88 Jewish Almanac.* Compiled and edited by Ivan T. Tilem. New York: Pacific Press, 1987. 516, 166p.

Part two, the *Yellow Pages*, is a directory listing 17,000 Jewish communal organizations and commercial establishments in the United States and Canada. A helpful alphabetical table of contents to the directory is provided which lists the headings —from advertising agencies to Zionist organizations.

261 *American-Jewish Media Directory.* Editor Ray Kestenbaum. Rego Park, NY: R.K. Associates, 1989. 204p.

This directory was written for the individual who wishes to put together an effective public relations campaign. It is divided into two sections: A. Print —which includes detailed information about the Jewish press, with special sections on the Jewish press of metropolitan New York, Los Angeles, and Washington,D. C., the Jewish student press, national Jewish publications, and Jewish news services. B. Media—which includes detailed information about 200 radio, broadcast, and cable TV programs in the United States and Canada.

MUSEUMS

262 Frazier, Nancy. *Jewish Museums of North America: A Guide to Collections, Artifacts and Memorabilia.* New York: Wiley, 1992. 242p.

This is a detailed description of over 100 collections of Jewish art, artifacts and memorabilia housed in such institutions as museums, historical societies and libraries. The directory is arranged by state. It includes a glossary and bibliography, and is indexed.

OVERVIEWS

263 *The Jews of North America.* Edited and Introduced by Moses Rischin. Detroit: Wayne State, 1987. 279p.

This book contains essays initially delivered at an international conference convened in 1983 by the Multicultural History Society of Ontario. It is divided into four parts: A. Modern Migration, i. e., from the 1880's to 1950. B. Continuity and Tradition, containing essays which examine how Jews in North America maintained their tradition, community and culture. C. The Fathers of Jewish Ethnic Culture, containing essays by Fred Matthews on the sociologist Louis Wirth; Robert M. Seltzer, on the Jewish historian Simon Dubnow; and William Toll on the Zionist intellectual Horace Kallen. D. Jews, Community and World Jewry, containing essays which discuss Canadian Zionism, Jewish philanthropy in the United States, the decline of small town Jewish communities, anti-Semitism in Canada, and the Canadian poet A. M. Klein. Each section is introduced by brief perceptive essays by Moses Rischin.

CANADA

See also this chapter, under Great Britain, North America and the United States for related materials.

ARCHIVAL RESOURCES

264 Tapper, Lawrence F. *Archival Sources for the Study of Canadian Jewry.* Ottawa: National Archives of Canada, 1987. 96, 102 p.

This guide, in English and French, contains a descriptive list of the collections of papers of Canadian Jews and of Canadian Jewish organizations that are found in the manuscript division at the National Archives. A

biographical sketch is provided for each of the individuals included in the
guide. In addition, a historical sketch is provided for each institution listed.

BIBLIOGRAPHY

265 Cukier, Golda. *Canadian Jewish Periodicals: A Revised Listing*. Montreal:
Collection of Jewish Canadiana, Jewish Public Library, 1978. 38 *l.*
> This list of Canadian Jewish periodicals is arranged by city of publication.
> Periodicals in Hebrew characters precede those in Latin characters. The
> following information is provided for each title, when available: A. Starting
> and closing date. B. Frequency. C. Purpose. Both Hebrew and Latin title
> indexes are included.

266 Davies, Raymond Arthur. *Printed Jewish Canadiana, 1685-1900*.
Montreal: L. Davies, 1955. 56p.
> "A tentative checklist, of books pamphlets, pictures, magazines, and
> newspaper articles ... written by or relating to Jews of Canada." The check
> list is arranged by author. Not indexed.

267 *Les Juifs du Québec: Bibliographie Rétrospective annotée, David Rome,
Judith Nefsky, Paul Obermeier*. Québec: Institut Québécois De Recherche
sur la Culture, 1981. 317p.
> This annotated bibliography lists 1,646 articles, literary works, films, etc.
> pertaining to all aspects of Jewish life in Quebec. The bibliography is
> divided into four sections: A. 1759-1880 B. 1880-1915 C. 1915-1945 D. 1945-
> 1981. Each section is further subdivided by topics, e. g., culture, society,
> education, immigration, Zionism, Christian-Jewish relations, Canadian-
> Jewish relations, the Holocaust, etc. It includes a name index.

268 Rome, David. *A Selected Bibliography of Jewish Canadiana*. Montreal:
Canadian Jewish Congress, 1959. 1v.

> This bibliography, arranged alphabetically by author, lists books and
> articles pertaining to such topics as Canadian Jewish history, institutions,
> religion, sociology, Jewish education, literature, etc. The entries are not
> annotated, and the bibliography lacks an index.

BIOGRAPHICAL DICTIONARIES

269 *Canadian Jewish Women of Today: Who's Who of Canadian Jewish Women*.
Downsview, Ont., J. E. S. L. Educational Projects, 1983. 142p.
> This work is divided into three parts: A. Two introductory essays, "The
> Role of Canadian Jewish Women in Historical Perspective," by Paula
> Draper, and "The Changing Role of Canadian Jewish Women", by Yaêl
> Gordon-Brym. B. Biographical sketches of about 300 prominent Canadian
> Jewish women. C. A listing of the biographees by professional field of their
> choice.

270 *Canadian Jewry Today: Who's Who in Canadian Jewry*. Edited by Edmond
Y. Lipsitz. Downsview, Ontario: J.E.S.L. Educational Projects, 1989.
198p.

This work is divided into three parts: A. Twelve essays by academicians about issues on "today's Jewish agenda" such as anti-Semitism in Canada, Jewish survival in small communities in Canada, and Jewish identity in a multicultural Canada. B. Biographical sketches of about 400 prominent Canadian Jewish men and women. C. "Who's What in Canadian Jewry", a listing of the biographees by professional field.

CANADIAN JEWISH LITERATURE

See also entry 349.

271 Fox, Chaim Leib. *Hundert Yor Yidishe un Hebraishe Literatur in Kanade.* Montreal: Kh. L. Fuks Bukh fond Komitet, 1980. 326p.

This bio-bibliographic lexicon lists over four hundred Canadian authors who wrote in Hebrew and Yiddish during the period beginning with 1880. A brief biographical sketch and a complete listing of works is given for each author. Sources are included in each entry.

272 Rome, David. *Jews in Canadian Literature: A Bibliography.* Montreal: The Canadian Jewish Congress and the Jewish Public Library, 1964. Rev. ed. 2v.

This is a bio-bibliographic dictionary of Canadian Jewish authors. The author evaluates each author's work and provides bibliographic citations. This work is supplemented by the author's *Recent Canadian Jewish Authors and la Langue Francaise* (Montreal: The Bronfman Collection of Jewish Canadiana at the Jewish Public Library, 1970). This bio-bibliographical dictionary lists an additional 42 Canadian Jewish authors who published their work in book form since 1964. The supplement, "La Langue Francaise," provides information about Jewish authors who have contributed to French Canadian letters.

HISTORICAL OVERVIEWS

273 Rosenberg, S. *The Jewish Community in Canada.* Toronto: McClelland & Stewart, 1970-71. 2v.

This is an illustrated history of the Canadian Jewish community from its beginning to the present. The author discusses the cultural growth and development of the Canadian Jewish community, as well as the contribution of Canadian Jews to Canadian literature, art and sciences. The study includes a glossary, bibliographic notes, a bibliography and an index.

274 Tulchinsky, Gerald. *Taking Root: the Origins of the Canadian Jewish Community.* Toronto, Ont.: Lester Publishing, 1992. 341p.

In this definitive history of the Canadian Jewish community from its beginning in the 1760's to the end of the First World War, Tulchinsky shows how the unique character of the Canadian Jewish experience reflects the political, economic, and social development of Canada. The study includes bibliographic references.

United States

Educational Institutions

275 *The Hillel Guide to Jewish Life on Campus: A Directory of Resources for Jewish College Students 1991/1992.* Washington, DC: B'nai B'rith Hillel Foundations, 1990. 129p.

This directory provides information pertaining to Jewish life at 453 institutions of higher learning in the United States and abroad (including Israel) that are serviced by Hillel. Information may be found on such topics as Jewish enrollment, Jewish studies courses and programs, facilities for kosher meals, religious services, social and cultural activities, housing, etc. The names of contact persons on each campus are given. The directory also lists other national Jewish organizations which provide programs for college students, and includes a ten year Jewish calendar.

Foundations

276 *Foundation Guide for Religious Grant Seekers.* Kerry A. Robinson, ed. 4th ed. Atlanta: Scholars Press, 1992. 287p.

This is a general listing of foundations with a history of religious grant-making. Of particular interest is the information about Jewish foundations. The *Guide* is arranged by state, and provides the following information about each foundation: name, address, telephone number, contact person, geographic giving pattern, and special interests. It also includes information on the grant-seeking process, facts about religious philanthropy, building constituency support, etc.

General

277 Rockland, Mae Schafter. *The New Jewish Yellow Pages: A Directory of Goods and Services.* Englewood, NJ: SBS Publishing, 1980. 271p.

This work lists hundreds of individuals, businesses, and agencies throughout the the United States, giving complete information about how to obtain their products and services. The *Directory* is divided into the following sections: A. Creating—calligraphy, pictures, folk art, etc. B. Learning—books, courses, Holocaust, media, museums, periodicals, programs, teaching aids C. Buying—antiques, art, gifts, etc.; Playing—camping, music, theater, games, travel, etc. D. Observing —charity, holidays and ceremonies, life cycle, mitzvot. The *Yellow Pages* includes more than 300 illustrations and an index.

278 *Directory of Jewish Federations, Welfare Funds and Community Councils.* New York: Council of Jewish Federations, 1986- .

This is an annual listing of the local central agencies of Jewish federations responsible for fundraising, allocations, distribution of funds, and coordination of local social services in the United States. The directory is arranged alphabetically by state, and then city. There are also entries for: Canada,

Australia, Europe, Latin America and South Africa. Each entry gives address, telephone number, executive director and president.

JEWISH ORGANIZATIONS

279 *American Jewish Organizations Directory.* 12th ed. New York: Frenkel Mailing Service (75 Montgomery St., New York, NY 10022), 1987. 231p.

This is a directory of synagogues, Jewish organizations and Jewish schools. The directory is arranged alphabetically by state and by city within each state. The institutions are listed under each city in the following order: A. Synagogues B. Jewish organizations C. Jewish schools. The only exception is Brooklyn, N.Y., for which Jewish organizations are listed in alphabetical order, and synagogues and schools are listed in zip-code order. Each entry gives the address, telephone number and names of each institution's officials.

280 *American Jewish Organizations with Offices in Israel: A Directory.* New York: Institute on American Jewish-Israel Relations. American Jewish Committee, 1987. 27p.

This is a listing of thirty-two American Jewish organizations that maintain offices in Israel. The activities of each organization are described in a brief paragraph, and its address and telephone number in the United States and Israel are given.

YEARBOOKS

281 *The American Jewish Yearbook.* New York: American Jewish Committee, 1899- .

The *Yearbook* is arranged in three parts: A. Essays about contemporary issues of concern to the Jewish community. B. An annual survey of world Jewish activity country by country, with emphasis on the United States. C. Directories, including a list of national Jewish organizations in the United States and Canada, a list of Jewish periodicals published in the United States and Canada, necrology, etc. Indexed.

282 —. *Index* to Volumes 1-50, 1899-1949, prepared by Elfrida C. Solis-Cohen. New York: Ktav, 1967.

283 *Jewish Book Annual.* New York: Jewish Book Council, 1942- .

This annual contains essays on literary topics, as well as annual listings of books published in the following areas: A. American Jewish Non-Fiction B. American Jewish Fiction C. Jewish Juvenile Books D. Hebrew Literature in America E. Yiddish Books F. Anglo-Jewish Books F. Selected Books on Judaica From Israel. Volume 50 (1992) includes a cumulative index for volumes 1-50.

HISTORICAL OVERVIEWS

284 *The Jewish People in America.* Henry L. Feingold, General Editor. Baltimore, MD.: Johns Hopkins University Press, 1992. 5v.

This series, sponsored by the American Jewish Historical Society, "offers a historical synthesis at once comprehensible to the intelligent lay leader and useful to the professional historian. Each of the volumes integrates common themes: the origins of Jewish immigrants, their experience of settling in America, their economic and social life, their religious and educational efforts, their political involvement and the change the American Jewish community experienced over time." Volume I, "A Time for Planting—The First Migration, 1654-1820," is by Eli Faber. Volume II, " A Time for Gathering—The Second Migration, 1820-1880, is by Hasia R. Diner. Volume III, " A Time for Building —The Third Migration, 1880-1920," is by Gerald Sorin. Volume IV. "A Time for Searching—Entering the Mainstream, 1920-1945," is by Henry Feingold. Volume 5, " A Time for Healing —American Jewry Since World War II, is by Edward Shapiro. The "Bibliographical Essay" in each volume enables the reader to further pursue the study of topics of interest. The volumes contain many illustrations and are indexed. ▌▌

For single volume historical overviews see such works as: *Zion in America*, by Henry L. Feingold (New York: Hippocrene Press, 1974. 357p.) and *Haven and Home: A History of the Jews in America*, by Abraham J. Karp. (New York: Schocken, 1986. 40lp.)

ARCHIVAL RESOURCES

285   American Jewish Archives. *Manuscript Catalog of the American Jewish Archives.* Boston, MA: G. K. Hall, 1971. 4v.

286   —. *First Supplement.* Boston, MA: G. K. Hall, 1978. 1v.

287   —. *Second Supplement.* Boston, MA: G. K. Hall, 1991. Microfiche.
This catalog provides access to the extensive manuscript collection housed at the American Jewish Archives. All items included are cataloged by author, title, geographic provenance and content, with numerous cross references to help researchers.

288   American Jewish Periodical Center. *Jewish Newspapers and Periodicals on Microfilm.* Cincinnati, OH: American Jewish Periodical Center, 1984. 158p.
The American Jewish Periodical Center, housed on the Campus of Hebrew Union College in Cincinnati, has set out to microfilm all American Jewish serials to 1925 and selected periodicals after that date. This, the third catalog issued by the Center, lists the American Jewish newspapers and periodicals on microfilm in its collection. It supersedes the first two catalogs (1957, 1960) issued by the Center. The catalog is arranged alphabetically by state and the titles are listed alphabetically by language group within the city of publication.

289   Clasper, James W. and M. Carolyn Dallenbach. *Guide to the Holdings of the American Jewish Archives.* Cincinnati, OH: American Jewish Archives, 1979. 211p.
This book provides a guide to the collections in the American Jewish Archives to June 1987. The *Guide* is divided into four sections: A. Manuscript Collections. In this section the authors list and briefly describe the collections for which the Archives houses the original copy (in paper or microfilm). The materials are arranged within three groups: a. Personal

papers b. Local organizations' records c. National organizations' records. B. Microfilms from Other repositories C. Theses, Dissertations, and Essays D. Special Files, e. g., correspondence, genealogies, wills, etc. These files are listed in the appendices. The index to this guide provides a cross-reference to all individuals, organizations, and subjects that are contained in all sections and appendices of the *Guide.*

290 Cleveland Jewish Archives. *A Guide to Jewish History Sources in the History Library of the Western Reserve Historical Society.* Cleveland: Western Reserve Historical Society, 1983. 92p.
This is a detailed guide to the manuscript collection, and photographic and printed material relating primarily to the history of the Jewish community in Cleveland.

291 Kohn, Gary J. *The Jewish Experience: A Guide to Manuscript Sources in the Library of Congress.* Cincinnati: American Jewish Archives, 1986. 166p.
This guide to the materials housed in the Manuscript Division of the Library of Congress pertaining to the study of Jewish history, is divided into three independent parts: A. Collections Section—"composed of entries of collection titles within the Manuscript Division of Jewish individuals or organizations" B. Individual and Corporate Section—"an index of prominent Jewish individuals and corporate entries represented by materials scattered throughout various collections in the Division's custody" C. Subject Section—a listing by broad subject of materials in the Manuscript Division pertaining to various aspects of Jewish history. The guide is indexed.

292 Rafael, Ruth Kelson. *The Western Jewish History Center: Guide to Archival and Oral History.* Berkeley, CA: Western Jewish Historical Center, Judah L. Magnes Memorial Museum, 1987. 207p.
This is a definitive, illustrated catalog of the archival and oral history collections of the Western Jewish History Center, the holder of the most significant collection on Jews of the Western United States. The guide lists 300 archival collections and 95 oral histories. The descriptive annotation for each entry includes historical or biographical background, a general description of contents, and detailed notes on items of special research interest. A glossary and name and subject indexes are appended.

ORAL HISTORY CATALOGS

See also entry 244.

293 American Jewish Committee. *Catalogue of Memoirs, William E. Wiener Oral History Library.* New York: American Jewish Committee, 1983-1985. 2v.
This is a descriptive catalog of part of the oral history catalog housed in the William E. Wiener Oral History Library of the American Jewish Committee. The catalog is divided into two sections: A. General Biography Collection B. Special Collections Arranged in Major Themes, e. g., American Jewish women of achievement, American Jews in Israel, Jews in sports, etc. In the first section individual American Jews "who shaped the society in which they live" are listed. In the second section individuals who are associated with a particular theme are listed by theme. The following

information is provided for each of the oral histories: A. The name of the interviewee B. Date of birth C. Occupation D. Synopsis of the interview E. Name of the interviewer F. Number of pages of the transcript G. Restrictions, if any. Volume 2 includes a cumulative index to both volumes.

294 *American Jewish Memoirs: Oral Documentation.* Edited by Geoffrey Wigoder. Jerusalem: Oral History Division, The Institute of Contemporary Jewry, The Hebrew University of Jerusalem, 1980. 88p.

> This booklet, issued on the occasion of the twentieth anniversary of the Oral History division, contains selected excerpts from interviews relating to Jewish history in the United States. The following are a few of the excerpts that are included: The New York Kehillah—Mordecai Kaplan; Aspects of American Zionist History —Robert Szold; A Jewish Chaplain in Dachau—Abraham J. Klausner.

BIBLIOGRAPHY

GENERAL

See also entry 884.

295 "American Jewish Studies: A Periodic Report of the Status of the Field." Compiled by Marc Lee Raphael. *American Jewish History* 68- . (1978/79-).

> The surveys that appear periodically may include the following: A. Conference calendar B. American Jewish studies courses, etc. C. Recent dissertations, etc. D. Dissertations in progress.

296 Brickman, William W. *The Jewish Community in America: An Annotated and Classified Bibliographic Guide.* New York: B. Franklin, 1977. 396p.

> This is a descriptive and critically annotated bibliography of items which shed light on the Jewish experience in America from the colonial period to the present. Among the topics included in the bibliography are: family life, society, religion, economics, industry, politics, education, literature, culture and foreign relations. Reprints of various documents and articles are to be found in the appendices.

297 Elazar, Daniel J. "Jewish Community Studies: A Selected Bibliography." in his *Community & Polity,* 394-399. Philadelphia: Jewish Publication Society, 1976.

> This is a selective list of current literature about local histories and demographic surveys. The list is arranged alphabetically by state and subdivided within each state by community.

298 Glanz, Rudolf. *The German Jews in America: An Annotated Bibliography Including Books, Pamphlets, and Articles of Special Interest.* Cincinnati: Hebrew Union College Press, 1969. 192p.

> This annotated bibliography covers the main period of German immigration, 1820-1880, and lists 2,527 relevant items. The following are among the major themes which are included in the bibliography: A. Immigration and acculturation to general American life B. Independent life as a Jewish group C. Assessments of the group by others, especially in comparison

with the achievement of other immigrant groups. It also references biographies of German Jews and is indexed.

299 Gurock, Jeffry. *American Jewish History: A Bibliographical Guide*. New York: Anti-Defamation League, 1983. 195p.
Gurock divides his bibliographic guide into two parts. The first part —The State of the field—discusses and evaluates books and articles which deal with the major problems, issues, and personalities of American Jewish history from the Colonial era to the present, as well as special topics, e. g., American Zionism, anti-Semitism, and American Jewish women's history. He also discusses and evaluates introductory and reference works. The second part —future directions —includes suggestions for further research, bibliographic notes, and a bibliography of the more than 800 books and articles which were discussed in the essay. The *Guide* includes author and title indexes.

300 Heilman, Samuel C. "The Sociology of American Jewry: The Last Ten Years." *Annual Review of Sociology*. 8 (1982): 135-160.
This bibliographic essay covers studies written during the past ten years about the American Jewish community from a sociological perspective. General analyses, as well as studies pertaining to specific topics, e. g., Jewish politics and social movements, Jewish identity and identification, are included in the survey.

301 *Jewish American Voluntary Organizations*. Edited by Michael N. Dobkowski. Westport, CT: Greenwood Press, 1986. 700p.
This source book contains historical sketches of 120 national and local voluntary social service, philanthropic, religious, political, cultural, Zionist, and social agencies and organizations that have played a major role in American Jewish life. The book is arranged alphabetically by the name of the organization. The authors of each article cite sources in which the user may find additional information about the organization. The appendices "include several essays on major issues of Jewish American organizational life; a chronology that juxtaposes the founding dates of the organizations with significant events in American Jewish history; organizational genealogies that list agency name changes and mergers; a listing of the organizations by category such as social, cultural and religious." Additional access is provided through a general index and cross references.

302 *Jewish Communal Services in the United States, 1960-1970: A Selected Bibliography*. Edited by Norman Linzer. New York: Commission on Synagogue Relations, Federation of Jewish Philanthropies, 1972. 296p.
This bibliography includes many subjects which are basic to an understanding of American Jewish life, e. g., the Jewish aged; Jewish education; Jewish family; intergroup relations; Israel and the American Jew; the Jewish component in Jewish communal service; the Rabbi, the Synagogue and the community; Jewish vocational services; Jewish youth. The section on Jewish youth includes materials on Jewish college students, Jewish youth organizations and publications of Jewish college youth. The bibliography is limited to the decade 1960-1970. The introduction by the editor " presents an overview of the range covered by each subject, and information about the researchers precedes the literary references."

303 *Jewish Immigrants of the Nazi Period in the USA*. Edited by Herbert A. Strauss. New York: K. G. Saur, 1978- .

A multi-volume collection of both primary and secondary materials pertaining to the immigration, resettlement, and acculturation in the United States of Jews from Germany who were uprooted by Nazi persecution. The following volumes have been published to-date: Volume 1. Archival Resources, compiled by Steven W. Siegel Volume 2. Classified and Annotated Bibliography of Books and Articles on the Immigration and Acculturation of Jews from Europe to the United States since 1933, compiled by Henry Friedlander Volume 3 Part I. Guide to the Oral History Collection of the Research Foundation for Jewish Immigration, New York Volume 3 Part 2. Classified List of Articles Concerning Emigration in German Jewish Periodicals, January 30,1933 to November 9, 1938, Compiled by Daniel R. Schwarz and Daniel S. Niederland Volume 5. The Individual and Collective Experience of German-Jewish Immigrants, 1933-1945; An Oral History Record. Compiled by Dennis Rohrbaugh with Antje Schubert 6. Essays on the History, Persecution, and Emigration of German Jews in the U. S. A. Compiled by Herbert A. Strauss with Antje Schubert.

304 *"Judaica Americana." American Jewish Historical Quarterly* 50 (1960/61)- .

This is an annotated classified bibliography of monographic and periodical literature pertaining to all aspects of Jewish history and culture in the Americas. The bibliography lists materials received by the American Jewish Historical Society, in Waltham MA. It was compiled until 1992 by the Society's Librarian, Dr. Nathan Kaganoff.

305 Karkhanis, Sharad. *Jewish Heritage in America: An Annotated Bibliography*. New York: Garland, 1988, 456p.

"Intended for the use of students, scholars and general readers... this fully annotated bibliography includes 1,100 selected sources (323 books and 777 articles from 88 popular and scholarly journals dating from 1925 to 1987) and presents the whole panorama of the Jewish heritage in America, portraying the historic beginnings, social conditions, cultural life, the Holocaust years, anti-Semitism, intellectual and literary contributions, religious traditions, political activism, dilemmas of assimilation and identity, and relations with Christians and blacks." (Intro.) It includes author, title, and subject indexes.

306 Korros, Alexandra S. and Jonathan D. Sarna. *American Synagogue History: A Bibliography and State-of-the Field Survey*. New York: M. Wiener, 1989, 285p.

This guide lists over 1,100 American synagogue histories. The work has four sections: a comprehensive bibliography of American synagogues and community histories arranged by state; a select bibliography of secondary sources; community histories that include information on various synagogues; a bibliography of American synagogue architecture. It includes an index of authors.

307 Lifschutz, Ezekiel. *Bibliografye fun Amerikaner un Kanader Yidisher Zikhroynes*. New York: YIVO, 1970. 76p.

This work is an annotated bibliography of published autobiographies and memoirs of Americans and Canadians. The bibliography is divided into three sections: A. Yiddish memoirs and autobiographies B. Hebrew memoirs and biographies C. English memoirs and autobiographies. The date of birth of each author is given. In addition, Lifschutz notes if an author is an immigrant by placing an *I* next to the author's name. The year of the author's arrival and country of origin are also noted.

308 Monson, Rela Geffen. "Sociology of the American Jewish Community." *Modern Judaism* 11 (1991): 147-156.
In this essay Monson synthesizes and analyzes the studies that were written in the 1980's pertaining to the sociological study of American Jewry and its institutions. The essay includes bibliographic notes.

309 Rischin, Moses. *An Inventory of American Jewish History.* Cambridge, MA: Harvard University Press, 1954. 66p.
The author evaluates published material pertaining to American Jewish history. The footnotes contain bibliographic references and suggestions for further research.

310 Sarna, Jonathan D. and Janet Liss. *Yahadut Amerikah: Bibliyografyah Nivheret shel Pirsumim be-'Ivrit.* Jerusalem: Hebrew Union College Jewish Institute of Religion; Hebrew University. The Institute of Contemporary Jewry, 1991. 109p.
This is a selective bibliography of books and articles in Hebrew, mostly written in the past 50 years, pertaining to American Jewry. The bibliography is arranged alphabetically by author and includes a title index.

311 —. "The American Jewish Experience." In *The Schocken Guide to Jewish Books*, edited by Barry W. Holtz, 108-127. New York: Schocken, 1992.
In this bibliographic essay, the author discusses books that have been written about the history of the Jews in the United States and studies about specific topics, e. g., anti-Semitism, religious movements, Sephardim.

312 —. "American Jewish History." *Modern Judaism* 10 (1990): 343-365.
In this essay, Sarna reviews the major works that were written in American Jewish history in the 1980's. He highlights areas that need further study. The essay includes bibliographic notes.

313 Stern, Malcolm H. "American Reform Judaism: A Bibliography." *American Jewish Historical Quarterly* 63 (1973/74): 120-137.
The bibliography is included in an appendix to the author's article "Reforming of Reform Judaism—Past, Present, and Future. It lists materials pertaining to the following subjects: A. History B. Institutions C. Biography D. Sociological studies E. Principles and practices F. Periodicals G. Congregational histories.

314 Weisbach, Lee Shai. "Jewish Communities of the United States on the Eve of Mass Migration: Some Comments on Geography and Bibliography" *American Jewish History* 78 (1988/89): 79-108.
Following an introductory essay, the author lists published historical studies of Jewish communities with a population of at least one hundred individuals on the eve of East European migration (1870).

See also entries 813-15.

315 Tumin, Melvin M. *An Inventory and Appraisal of Research on American Anti-Semitism.* New York: Freedom Books, 1961. 185p.
"The primary purpose of this volume is to present a series of digest researches, theories, hypotheses about anti-Semitism in America. The secondary purpose is to try, in the statements that precede each section of digests, to state the major issues at stake and some of the applications that can be drawn from the material that is digested." The bulk of the material was published after 1930. The following are among the subjects that are discussed: A. Who are the anti-Semites B. Jewish traits C. The identifiability of Jews D. The nature and causes of anti-Semitism E.Theories and speculation on the causes of anti-Semitism.

CULTS

316 Porter, Jack Nusan. *Jews and the Cults: Bibliography/Resource Guide.* Fresh Meadows, NY: Biblio Press, 1981. 49p.
This annotated bibliography "guides readers to a variety of points of view on Jews and cults in both popular and professional journals."

DEMOGRAPHY

317 Cohn, John M. "Demographic Studies of Jewish Communities in the United States: A Bibliographic Introduction and Survey." *American Jewish Archives* 32 (April 1980): 35-51.
The bibliography consists of an annotated list of c. 80 items in which demographic data is of primary concern. The items were published " principally in the 50's and 60's". The bibliography is divided into two parts: A. "A selected listing of related ancillary writings which would interest readers of community surveys" B. Surveys.

318 Kosmin, Barry A. *Highlights of the CJF 1990 National Jewish Population Survey.* New York: Council of Jewish Federations, 1991. 39 p.
This pamphlet contains the highlights of the data gathered from 2,441 telephone interviews of members of households "containing at least one person identified as currently or previously Jewish." The data is arranged in the following broad categories: A. Demography B. Geography C. Jewish Identity. Numerous tables, charts, and maps are included., Issues relating to the sampling are discussed in a "Methodological Appendix."

319 Marcus, Jacob Rader. *To Count A People: American Jewish Population Data, 1585-1984.* Lanham, MD: University Press of America, 1990. 274p.
This is a collection of population statistics from a variety of sources. The data is arranged in three sections: A. State B. Local communities within each state C. United States. This work includes a geographic index.

320 Cline, Scott. "Jewish Ethnic Interaction: A Bibliographical Essay." *American Jewish History* 77 (1987/88): 135-154.
"A review of the literature treating Jewish interaction with other ethnic groups."

321 Davis, Lenwood G. *Black-Jewish Relations in the United States: A Selected Bibliography.* Westport, CT: Greenwood Press, 1984. 130p.
This work is a selective annotated bibliography listing major books and pamphlets, general works, dissertations and theses, as well as articles pertaining to Black-Jewish relations in the United States beginning with the year 1752 to the present. In the introduction, the compiler presents a historical overview that relates to the significant periods in this relationship and shows how Black-Jewish relationships have changed over the years. It includes an author index.

322 Levtow, Patricia. *Black-Jewish Relations in the U.S.* New York: American Jewish Committee, 1978. 26p.
This is one in a series of selected annotated bibliographies of books, pamphlets and articles pertaining to Black-Jewish relations published by the American Jewish committee. This pamphlet lists materials pertaining to Black-Jewish relations in the 70's. It includes an index of titles.

HOLOCAUST

See also Chapter 18.

323 Lipstadt, Deborah. "America and the Holocaust." *Modern Judaism* 10 (1990): 283-296.
Lipstadt reviews the major studies that have been written pertaining to such subjects as the rescue of Jews, American public opinion, the response of the American religious establishment, the reaction of American Jewry, the punishment of Nazi criminals, and remembrance. The essay includes bibliographic notes.

JEWISH CHRISTIANS

324 Pruter, Karl. *Jewish Christians in the United States: A Bibliography.* New York: Garland Publishing, 1987. 192p.
This is a bibliography of books, pamphlets, tracts, and periodicals published by various organizations that are currently engaged in Jewish evangelism, i.e. missionary efforts aimed at converting Jews to Christianity. Each organization is identified, and the literature that it has produced is listed. The remainder of the work provides the reader with an historical overview of the evangelical movement, which began in the 19th century. Publications pertaining to the historical development of the evangelical movement, materials in support of Jewish missions, as well as publications on Christian-Jewish relations, are also cited. The bibliography includes an author index.

325 *Contemporary Jewish Philanthropy in America.* Edited by Barry A. Kosmin and Paul Ritterband. Savage, MD: Rowman & Littlefield, 1991. 254p.
This survey includes fifteen essay by noted scholars in the following areas: A. Theory and background B. General philanthropy C. Special philanthropy D. Clients. Each essay includes a bibliography which enables the reader to pursue further research on the subject. In addition the collection also includes a general bibliography.

PUBLICATIONS

326 Rosenbach, Abraham S. W. *An American Jewish Bibliography Being a List of Books and Pamphlets by Jews or Relating to Them Printed in the United States from the Establishment of the Press in the Colonies Until 1850.* Baltimore: American Jewish Historical Society, 1926. 486p.
This standard work, used by scholars and bibliographers for citing early American imprints, was published as volume 30 of the *Publications* of the American Jewish Historical Society. It contains a detailed, chronologically arranged list of 691 books printed in the United States between 1640-1850 by Jews or relating to them. Rosenbach provides a full bibliographic description for each item cited, and notes the location of extant copies in public and private libraries. He also notes the first use of Hebrew type in each locality. Facsimiles of title pages from the works cited in the bibliography and a detailed index are included. The bibliography is supplemented by: Hebrew Union College—Jewish Institute of Religion Library. *Jewish Americana: A Catalogue of Books.* Cincinnati: American Jewish Archives, 1954; Wolf, Edwin. "Some Unrecorded American Judaica Printed Before 1851." In *Essays in American Jewish History to commemorate the Tenth Anniversary of the American Jewish Archives,* 187-245. Cincinnati, 1958; Kaganoff, Nathan M. "Supplement III: Judaica Americana Printed Before 1851." In *Studies in Jewish Bibliography, History, and Literature in Honor of I. Edward Kiev,* Edited by Charles Berlin, 177-209. New York, 1971. In addition, the following two bibliographies have been compiled: Levine, Allen E. *An American Jewish Bibliography: A List of Books and Pamphlets by Jews or Relating to them Printed in the United States from 1851-1875.* (Cincinnati: American Jewish Archives, 1959), which are in the possession of the Klau Library, and an unpublished preliminary compilation prepared by Leopold Naum Friedmann listing the holdings of the American Jewish Historical Society for the same period.

327 Singerman, Robert. *Judaica Americana: A Bibliography of Publications to 1900.* New York: Greenwood Press, 1990. 2v.
Singerman lists and provides full bibliographic descriptions for 6,500 books, pamphlets and serials published in the United States 1640-1900. In addition, he includes locations for all known copies of a work, and identifies each work with its listing in earlier Jewish, as well as, classic American reference works. Only a portion of the material in Rosenbach's *An American Jewish Bibliography* and the supplements to it (see above) have been included in this bibliography because Singerman chose to include, with few exceptions, only works dealing with American Jewish history or books of Jewish content. A "Union List of Nineteenth Century Jewish Serials Published in the United States" is included in an appendix. The Union List is sub-divided by language—English, French ,German, He-

brew, Yiddish. The detailed index provides access by author, title, broad subject area, place of publication (by state broken down by city), and individual publisher and printer.

328 Cogan, Sarah. *The Jews of Los Angeles: An Annotated Bibliography.* Berkeley, CA: Western Jewish History Center, Judah L. Magnes Museum, 1980. 237p.
This annotated bibliography lists general books and articles about all aspects of Jewish life in the city and county of Los angeles from the mid-nineteenth century through World War II. It includes a chapter "Works on the Motion Picture Industry," and is indexed.

329 —. *The Jews of San Francisco and the Greater Bay Area: An Annotated Bibliography.* Berkeley, CA: Western Jewish History Center, Judah L. Magnes Museum, 1973. 127p.
The author lists primary resources for the period 1849-1919, as well as popular and scholarly works pertaining to all aspects of Jewish life. Indexed.

330 —. *Pioneer Jews of the California Mother Lode, 1849-1880: An Annotated Bibliography.* Berkeley, CA: Western Jewish History Center, Judah L. Magnes Memorial Museum, 1968. 54p.
This is a bibliography of 183 primary and secondary sources.

331 Stern, Norton B. *California Jewish History: A Descriptive Bibliography, Over Five Hundred Fifty Works for the Period Gold Rush to Post World War I.* Glendale, CA: Arthur H. Clark, 1967. 175p.
This is an annotated bibliography of books, periodical articles, and unpublished works. It includes a listing of California Jewish newspapers in an appendix, and a name and subject index.

See also entries 858-64.

332 Marcus, Jacob Rader. *The American Jewish Woman, 1654-1980.* New York: Ktav, 1981. 231p.
The "Bibliographic Note" contains a bibliographic essay by the author about the sources and literature he employed in this study. He also lists additional materials for those students who wish to carry on research in the field.

333 *American Jewish Biographies.* Murray Polner, editor. New York: Facts on File, 1982. 493p.
This dictionary includes short biographies of over 400 prominent Jews "who have distinguished themselves either in American life or American

Jewish life." Many of the entries include suggestions for further reading. The dictionary also includes "A Selected Bibliography of American Jewish Life," and a general index.

334 Nadell, Pamela S. *Conservative Judaism in America: A Biographical Dictionary and Sourcebook.* New York: Greenwood Press, 1988. 409p.
This, the first in a series of three volumes on American Judaism (see *Reform Judaism* below), contains sketches of the lives of 130 leaders in the Conservative movement. Each biographical sketch evaluates the figure's contributions to the movement and includes a bibliography of major writings by and about the individual. The dictionary also includes essays on the Jewish Theological Seminary of America, The Rabbinical Seminary, and the United Synagogue of America. A listing of the executive officers (including the dates they held office) of the major Conservative and Reconstructionist institutions are included in the appendices. A glossary, a thematically arranged bibliography covering such topics as memoirs, autobiographies, biographies, collections of sermons, and synagogue histories, and a general index are also included.

335 *Reform Judaism in America: A Biographical Dictionary and Sourcebook.* Edited by Kerry M. Olitzky, Lance J. Sussman and Malcolm H. Stern. Westport, CT.: Greenwood Press, 1993. 343p.
This, the second in a series of three volumes on American Judaism (see Nadel above), contains sketches of the lives of 170 leaders in American Reform Judaism, from 1824 to 1976. Each biographical sketch evaluates the figure's contribution to the movement and includes a bibliography of major writings by and about the individual. The dictionary also includes essays on the Union of American Hebrew Congregations, Hebrew Union College—Jewish Institute of Religion and the Central Conference of American Rabbis. A listing of the executive officers (including the dates they held office) of the major institutions of the movement are included in the appendices. A thematically arranged bibliography covering such topics as memoirs, autobiographies, biographies, and a general index are also included.

336 Rosenbloom, Joseph R. *A Biographical Dictionary of Early American Jews: Colonial Times through 1800.* Lexington: University of Kentucky Press, 1960. 175p.
Every person identifiable as a Jew in America before 1800 is included in this dictionary. Each entry may include the following information, when known: birth and death dates, country of origin, date of arrival, parentage, and occupation. Each entry includes bibliographical sources.

337 Schwartz, B. *Sefer Artsot ha-Hayim.* Brooklyn, New York: The Author, 1992. 131p.
This bio-bibliographical dictionary is divided into two parts: A. Ma'arekhet ha-Gedolim—A biographical dictionary which lists "Orthodox Rabbis" who settled or worked in the Americas B. Ma'arekhet ha-Sefarim—A descriptive bibliography of Rabbinic works composed in the Americas. Many Rabbis whose works are listed in the second section are not listed in the first section. The focus of the work is on the United States. The book is valuable because it provides bio-bibliographical information about the Orthodox Rabbinate in the Americas and its literary creativity.

338 *Who's Who in American Jewry.* Los Angeles: Standard Who's Who, 1980-
To-date only the 1980 edition has been published. It is divided into two
sections: A. A biographical dictionary of over 6,000 prominent Jewish men
and women in the United States and Canada B. *The Directory of American
Jewish Institutions.* The directory lists approximately 10,000 Jewish organizations in four categories:A. Organizational B. Synagogues C. Educational
D. Youth groups. Each entry includes the name of the institution, regional
branch offices, address, zip code, telephone number, and in most cases, the
name and title of one or more executive officers. Listings in the *Directory* are
by State (Province), alphabetical by city, and alphabetical by name within
a city.

339 *Who's Who in American Jewry.* New York: The Jewish Biographical
Bureau, 1927-1938.
Editions in this series appeared in 1926, 1928, and 1938/39. This biographi-
cal dictionary remains useful for the period covered.

CHRONOLOGY

340 *The Jews in America, 1621-1970: A Chronology and Fact Book.* Irving J.
Sloan, compiler and editor. Dobbs Ferry, NY: Oceana Publications,
1971. 191p.
This sourcebook is divided into two sections: A The Jews in America—a
chronology covering the period from 1621-1970 B. "Selected Documents of
American Jewry." The appendices include: A. Estimated American Jewish
population statistics by state based on data from the U. S. Bureau of the
Census (1969) B. A selected and annotated bibliography C. An annotated
list of audio-visual materials on American Jewish life and history D. A list
of American Jewish civic organizations, providing for each the date of its
founding and location E. A list of American Jewish newspapers and
periodicals arranged by state. A name index is included to facilitate access.

ENCYCLOPEDIAS

341 *Jewish-American History and Culture: An Encyclopedia.* Edited by Jack
Fischel and Sanford Pinsker. New York: Garland, 1992. 710 p.
This illustrated *Encyclopedia* is a one volume comprehensive reference
work which contains authoritative signed articles. The articles survey the
entire range of American Jewish life and achievements, i. e., religious
institutions, communal organizations, secular activities, cultural contributions. They provide factual information, as well as, commentary and
analyses. Each entry in the *Encyclopedia* contains an up to date bibliography
for researching topics in greater depth. Cross references enable the user to
broaden or narrow an information search. An extensive general index
(name/subject) helps readers find a particular person, event, etc., even if it
is covered in an entry on another subject.

INDEXES (PERIODICAL LITERATURE)

See also entry 305.

342 Brunkow, Robert de V. *Religion and Society in North America: An
Annotated Bibliography.* Santa Barbara, CA: ABC-CLIO, 1983. 515p.

This bibliography "provides the scholar, the researcher, and student of religion with a convenient guide to the extensive range of periodical literature on the history of religion in the United States and Canada since the Seventeenth century." It deals more fully with the religious aspects of the Jewish experience in America than does the aforementioned work.

343 *The Jewish Experience in America: A Historical Bibliography.* Santa Barbara, CA: ABC-CLIO, 1983. 190p.

This bibliography "includes 827 article abstracts selected from more than 2,000 Journals in 42 languages, published in 90 countries. The abstracts, which cover journal literature from 1973 through 1979, were prepared by a worldwide network of scholars. Abstracts are arranged alphabetically by author. All non-English article titles have been translated into English, and all abstracts are written in English, thereby providing the student and scholar with access to scholarship from all over the world." A full subject index is also provided.

344 Marcus, Jacob Rader. *An Index to Scientific Articles of American Jewish History.* Cincinnati: American Jewish Archives, 1971. 240p.

Marcus has prepared an indispensable index to scholarly articles dealing with the life, culture and history of American Jews that were published in thirteen scholarly Jewish periodicals between 1892 and 1968. Each article is listed by author, title and subject. The following are among the periodicals that are indexed: *American Jewish Archives* (1-20,1948-1968), *American Jewish Historical Society Quarterly* (1-57, 1892-1968), *Historia Judaica* (1-23, 1938-1961), *Michigan Jewish History* (1-8 , 1960-1968), *The Record* (1-3, 1966-1968) *Rhode Island Jewish Historical Notes* (1-4, 1946-1965).

AMERICAN JEWISH LITERATURE

345 Berger, Alan L. "American Jewish Fiction." *Modern Judaism* 10 (1990): 221-241.

"This essay discusses literary portrayals of orthodoxy, the *Shoah,* and the Jewish theological Imagination. In addition the role of literary criticism is evaluated. The discussion concludes by suggesting directions that American Jewish Literature is likely to take in the decade of the nineties." The essay includes bibliographic notes.

346 Blackman, Murray. *A Guide to Jewish Themes in American Fiction, 1940-1980.* Metuchen, NJ: Scarecrow Press, 1981. 266p.

This *Guide* contains an annotated bibliography of all works of American fiction written from 1940-1980 that relate to "Jews and Judaism," and an alphabetically arranged thematic index (c. 300 subjects) to this material. Blackman prepared the thematic index as a tool to be used in adult Jewish education courses. He offers suggestions on the use of fiction in adult education programs and on applying the thematic index to Jewish programming. The *Guide* includes a title index.

347 Cronin, Gloria L., Blaine H. Hall, and Connie Lamb. *Jewish-American Fiction Writers: An Annotated Bibliography.* New York: Garland Publishing, 1991. 1,233p.

Charles Angoff, Mary Antin, Arthur A. Cohen, Howard Fast, Fannie Hurst, Meyer Levin, Cynthia Ozick, Leon Uris, and Anzia Yezierska are among the sixty-two "Jewish-American" authors of the nineteenth and twentieth centuries who are included in this dictionary of Jewish-American fiction. The entry for each author includes: A. Primary Sources, i. e., a listing of the authors, novels , collected works, short fiction in anthologies, and short fiction in periodicals B. Secondary Sources, i. e., an annotated list of books, articles and chapters, interviews, biographical sources, bibliographies and dissertations. The compilers have also listed articles and books on the subject of Jewish American fiction and fiction writers in a "General Sources " section at the beginning of the dictionary.

348 *Handbook of American-Jewish Literature: An Analytical Guide to Topics, Themes and Sources.* Lewis Fried, Editor-in-Chief. New York: Greenwood Press, 1988. 539p.

The *Handbook* contains a collection of essays by noted scholars about "the rise of American-Jewish letters, literature, theology, and cultural meditation from approximately 1880 to the present." It includes essays on such topics as women poets in Yiddish, American-Jewish poetry, American-Jewish drama, American-Jewish autobiography, the Holocaust and its historiography, and fiction of the Holocaust. The book's purpose is twofold: "to acquaint the general reader with the major subjects and themes of American-Jewish literature and to renew the scholar's familiarity with this material and its interpretation." Each essay includes a bibliography of sources, as well as (where necessary) a list of additional readings to guide the reader's study. In addition the work includes an overall bibliography and a general index.

349 Nadel, Ira Bruce. *Jewish Writers of North America.* Detroit: Gale Research, 1981. 493p.

This bibliography of Canadian and American Jewish authors is divided into the following four parts: A. General reference guides B. Poets C. Novelists and short-story writers D. Dramatists. The general reference section consists of an annotated bibliography of general reference materials, as well as materials on such subjects as Canadian and American literary history, American and Canadian literary criticism, and American and Canadian anthologies. The remaining sections include bio-bibliographies of 118 Canadian and American Jewish authors. The bio-bibliographies include works by and about the authors. The fourth section," Dramatists", also includes a general bibliography. In addition, a bibliography consisting of: A. Histories and criticism in English: American and Canadian Yiddish writing B. Anthologies of American and Canadian Yiddish literature in translation is included in an appendix. The author also includes a checklist of additional American and Canadian Jewish authors. The bibliography includes author, title, and subject indices.

350 *Twentieth-Century American-Jewish Fiction Writers.* Edited by Daniel Walden. Detroit: Gale Research, 1984. 367p.

This bio-bibliographical dictionary, volume 28 of the *Dictionary of Literary Biography*, contains essays on fifty-one authors "whose novels and short stories deal with or come out of their American-Jewish experience." Abraham Cahan, Ben Hecht, Harry Kemelman, Ludwig Lewisohn, Charles Reznikoff, and I. B. Singer are among the authors whose works are discussed. The birth and death date (when applicable), a list and discussion of the author's works, and bibliographical references are included in each entry. The location of the author's papers is also noted, if known.

LATIN AMERICA

See also this chapter, under Great Britain for materials pertaining to the West Indies.

BIBLIOGRAPHY

351 *Latin America Jewish Studies: An Annotated Guide to the Literature.* Compiled by Judith Laikin Elkin and Ana Lya Sater. New York: Greenwood Press, 1990. 239p.

> This is a classified and annotated guide to research on Latin American Jewish studies. Latin America covers the following regions: South America, Central America, the West Indies, the Caribbean area, and Middle America. The guide is divided into two parts: Part I list 773 monographs, dissertations and articles published from 1970 to 1986. Part II "lists, describes, and evaluates holdings of over 200 Latin American Jewish periodicals at the University of California, Los Angeles . . .; American Jewish Historical Society . . .; Judah L. Magnes Museum . . .; the Benson Library of the University of Texas at Austin; and the Price Library of Judaica at the University of Florida, Gainesville." There are author and title indexes to part I, and a subject index to part II.

352 *Oral Documents from Latin America.* Jerusalem: Hebrew University, Institute of Contemporary Jewry, Latin American Division, Oral History Division, 1987. 79p.

> This descriptive catalog of the Oral History Division's collection pertaining to Latin American Jewry provides information about such subjects as Jewish education in Latin America, Cuban Jewry, the history of the Jewish community in Argentina, and anti-Semitism in Argentina. The catalog includes a brief biographical sketch of each interviewee.

353 *Resources for Latin American Jewish Studies.* Judith Laikin Elkin, Editor. Ann Arbor, MI: LAJSA, 1984. 60p.

> This is a collection of expanded articles that were presented as papers at the first conference of Latin American Jewish Studies Association in 1982. This collection provides the researcher with needed bibliographic and archival tools to study Latin American Jewry. Included are: "Using Jewish Reference Sources for the Study of Latin American Jewry: A Bibliography," by Arnona Rudavsky; "United States Archival Resources for the Study of Jews in Latin America," by Thomas Niehaus and Maria Hernandez-Lehmann; "Disappearing Memories: the Loss of Jewish Records in Latin America," by Robert Levine; "U. S. Collections on Latin American Jews," compiled by Richard Woods and Arnona Rudavsky.

354 Sable, Martin. *Latin American Jewry: A Research Guide.* Cincinnati: Hebrew Union College Press, 1978. 633p.

> This is a topically arranged bibliography of scholarly and popular materials "covering almost all aspects of the impact of Jewry in and on Latin America and its individual nations, regions and places from 1492 to 1974." Included is a directory of general associations and organizations. It is indexed, but not annotated.

ARGENTINA

355 *Bibliografia Tematica Sobre Judaismo Argentino.* Buenos Aires: Centro de Documentacion e Informacion sobre Judaismo Argentino "Marc Turkow", 1984- .

This series of bibliographies provides access to materials pertaining to all aspects of Jewish life in Argentina. The following volumes have been published to-date: *Educacion Judia en la Argentina* (1984) lists articles in Spanish and Yiddish about various aspects of Jewish Education in Argentina; *Revistas Judeo Argentinas* (1984) lists articles in Spanish and Yiddish pertaining to all aspects of Jewish studies; *Antisemitismo en la Argentina, 1909-1929* (1985) lists articles in Spanish and Yiddish pertaining to anti-Semitism in Argentina; *El Movimiento Obrero Judio en la Argentina* (1987) lists articles in Spanish and Yiddish pertaining to the Jewish labor movement in Argentina.

BRAZIL

356 Wolff, Egon and Frieda Wolff. *Diccionário Biográfico.* Rio de Janeiro: E. F. Wolff, 1986- .

This dictionary contains biographical sketches of Jews and Marranos in Brazil. The entries include bibliographic references. The data for the entries are based on records of Jewish burial societies, marriage and birth records of communal organizations, records of the "visiting" Inquisition in Portugal from 1536 to 1773. Bibliographic sources are cited following each entry. The following seven volumes have been published to-date: 1. Judaizantes e judeus no Brazil, 1500-1808 2. Judeos no Brasil, século XIX 3. Testamentos e inventários 4. Processos de naturilzacão de israelitas século XIX 5. Judáismo e judeus na bibliografia em língua portugesa 6. Genealogìas judaìcas 7. Processos de Inquiscão de Lisboa referentes a persoas nescidas ou residentes no Brasil e outros estudos.

ASIA

See also entry 248.

357 Attal, Robert. "Yehude ha-Mizrah u-Tsefon Afrikah: Bibliografyah Mu'eret, 1974-1976." *Sefunot* 1 (16) (1979): 401-495.

CHINA

358 Leventhal, Dennis A. *Sino-Judaic Studies: Whence and Whither: An Essay and Bibliography.* Hong Kong: Jewish Historical Society of Hong Kong, 1985. 99p

This work includes a brief essay on the history of the Jews in China. Of particular importance to the Judaica reference librarian is the bibliography of books and articles in both Western languages and Chinese on the Jewish experience in China.

359 Loewenthal, Rudolf. *The Sino-Judaic Bibliographies of Rudolf Loewenthal.* Edited by Michael Pollak. Cincinnati: Hebrew Union College Press in association with the Sino-Judaic Institute, Palo Alto, California, 1988. 398p.

This is a lithographic reprint of the following works by Rudolf Loewenthal published originally in Beijing, 1939-1946: A. The Jews in China: A Bibliography (1939) B. The Jews in China: An Annotated Bibliography (1940) C. The Early Jews in China: A Supplementary Bibliography (1946). Only the Introduction and Preface of the 1939 edition were reprinted, because the entries in this bibliography were incorporated into the 1940 edition of the bibliography.

INDIA

See also this chapter, under Great Britain for related materials.

360 Katz, Nathan. "An Annotated Bibliography About Indian Jews." *Kol Bina* 8, no. 1 (1991): 6-33.

This annotated bibliography is organized in the following sections: Indian Jewry in General II. Cochin Jews, III. The Bene Israel IV. Mughal Jews V. Baghdadi Jews VI. Ashkenazim in India VII. Tribal Jews. The author lists both primary works, as well as secondary works, such as accounts by Jewish travelers and works of modern scholarship.

AUSTRALIA / NEW ZEALAND

361 *Archive of Australian Judaica.* Sydney: Archive of Australian Judaica, 1985- .

This series of pamphlets provides detailed descriptions of the cataloged collections housed in the Archive. The latest pamphlet, compiled by Marianne Dacy, describes "Holdings To 1991/2."

362 Dacy, Marianne. *Periodical Publications from the Australian Jewish Community: A Union List.* Sydney: University of Sydney, Archive of Australian Judaica, 1986 160p.

Dacy provides full bibliographic descriptions for over 300 Jewish periodicals, as well as over 100 organizational annual reports and yearbooks that are published in Australia and New Zealand. She notes the content of each item and indicates where these periodicals can be found. Titles are listed alphabetically under each place of publication. The index to periodicals provides subject access to these materials. The bibliography includes an introductory essay which discusses the history of Australian Jewry and Australian Jewish periodicals.

363 Liberman, Serge. *Bibliography of Australian Judaica.* Sydney: Mandelbaum Trust and the University of Sydney Library, 1991. 257p.

This edition represents a "re-designed" and "re-edited" version of a work first published in 1987. It is a comprehensive classified bibliography of materials pertaining to all aspects of Jewish life in Australia and New

Zealand. Part One lists materials pertaining to such topics as: Creative Writing by Jews; Jews in Australian Literature; The Arts; and Education. Part Two includes such subjects as: Autobiography and Biography; Genealogy; History of the Jews in Australia; Politics, World War I and II, Zionism; Jewish Visitors to Australia. Part Three includes author and title indexes.

EUROPE

See also entries 149, 179, 248-49 and 507.

BIBLIOGRAPHY

364 Baker, Zachary M. *Bibliography of Eastern European Memorial (Yizkor) Books*. Edited by Steven W. Siegel. New York: Jewish Genealogical Society, 1992. 51p.

This listing of books commemorating Jewish communities of Eastern Europe that were destroyed during the Second World War, is arranged alphabetically by the name of the community. The name of the country in which the community was located in the interwar period is noted in parentheses following the community's name. The romanized form of the original Hebrew or Yiddish titles is given. Cross references direct the user to the form of the name of the community that is used. The call number and location of each Yizkor book in the following six Judaica libraries in New York City are noted: Bund Archive of the Jewish Labor Movement, Jewish Theological Seminary Library, New York Public Library. Jewish Division, Yeshiva University Library, YIVO, and Hebrew Union College. This edition supersedes the edition of this bibliography which was published in *Genealogical Resources in the New York Metropolitan Area*, edited by Estelle M. Guzik. (New York: Jewish Genealogical Society, 1989).

ENCYCLOPEDIAS

365 *Pinkas ha-Kehilot; Entsiklopedyah shel ha-Yishuvim ha-Yehudiyim le-min Hivasdam ve'ad le-Ahar Shoat Milhemet ha-'Olam ha-Sheniyah*. Jerusalem: Yad Vashem, 1972- .

This multi-volume encyclopedia provides the reader with an overview of the history of the Jews in various European communities, and their economic and cultural life. Each volume pertains to a country or to a specific region within a country and contains an essay about the Jews in the areas covered. The essays are followed by brief bibliographies. Each volume also includes charts, maps, photographs, a general bibliography, and place and name indexes. The following volumes have been published to-date: A. Germany: v.1 Bavaria (1972) v.2 Württemberg, Hohenzollern, Baden (1986) v.3 Hesse, Hesse-Nassau, Frankfort (1992) B. Hungary (1976) C. Latvia & Estonia (1988) D. Netherlands (1985) E. Poland: v.2 Eastern Galicia (1980) v.3 Western Galicia & Silesia (1984) v. 4 Warsaw & its Regions(1989) v.5 Volhynia & Polesie (1990) F. Rumania (2v., 1969-80).

366 *Church, State and the Jews in the Middle Ages.* Edited by Robert Chazan. New York: Behrman House, 1979 309p.

This reader contains primary source materials in English translation which shed light on Jewish life in the Middle Ages primarily in Spain, southern and northern France, Italy, England, Germany and Poland. The Catholic church was a dominant force in these countries. The documents are arranged into six chapters: A. Formal position of the Church B. The charters of the state C. Protection of the Jews D. Ecclesiastical limitations E. Missionizing among the Jews F. Governmental persecution. Suggestions for further reading, a list of sources, and an index are included at the end of the volume.

367 Marcus, Jacob Rader. *The Jew in the Medieval World.* New York: Hebrew Union College Press, 1990. 504p.

This reprint edition of a standard reader includes documents translated into English which portray aspects of Jewish social, religious and intellectual life in the medieval Christian world. The book is divided into three sections: A. The state and the Jew B. The Church and the Jew C. Jewry and the individual Jew. Marcus introduces each document and includes explanatory notes when necessary. Bibliographies generally follow each item. They refer the reader to standard textbooks and suggest additional literature and sources for the more advanced student. A bibliography of "References to Sources" and a general index are included at the end of the volume.

FRANCE

See also entry 508.

ARCHIVAL RESOURCES

368 *Documents Modernes sur les Juifs XVIe-XXe Siècles.* Under the Direction of Bernhard Blumenkranz, 1979- .

Volume one, *Dépôts Parisiens,* the first in a projected series of volumes, lists documents pertaining to the Jews in France for the period beginning with the sixteenth century until the twentieth century. The documents are housed in various archives in Paris, e. g., the Archives of the Archdiocese, the Ministry of Foreign Affairs, the National Archives, the Bibliotheque Nationale. They are listed under the institution at which they are housed. A general index is included in the volume.

369 Kohn, Roger S. *An Inventory to the French Jewish Communities Record Group, 1648-1946.* New York: Jewish Theological Seminary of America, 1991. 295 p.

This inventory provides access to a collection of documents concerning the French Jewish communities, which was acquired by the Jewish Theological Seminary of America from Zosa Szajkowski. The materials shed light on how the French Jewish community reacted to the French Revolution and Emancipation. They also provide information on major Jewish figures during the French Revolution and the First Empire, as well as on rabbinical and lay leaders in the last two centuries. The inventory includes an index of proper names and a chronological index. In addition cross references are provided to the following bibliographical works by Zosa Szajkowski: *Agricultural Credit and Napoleon's anti-Jewish Decrees* (New York, 1953); *Economic Status of the Jews in Alsace, Metz and Lorraine (1648-1789)* (New York, 1954); *Franco-Judaica: An Analytical Bibliography of Books, Pamphlets, Decrees, Briefs, and Other Printed Documents Pertaining to the Jews in France* (New York, 1962); *Jews and the French Revolutions of 1789, 1830 and 1848* (New York,1970).

BIBLIOGRAPHY

370 Blumenkranz, Bernhard. *Bibliographie des Juifs en France*. Paris: E. Privat, 1974. 349p.
This is a revised and corrected edition of the author's 1961 bibliography. The present edition is topically arranged, and consists of over 4,000 items, mostly articles on such aspects of Jewish life in France as history, Jewish culture, biography, and Jewish institutions. It is indexed.

371 Gross, Heinrich. *Gallia Judaica: Dictionnaire Géographique de la France d'après les Sources Rabbiniques*. Amsterdam: Philo Press, 1969. 766, 37p.
Gross's geographical dictionary of France, originally published in 1897, is based on Rabbinic sources. It is a basic resource for the study of the French Jewish community, the rabbinate and rabbinic literature in medieval times. This reprint edition includes additional notes and corrections by Simon Schwarzfuchs. The Dictionary includes place and name indexes in Hebrew, indexes of names and cities in Latin characters, Hebrew title and non-Hebrew title indexes.

372 Szajkowski, Zosa. *Franco-Judaica: An Analytical Bibliography of Books, Pamphlets, Decrees, Briefs and Other Printed Documents Pertaining to the Jews in France 1500-1788*. New York: American Academy for Jewish Research, 1962. 160p.
This bibliography of books, pamphlets, and a variety of documents printed from 1500-1788 is arranged, with few exceptions, chronologically according to geographical Jewish centers. Seven of the thirty chapters are devoted to the legal status of the Jews in various French provinces. The work includes indices of authors, subjects, names of persons and places.

373 Weinberg, David. "French Jewish History." *Modern Judaism* 10 (1990): 379-395.
Weinberg reviews the major areas of research pertaining to French Jewry during the decade of the 1980's, e. g., the Holocaust, anti-Semitism, North African Jewry. He also notes areas of research desiderata. The essay includes bibliographic notes.

BIOGRAPHICAL DICTIONARIES

374 Cavignac, Jean. *Dictionnaire du Judaisme Bordelais au XVIIIe et XIXe Siècles: Biographies, Généalogies, Professions, Institutions*. Bordeaux: Archives Départmentales de la Gironde, 1987. 305 p.
This dictionary provides the user with detailed biographical sketches of Jews who lived in Bordeaux during the 18th and 19th centuries. The author

also includes in the dictionary 53 family trees, a list of professions that Jews engaged in, and information about Jewish communal institutions.

GERMANY (INCLUDING CENTRAL EUROPE)

ARCHIVAL RESOURCES

375 Leo Baeck Institute. Library and Archives. *Catalog of the Archival Collections.* Tübingen: J.C.B. Mohr, 1990. 409p.
This is a catalog of the over 4,000 public and family archival collections housed at the Institute. It is divided into two sections: a) 284 major collections, i.e. collections that contain more than 100 items, and b) 3,285 small collections. The major collections are described in full and indexed. All collections acquired through 1988 are included. The catalog is an invaluable resource for the student of modern German-Jewish history and culture.

BIBLIOGRAPHY

376 "Bibliography of Hebrew and Yiddish Publications on German Jewry, 1950-1955." Compiled by G. Ormann. Leo Baeck Institute. *Yearbook* 1 (1956): 447-466.
This partially annotated classified bibliography lists publications on such topics as: A. Theology and Philosophy (Jewish) B. Philosophers of Jewish origin C. History 1750-1955 D. Biography and Autobiography E. Hebrew Literature in Central Europe F. Yiddish Fiction. The bibliography includes an "Index of Names to the Hebrew Bibliography."

377 Eichstädt, Volkmar. *Bibliographie zur Geschichte der Judenfrage.* Westmead: Gregg International, 1969. 267p.

This bibliography, planned as a three volume work, was published originally in 1938. It was commissioned by the Nazi Reichsinstitut für Geschichte des neuen Deutschlands. The bibliography lists 3,016 books, pamphlets, journal articles and chapters in books, published between 1750-1848, that deal with a variety of political issues pertaining to the Jews in Germany during this period. The following are among the topics covered by this bibliography: tolerance of the Jews, civil reforms, emancipation of the Jews, and the "Jewish Question." A star denotes that the item was written by a Jew. A question mark denotes that the author of a cited item may be Jewish. The bibliography includes an author/title index and a list of the periodicals cited. Volumes 2-3 were never published.

378 *Germania Judaica.* Nach dem Tode von Markus Brann hrsg. von Ismar Elbogen, Aron Freimann, und H. Tykocinski. Tübingen: J. C. B. Mohr, 1963- .
This gazetteer documents the history of Jewish settlement in various communities throughout Germany from the earliest times (c. 10th century) to 1519. Each entry includes "Sources" (archival, etc.) and a bibliography for further study. The following volumes have been published to date:

Volume 1, covers the period from the earliest settlement of the Jews in Germany to 1238. This volume is a reprint of the 1934 edition and includes additions and corrections by Zvi Avneri. It also includes author, name and place indices. Volume 2, edited by Zvi Avneri, was published in 1968. Prior to the publication of this volume, Avneri updated the materials which had been gathered before World War II. The volume includes author, name and place indices. Volume 3, part 1, edited by Aryeh Maimon, was published in 1987. It covers the period 1350-1519 and includes to-date, the letters Aach-Lychen.

379 "The Jews of Weimar." In *The Weimar Republic: A Historical Bibliography*, 154-167. Santa Barbara, CA: ABC Clio Information Services, 1984.
This chapter lists 62 articles pertaining to various aspects of Jewish life in Germany during the Weimar Republic. The entries are annotated.

380 Magnus, Shulamit S. "German Jewish History." *Modern Judaism* 11 (1991): 125-146.
Magnus briefly reviews the scholarly publications that have been written in the past ten years pertaining to German Jewish history and notes the trends in the field. The essay includes bibliographic notes.

381 "Post War Publications on German Jewry: Books and Articles." Leo Baeck Institute. *Yearbook* 1- . (1956-)
This annual classified bibliography lists publications on such topics as: A. History B. The Nazi Period C. Post War D. Judaism F. Zionism and Israel G. Autobiography, Memoirs, and Letters H. Fiction and Poetry. The bibliography includes an index of Names, Places and Organizations.

382 Schembs, Hans Otto. *Bibliographie zur Geschichte der Frankfurter Juden, 1781-1945*. Frankfurt a/M: W. Kramer, 1978. 680p.
Schembs has compiled a comprehensive classified bibliography pertaining to the Jews of Frankfurt. Archival material, as well as, monographs, and articles that have been published in Germany and elsewhere in many different languages are listed. The Bibliography consists of two major sections: I. Subject matter. II. Biography In the first section, materials are arranged in fifteen broad subject, e. g., History of Frankfurt Jewry, Emancipation (1781-1864), Assimilation, Anti-Semitism, Zionism (1866-1933), Persecution (1933-1945), Education, Art. The second section includes an alphabetical listing of Jews or individuals of Jewish descent who are associated with Frankfurt. Each entry includes: the birth and death date (where applicable and available), occupation and bibliographical references. The bibliography includes author and name (to the subject section) indices. See "Biographisches Lexikon der Juden in den Bereichen" below.

383 Wiener Library. *Catalogue Series*. Numbers 1-7. London: For the Wiener Library By Vallentine & Mitchell, 1958-1978.
The Wiener Library, now at Tel-Aviv University, houses an extensive collection of materials pertaining to "German speaking" Jewry from the very beginnings of Jewish history in Central Europe to the present time. The bulk of the collection pertaining to German Jewry relates to the post-emancipation period. In addition, the Library collects materials pertaining to contemporary German history, with particular emphasis on such topics

as prejudice and racism, the Nazi party and resistance to it. The Library's *Catalogue Series* provides access to the materials in the collection.

The following volumes are included in the series: No. 1 Persecution and Resistance under the Nazis. No. 2 From Weimar to Hitler-Germany 1918-1933 (2nd rev. enl. ed. 1964). This catalogue includes works pertaining to anti-Semitism and the German-Jewish communities during the Weimar period. No.3 German Jewry —Its History, Life and Culture (1958). No.4 After Hitler—Germany, 1945-1963 (1963). This catalogue includes works pertaining to the German-Jewish communities after World War II, and restitution and compensation by the Federal Republic of Germany. No.5 Prejudice—Racist, Religious, Nationalist (1971). This catalogue includes materials pertaining to racial theories, the Dreyfus case, anti-Semitism and defence, antisemitica, and anti-Zionism. No.6 German Jewry—Its History, Life and Culture (2nd rev. enl. ed. 1978). This revised catalogue (No. 3) lists materials under the following broad subject areas: A. Reference Books B. History, including Regional and Communal History C. Jewish Life and Thought D. Integration —Assimilation—ionism E. Biography F. Participation in Cultural Life G. Participation in Economic, Political and Social Life H. Central European Jews as Emigrants and Expatriates I. Periodicals. Each subject area is further subdivided. No.7 Prejudice —Racist, Religious, Nationalist (2nd rev. enl. ed. 1978). This catalogue is a reprint of Catalogue No. 1, and includes "New Material and Amendments." It lists materials pertaining to the persecution of Jews in individual cities and regions of Nazi Germany, the Eichmann trial, the controversy on the role of Pope Pius XII, and the after-effects on the health of the persecuted. The following materials are included in an appendix: A. Periodicals of Germans in Exile B. Illegal Pamphlets and Periodicals C. Alphabetical List of Concentration Camps Mentioned in the Text. All the volumes in the *Catalogue Series* are indexed.

384 Wiesemann, Falk. *Bibliographie zur Geschichte de Juden in Bayern.* Munich: K. G. Saur, 1989. 263 p.

This classified bibliography lists more than 2,913 books and articles pertaining to the history and culture of Bavarian Jewry. The materials are arranged in 29 broad subject areas, e. g., history, local history, demography, anti-Semitism, emancipation, the rabbinate, the synagogue, ritual. A biography section provides bibliographic sources for individual Bavarian Jews and families. The bibliography includes name, place, subject and author indices.

BIOGRAPHICAL DICTIONARIES

385 "Biographisches Lexikon der Juden in den Bereichen: Wissenschaft, Kultur, Bildung, Öfentlichtkeitsarbeit in Frankfurt a/M." Edited by Hans Otto Schembs. In *Geschichte der Frankfurter Juden seit der Französichen Revolution,* by Paul Arnsberg, 3, 12-526. Darmstadt: Edward Roether Verlag, 1983.

This dictionary includes biographical sketches of Frankfurt Jews who gained prominence in the arts, literature, the sciences, publishing, etc. Each entry includes a list of sources, and may include a portrait. A list of Jews active in municipal politics in Frankfurt is included in an appendix. See the editor's *Bibliographie zur Geschichte der Frankfurter Juden* above.

386 Heuer, Renata. *Bibliographia Judaica: Verzeichnis Jüdischer Autoren Deutscher Sprache.* Frankfurt /Main: Campus Verlag, 1982- .
This work is part of a bibliographic project that is intended to provide biographical information about the lives and careers of German speaking Jews (or of Jewish descent) who were active in such fields as literature, journalism, art, music, and science. The following information is provided for each individual: A. Place of birth B. Birth and death date C. Area of main activity. To-date three volumes (A-Z) have been published.

387 *International Biographical Dictionary of Central European Emigrés 1933-1945=Biographisches Handbuch der Deutschsprachigen Emigration nach 1933.* Edited by Herbert A. Strauss. Munich: K. G. Saur, 1980-1983. 3v.
This biographical dictionary describes the lives and works of 8,700 German emigrés who were forced to flee Nazi persecution. Volume 1 depicts the lives of individuals who were active in government, business, and public life. Volume 2 includes individuals who contributed the arts, sciences, and literature. Both volumes include scholarly introductions assessing the social and cultural consequences of this historic migration, for Germany and for the countries that finally accepted the Central-European emigrants. Volume 3, The Index, includes the following indices: A. Names, pseudonyms, cover names, and name changes B. Countries of intermediate emigration and final settlement C. Occupations D. Parties, associations, institutions E. Parliaments and governments F. Nobel Prize Winners.

388 Walk, Joseph. *Kurzbiographien zur Geschcichte der Juden, 1918-1945.* Jerusalem: Leo Baeck Institute; Munich: K. G. Saur, 1988. 452p.
This biographical dictionary in German, provides the user with brief biographical sketches of 4,000 Jews born in Germany and who lived there most of their lives. The individuals who are included in the dictionary, were active in the political, scientific, cultural arenas or who were active in the Jewish community or Jewish organizational life. Each entry includes full name, birth and death dates, title and occupation, short biographical description and a list of bibliographic sources.

LIBRARY CATALOGS
See also entry 214.

389 Leo Baeck Institute. Library and Archives. *Katalog.* Band I. Tubingen: J.C.B. Mohr, 1970- .
The first volume of the catalog represents the library's holdings in the following subjects: German Jewish communities; newspapers and other serial publications; memoirs, biographies, and autobiographies. The catalog is a first step towards a comprehensive bibliography on German Jewry. No other volumes have been published to-date.

GREECE
See also entry 154.

390 Attal, Robert. *Yahadut Yavan.* Jerusalem: Ben-Zvi Institute, 1984. 215p.
This bibliography contains 2,294 citations from books and articles concerning Jewish life in Greece. The bibliography is limited to Greece as defined

by its present borders, and covers the period from 1492 to the present. Special attention is focused on the Jewish settlement in Salonica. The appendices include citations pertaining to various Jewish communities in Greece from *El Tiempo* (Istanbul) and *La Epoca* (Salonica), the major Ladino newspapers. The bibliography includes a name, place and subject index.

GREAT BRITAIN

BIBLIOGRAPHY

391 Endelman, Todd M. "English Jewish History." *Modern Judaism* 11 (1991): 91-109.
Endelman reviews the trends in recent scholarship pertaining to the history of English Jewry. He notes areas that need to be studied. The essay includes bibliographic notes.

392 Jacobs, Joseph and Lucien Wolf. *Bibliotheca Anglo-Judaica: A Bibliographic Guide.* London: Jewish Chronicle, 1888. 231p.
This classified bibliography lists 2,164 items pertaining to the history of the Jews in England from their earliest settlement to 1886.

393 *Jewish Books in Whitechapel: A Bibliography of Narodczky's Press.* Compiled by Moshe Sanders. Edited by Marion Aproot. London: Duckworth, 1991. 220p.
This chronologically arranged bibliography provides full bibliographic descriptions of 578 books published by the Narod Press between 1901 and 1971. The largest categories of publications are about Judaism, Zionism, and Yiddish literature. This publication sheds light on literary creativity in Yiddish during this period.

394 Lehmann, Ruth Pauline. *Anglo-Jewish Bibliography, 1937-1970.* London: Jewish Historical Society of England, 1973. 364p.
This classified bibliographic guide lists close to 5,000 books, pamphlets, journal articles, chapters of related content from non-Judaic books, etc., pertaining to all aspects of Anglo-Jewish history and culture. This work completes and updates the author's *Nova Bibliotheca.* It features new sections and subsections, and a new system of annotation. Materials pertaining to the Jews in the Commonwealth, Dependencies and the Union of South Africa are listed. Indexed.

395 —. *Anglo-Jewish Bibliography, 1971-1990.* Compiled by Ruth P. Goldschmidt-Lehmann; edited and augmented by Stephen W. Massil, and Peter Shmuel Salinger. London: Jewish Historical Society of England, 1992. 377p.
This *Bibliography* continues its predecessor, and is similar to it in format and arrangement. However, a number of changes have been introduced to reflect the increasing interest of scholars and lay readers in sociological research and communal history, as well as in the conferences and exhibitions held during the period. A section on the Commonwealth (Past and Present), has been eliminated. The inclusion of thesis material has enriched the content of this work.

396 —. *Nova Bibliotheca Anglo-Judaica.* London: Jewish Historical Society of England, 1961. 232p.

This bibliographic guide lists c. 1,700 items pertaining to all aspects of Anglo-Jewish history and culture. It follows the arrangement of Roth's *Magna.* The guide completes and updates the first section (Histories) of the *Magna* to 1960. The *Nova* includes a chapter on the History of the Jews in England after 1937. Materials pertaining to the Jews in the Commonwealth, Dependencies and the Union of South Africa are listed. Indexed.

397 Roth, Cecil. *Magna Bibliotheca Anglo-Judaica: A Bibliographical Guide to Anglo-Jewish History.* New ed. rev. and enl. London: Jewish Historical Society of England, University College, 1937. 464p.

This classified bibliographic guide lists 2,959 items. The bibliography is divided into two main parts: A. Histories B. Historical materials. In the former section, Roth continues the work of Jacobs and Wolf (see above), by listing current materials pertaining to all aspects of Anglo-Jewish history and culture. In the latter section, Roth lists "works illustrative of Anglo-Jewish history and intellectual life" that were published to 1837. Materials pertaining to Jews in the British "Dominions and Dependencies" are also listed. Indexed.

BIOGRAPHICAL DICTIONARIES

398 Goldschmidt-Lehmann, Ruth P. *A Bibliography of Anglo-Jewish Medical Biography.* Jerusalem, 1988. 108p.

This bibliography is a supplement to *Korot* (volume 9), a journal devoted the history of Jewish medicine. It sheds light on the Jewish contribution to the medical profession in Great Britain from medieval times to the present. The bibliography is divided into two parts: A. A bibliography of "Jewish and non-Jewish reference works and secondary sources" B. An alphabetical listing of Anglo-Jewish doctors. The compiler notes the birth and death dates, as well as title of each physician when available. This is followed by a bibliography of articles describing the doctor's career.

399 Prager, Leonard. *Yiddish Culture in Britain: A Guide.* Frankfurt a/M: P. Lang, 1990.

This book is largely a bio-bibliographical dictionary. The introductory essay deals with such subjects as religious life and Yiddish, Yiddish and Zionism / Territorialism, the Yiddish press, Yiddish theater in Britain, Yiddish in British sociolinguistics. The guide includes a list of references. Not indexed.

YEARBOOKS

400 *Jewish Yearbook.* Edited by Michael Wallace. London: Jewish Chronicle, 1986- .

This annual's features include a summary of the important events of the previous year that were important to the Jewish community, a book list, a "Who's Who," and a "Necrology," as well as directories of Jewish institutions and organizations in Great Britain and the Commonwealth, international Jewish organizations, and the Anglo-Jewish press. Indexed.

401 *Zionist Yearbook.* Edited by Jane Moonman. London: Zionist Federation of Great Britain & Ireland, 1951- .
This annual includes feature articles related to Zionism, directory information about organizations and institutions in Great Britain, Israel and elsewhere, demographic data and statistics pertaining to Israel, a "Who's Who," and "Obituaries". The *Yearbook* is indexed.

HUNGARY

402 Braham, Randolph L. *The Hungarian Jewish Catastrophe: A Selected and Annotated Bibliography.* New York: Social Science Monographs and Institute for Holocaust Studies of the City University of New York, 1984. 501p.
After a brief introduction about the Holocaust in Hungary, Braham lists 3,000 items in a variety of languages relating to this subject. The entries are grouped in the following four chapters: A. General Reference Works B. Background of the Holocaust C. The Holocaust D. Post War Era. The chapters are arranged in historical-chronological order. Each chapter consists of divisions and subdivisions within which entries are arranged in alphabetical order. Brief annotations are supplied when a title is not indicative of the content matter. The inclusion of the following indexes facilitates the use of the bibliography: A. Personal and corporate author's index B. Name index C. Geographic index D. Subject index.

403 Haraszti, György. *Magyar Zsidó Levéltári Repertórium.* Budapest: MTA Judaisztikai Kutatócsoport, 1993- .
"The objective of the present first volume of the *Directory of Archival Holdings Relating to the History of Jews in Hungary* is to survey all the documents in public or institutional Hungarian archives and manuscript collections ... and to list and describe these documents according to the annotated catalogs ... published by the archives themselves in the period after World War II and available for students and the general public." The archival holdings in collections managed by the Jewish Community or the Community's institutions are dealt with in a separate chapter. The following indexes are included in the Directory: Index of place names, Index of personal names, Index of institutions, and Index of subjects.

ITALY

See also entry 153.

BIBLIOGRAPHY

404 *Bibliotheca Italo-Ebraica: Bibliografia per la Storia Degli Ebre in Italia, 1964-1973.* Compiled by Aldo Luzzatto and Moshe Moldavi; Edited by Daniel Carpi. Rome: Carucci, 1982. 251 p.
This bibliography continues Milano's *Bibliotheca Historica.* It lists 2,538 books, articles, pamphlets, encyclopedia articles, and chapters from books in various languages that deal with a wide range of topics pertaining to Jewish life in Italy beginning with the Roman period to-date. The bibliography also includes materials which shed light on the life of the Jews in the former Italian colonies and on Italian Jewry in Israel. It is arranged alphabetically by author, and includes geographic, author, and subject

indexes. A listing of sources from which the citations were taken is also included.

405 *Biblioteca Italo-Ebraica: Bibliografia per la Storia degli Ebrei in Italia, 1974-1985*, by Aldo Luzzatto. Milan: Franco Angeli, 1989. 258p.
This multilingual bibliography continues the aforementioned work.

406 *Cultura Ebraica in Emilia-Romagna*. Edited by Simonetta M. Bondoni and Giulio Busi. Rimni: Luisè Editore, 1987. 706p.
This catalog of ritual objects, Torah ornaments, etc. sheds light on aspects of the cultural life of the Jews in Emilia-Romagna during the past 500 years. "Of special interest are the surveys of illuminated manuscripts and early printed books in the region, and documents —etters, privileges, statutes-all evidence of the active participation of the Jews in general Italian material culture." The catalog includes an extensive bibliography.

407 Milano, Attilio. *Bibliotheca Historica Italo-Judaica*. Florence: Sansoni, 1954. 209p.

408 —. *Supplemento, 1954-1963*. Florence: Sansoni, 1964. 82p.
This is a bibliography of books and articles pertaining to various aspects of Italian-Jewish history. It includes geographical, subject and author indexes.

409 Romano, Giorgio. *Bibliografia Italo-Ebraica (1848-1977)*. Florence: L. S. Olschki, 1979. 208 p.
This is a bibliography of 2,095 books in Italian pertaining to all aspects of Judaica, Hebrew literature, and Israel. The bibliography consists of two parts: A. Books written in Italian B. Books translated into Italian. The materials in both parts are listed alphabetically by author. The bibliography includes an index of authors, editors and translators, pseudonyms used by Italian authors whose works are cited, and pseudonyms of authors whose works were translated into Italian.

THE NETHERLANDS

410 Coppenhagen, Jacob H. *De Israelitische 'Kerk' en der Staat deer Nederlanden: hun Betrekkingen Tussen 1814 en 1870*. Amsterdam: Nederlands-Israelietisch Kerkgenootschap, 1988. 198p.
This classified bibliography lists materials which shed light on the relationship between the Dutch government and the various local Jewish communities in the Netherlands during the period from 1814 to 1870. The Portuguese community, the Ashkenazi community, and Jews in the Dutch West Indies are among the topics included in this work. Indexes of persons and places facilitate the use of the work.

ARCHIVAL RESOURCES

411 *Guide to the Sources for the History of the Jews in Poland in the Central Archives.* Compiled by A. Teller. Jerusalem: The Central Archives for the History of the Jewish People, 1988. 100p.

This is a geographically arranged guide to archival materials, original and photocopied, that are housed in the Central Archives for the History of the Jewish People. Only communities that were part of Poland in the inter-war period are covered.

BIBLIOGRAPHY

412 Friedman, Philip. "Polish Jewish Historiography Between the Two Wars (1918-1939)." In *Jewish Social Studies*, 11, 4 (1949): 373-408.

"The purpose of this article is to provide a picture of Jewish historical writing in Poland between 1918 and 1939. It is not intended as a comprehensive bibliography but rather as a survey of the achievements of the various historical schools, and of the currents and kinds of problems studied." The article includes detailed bibliographic footnotes.

413 Goldberg-Mulkiewicz, Olga. *Ethnographic Topics Relating to Jews in Polish Studies.* Jerusalem: Magnes Press, 1989. 67p.

The author, in chapters one and two, discusses the growing interest in researching Jewish topics in Polish ethnographic scholarship prior to World War I and in the interwar period. She also discusses the range of subjects contained in studies published in Polish. The bibliography in chapter three lists works published from 1887-1983 which contain ethnographic material pertaining to Polish Jewish culture. A list of relevant periodicals, and an index of names are included.

414 Hundert, Gershon David and Gershon C. Bacon. *The Jews in Poland and Russia: Bibliographical Essays.* Bloomfield: Indiana University Press, 1984. 276p.

This book comprises two bibliographic essays, "The Jews in Poland-Lithuania from the 12th Century to the First Partition," by Gershon David Hundert, and "East European Jewry from the First Partition on Poland to the Present," by Gershon C. Bacon. Both essays concentrate on listing the most recent and important works, with an emphasis on works in Western languages, particularly English.

415 —. "Polish Jewish History." *Modern Judaism* 10 (1990): 259-270.

Hundert describes the historical literature which has appeared since the publication of his bibliographical essay in 1984. He suggests areas in need of study. The essay includes bibliographic notes.

416 "Jews." In *Eastern European National Minorities 1919-1980: A Handbook,* by Stephen M. Horak, 55-57, 79-92. Littleton, CO: Libraries Unlimited, 1985.

This annotated bibliography lists 85 items pertaining to history of the Jews in Poland.

417 "Jews." In *Galicia: A Historical Survey and Bibliographic Guide,* by Paul Robert Magocsi, 227-244. Toronto: Canadian Institute of Ukrainian Studies, 1983.

This essay contains a brief survey of the literature pertaining to the Jews of Galicia. It includes extensive bibliographic footnotes.

418 Lerski, Jerzy Jan and Halina T. Lerski. *Jewish-Polish Coexistence, 1772-1939.* Westport, CT: Greenwood Press, 1986. 230p.

This is a topical bibliography enumerating 2,778 books, pamphlets, brochures, and articles in journals pertaining to the interactions between Jews and Poles, as well as other ethnic groups who resided in multinational Poland, e.g. Germans, Ukrainians, and Byelorussians. The authors cover the period from the first partition in 1772 until the eve of the Nazi invasion. Sections containing citations to biographical materials and shtetlekh are included. Unlike Majer Balaban's *Bibliografia Historii Zydow w Polsce ...* (Warsaw, 1939), which is limited largely to Polish-language materials, and Gershon Bacon's and David Hundert's *The Jews in Poland and Russia* (Bloomington: Indiana University Press, 1984), which is limited primarily to English-language materials, this work includes materials written in a variety of languages. It is also more current than the former and more comprehensive in its coverage of this period than the latter. The bibliography includes an index of authors and editors.

419 Korsch, Boris. *Soviet Publications on Judaism and the State of Israel.* New York: Garland, 1990. 126p.

This is a comprehensive, annotated bibliography of 386 publications by the Communist Party of the Soviet Union (CPSU), the Soviet government, and different party agencies on Judaism, Zionism, and the State of Israel. The bibliography lists publications that were published between 1984-1988. The materials included in the bibliography are reflective of soviet ideology and policy towards Jews during these years. It contains an author Index.

420 Luckert, Yelena. *Soviet Jewish History: An Annotated Bibliography.* New York: Garland, 1992. 271p.

This selective annotated bibliography, arranged thematically, lists 1,446 items pertaining to various aspects of Jewish life in the Soviet Union. The author lists scholarly works, bibliographies, periodicals, political propaganda pamphlets, personal accounts, court transcripts, belles lettres, and musical scores in the bibliography. The following are a few of the topics covered in the bibliography: The Stalin era; The Soviet Jewry issue abroad; The Soviet government campaign against emigration and Israel; Gorbachev and Glasnost; Jews in Soviet intellectual and cultural life, and anti-Semitism. There is an author index.

421 Mendelsohn, Ezra. *Yehude Mizrah Merkaz Eropah ben Shete Milhamot ha-'Olam.* Jerusalem: Zalman Shazar Institute, 1978. 62p.

This work is a selected bibliography of books and articles written primarily in Hebrew, Yiddish, and English pertaining to the Jews who lived in East Central Europe between the wars. Preference for inclusion was given to materials that deal with history, economics, the society, and anti-Semitism.

The bibliography is arranged by country with a topical division under each country. There are author indexes.

422 Merowitz, Morton J. "Once a Jew, Always a German: An Annotated Bibliography of English-Language Materials on Polish-Jewish Relations and History Prior to 1939." *Polish Review* 30 (1985): 185-202.

423 Orbach, Alexander. "Russian Jewish History." *Modern Judaism* 10 (1990): 325-342.
    Orbach reviews the scholarly literature that has been written in the 1980's pertaining to the experience of Russia's Jews in both the Czarist and Soviet periods. The essay includes bibliographic notes.

424 Pilarczyk, Krysztof. *Przewodnik po Bibliografiach Polskich Judaików=Guide to Bibliographies of Polish Judaica*. Krakow: Uniwersytet Jagiellonski Miedzywydziazowy Zakyad Historii i Kultury Zydow w Polsce, 1992. 222p.
    This classified bibliography covers the period from the 17th century till the end of 1990. It is divided into the following two parts (each further subdivided): "A. Directory publications and card index with Polono-Judaica in structural repartition B. Bibliographical materials in thematic order." The materials in the first part are arranged according to the form of publication, e. g., basic bibliographies of bibliographies of Judaica and Polonica, bio-bibliographies, guides to library and archive collections of Polish Judaica. The second part includes reference books concerning the history of the Jews of Poland, lists of reference books concerning Polono-Judaica from fields of literature, theatre and film, etc. The bibliography includes an index of names, pseudonyms, cryronyms and an index of geographical names.

425 Pinkus, Binyamim. *Yahadut Berit ha-Mo'atsot, 1917-1973*. Jerusalem: Merkaz Zalman Shazar, 1974. 79p.
    This ia a topically arranged bibliography of books and articles written primarily in Hebrew, English, and French that were published after World War II and deal with various aspects of Jewish life in the Soviet Union and related topics, e. g., Soviet-Israeli relations.

426 Schoenburg, Nancy and Stuart Schoenburg. *Lithuanian Jewish Communities*. New York: Garland, 1991. 502p.
    This book is based in part on *Yahadut Lita* (Tel-Aviv: Am ha-Sefer, 1959-1984). Chapter 1 "An Historical Perspective" provides the reader with an overview of the history of Lithuanian Jewry. Chapter 2, "Jewish Communities of Lita," contains brief articles on individual Lithuanian towns and villages arranged alphabetically by Yiddish name (in transliteration). The book includes the following three appendices: A. A list of towns included in Chapter two. The following information is given for each town: Yiddish name (in transliteration); map key; current name; other name B. Lists of Lithuanian Jews C. Sources and information that can be useful in researching Lithuanian Jewish genealogy.

427 *Source Book on Soviet Jewry: An Annotated Bibliography*. Compiled by Sylvia Orenstein. New York: American Jewish Committee, 1981. 116p.

This annotated bibliography contains 650 books, pamphlets, articles, journals, and documents dealing with: Life in the Soviet Union; Government policy towards Jews, Zionism and Israel; anti-Semitism; Response abroad; Resettlement in Israel, the United States, and elsewhere. This is the most comprehensive compilation to date on the subject. It was issued in cooperation with the National Conference on Soviet Jewry. Material was chosen on the basis of interest to both the general reader and the scholar. It is indexed.

BIOGRAPHICAL DICTIONARIES

428 Wunder, Meir. *Meore Galitsyah.* Jerusalem: Institute for the Commemoration of Galician Jewry, 1978 -.
This dictionary provides detailed biographical sketches of rabbis and scholars who were born in Galicia, were active there or whose works were published there. It also includes a bibliography, a list of family names (in Hebrew, Yiddish and English), a list of Galician communities (in Hebrew Yiddish and English), a list of memorial books of Galician communities, an index of books written by Galician scholars and a general index. The inclusion of portraits, genealogical charts, facsimiles of manuscripts and documents have added to the value of this useful reference work. To-date four volumes (aleph-resh [Rakover]) have been published.

GAZETTEERS

429 Cohen, Chester G. *Shtetl Finder.* Los Angeles: Periday Co., 1980. 145p.
This is a list of "Jewish communities in the 19th and early 20th centuries in the Pale of Settlement of Russia and Poland, and in Lithuania, Latvia, Galicia, and Bukovina, with names of residents."

430 Kagan, Berl. *Yidishe Shtet, Shtetlekh, un Dorfishe Yishuvim in Lite biz 1918=Jewish Cities, Towns and Villages in Lithuania until 1918.* Brooklyn, NY: Kagan, 1991. 791p.
This gazetteer is divided into two sections: A. Cities and Towns B. Villages. The entries in each section are arranged alphabetically by the Yiddish name of the community. The official name of the community is also given. The author includes the following following information in each entry: A. A brief historical overview of Jewish settlement until 1918 B. Biographical sketches of Jewish notables and rabbinic figures C. Bibliography of sources. The gazeteer includes an index of towns and people.

ROMANIA

431 *Bibliography of the Jews of Romania.* Compiled by Jean Ancel and Victor Eskenasy. Ramat Aviv: The Goldstein-Goren Centre for the History of the Jews in Romania, Diaspora Research Institute, Tel-Aviv University, 1991. 50, 125 p.
This bibliography lists in alphabetical order by author over two thousand items pertaining to all aspects of Jewish life in Romania. The Bibliography is divided into two parts: A. Materials in Latin alphabets (including some Yiddish language material in Latin transcription) B. Materials in Hebrew

characters (including some Yiddish language material). Both lists are followed by an index of names, places and subjects.

432 Kohen, Yitshak Yosef. *Hakhme Transilvanyah.* Jerusalem: Mekhon Yerushalayim, 1988/89. 298, 280p.
This bio-bibliographical dictionary lists over 800 rabbis and scholars who contributed to Torah scholarship. It includes a discussion of the history of the Jews in Transylvania from 1630 to 1944 and a gazetteer of the Jewish communities in Transylvania.

SPAIN / PORTUGAL

433 Singerman, Robert. *The Jews in Spain and Portugal: A Bibliography.* New York: Garland Publishing, 1975. 364p.
This classified bibliography lists over 5,000 published items pertaining to "the Jewish presence in Spain and Portugal from antiquity to the present day." Emphasis is placed on Jewish history and culture. Indexed.

434 —. *Spanish and Portuguese Jewry: A Classified Bibliography.* Westport, CT: Greenwood Press, 1993. 720p.
The present work extends to 1992 and concludes the author's aforementioned work on Spanish and Portuguese Jewry. It, like its predecessor, pays close attention to local Jewish history, Jewish Christian polemics, and the portrayal of Spanish and Portuguese Jews in literature. "Corrigenda and Notes: *The Jews in Spain and Portugal: A Bibliography,*" are included in an appendix. Indexed

CHAPTER 16

ISRAEL / PALESTINE

See Chapter 15 and entries 89-98.

A. ARCHIVAL RESOURCES

435 Alsberg, P. A. *The Israel State Archives.* Jerusalem: Israel Archives Association in cooperation with the Israel State Archives, 1991. 106p.
This is a listing of the record groups in the State Archives pertaining to Palestine under Turkish and British rule, The State of Israel and its institutions, non-governmental records, as well as private papers and collections. Indexed.

436 *Guide to America—Holy Land Studies.* Edited by Nathan M. Kaganoff. New York: Arno Press, 1980-1984. 4v. (vols. 2-4, New York: Praeger, 1982-1984).
These descriptive catalogs are "designed to provide the serious student with a guide to primary source material reflecting the relationship of the United States and the Holy Land from the early 19th century until 1948. Each volume includes materials pertaining to an aspect of Holy Land Studies. Volume 1, "American Presence in the Holy Land" contains descriptions of manuscript and archival collections that relate to permanent as well as occasional identification with the Land, individual and institutional settlement, and pilgrimage and service. Volume 2 describes manuscript and archival collections that relate to " Political Relations and American Zionism." Volume 3 describes manuscript and archival collections relating to "economic relations and philanthropy". Volume 4 focuses on record groups in British and Turkish repositories, and on sections in Israeli archives not recorded in previous volumes. The manuscript and archival collections are arranged alphabetically within each volume. Each entry includes a biographical note (for personal papers) or a historical note (for organizational collections), a full description of the collection, its location and information pertaining to access and photocopying. Each volume contains a general index.

437 *Guide to the Archives in Israel.* Edited by P. A. Alsberg. Jerusalem: Israel Archives Association, 1973. 257p.
"This *Guide to the Archives in Israel* contains twenty-one short surveys and lists institutions which have in their custody archival material occupying some forty-five kilometers of shelving." Among the institutions included are the Israel State Archives, The Central Zionist Archives, The Archives of Religious Zionism, and the Central Archives for the History of the Jewish People. Each survey includes the address of the institution, its address, the name of the director, hours, a description of the institution's collection, and a listing of the record groups.

438 Jones, Philip. *Britain and Palestine, 1914-1948: Archival Sources for the History of the British Mandate.* Oxford: Oxford Univ. Press, 1979. 246p.

This book constitutes the findings of a survey sponsored by the British Academy. It lists and briefly describes "unpublished papers and records of those individuals and organizations, whose base was in Britain, that had involvement in events in Palestine during the first half of this century." The materials described are housed in university libraries, local record offices, military museums, and national repositories of archives in Britain. The materials are arranged alphabetically in two sections: A. Personal papers B. Organizational records. Each entry includes: information pertaining to location and access; biographical information or an historical note (for organizational archives); the number of files; the main dates; the principal correspondents; and subject matter (where possible). The book includes notes on archives in: Israel, The Arab Countries, The United States and The League of Nations, a guide to selected libraries and record offices in Britain, and a list of relevant documents in the Public Record Office and other official repositories in Britain.

439 *With Eyes Toward Zion*. Edited by Moshe Davis. New York: Arno Press, 1977- . (Vols. 2- . New York: Praeger, 1986- .)
The first two volumes in this series contain expanded versions of papers presented at the Scholars Colloquia on American Holy Land Studies. The third volume is based on papers from the July, 1990 Workshop of the International Center for University Teaching of Jewish Civilization. The papers presented at the first colloquium (1975) deal with a variety of subjects pertaining to the relationship between the United States and the Holy Land from Colonial times to the establishment of the State of Israel. The second colloquium (1983) focuses on "Themes and Sources in the Archives of the United States, Great Britain, Turkey and Israel." The third volume includes papers on the subject " Western Societies and the Holy Land." The following articles deal with archival resources: " Records in the National Archives Relating to America and the Holy Land," by Milton O. Gustafson (v. 1, p.129-152); "America-Holy Land Material in British Archives, 1820-1930," by Vivian D. Lipman (v.2, p. 25-56) ; "America-Holy Land Source Material in Israeli Archives: A Progress Report," by Menahem Kaufman (v.2, p.207-229); "French Archives as a Source for the Study of France-Holy Land Relations," by Ran Aaronsohn (v. 3, p. 137-146); " Sources for Germany-Holy Land Studies in the Late Ottoman Period: German Libraries and Archives," by Haim Goren (v.3, p. 170-178).

B. ATLASES AND GAZETTEERS
See also Chapter 15 and entry 626.

440 Ariel, Israel. *Atlas Erets Yisrael li-Gevuloteha 'al pi ha-Mekorot: Yesodot ve-Heker*. Jerusalem: Cana, 1988- .
This atlas, through maps and illustrations, depicts the boundaries of "Erets Yisrael" through the ages based on biblical and rabbinic sources. One volume has been published to-date.

441 *Atlas Karta le-Toldot Erets-Yisrael*. Jerusalem: Karta, 1964-1972. 5v.
This illustrated atlas depicts the history of the Jews in Palestine from antiquity to the present. It consists of the following parts: 1. Aharoni, Yohanan. *Atlas Karta li-Tekufat ha-Mikra* (1964) covering the period from c. 5, 000 B.C.E. to c.440 B.C.E. A geographic index is included. 2. Avi-Yonah, Michael. *Atlas Karta li-Tekufat Bayit Sheni, ha-Mishnah, veha-Talmud* (1966). covering the period from 500 B.C.E. until 500 C.E. 3. Gihon, Mordekhai.

Atlas Karta le-Toldot Erets Yisra'el mi-Betar ve-'ad Tel-Hai: Historyah Tsevait
(1969) a military history covering the period from antiquity to the twentieth
century 4. Wallach, Jehuda Lothar. *Atlas Karta le-Toldot Erets-Yisrael me-
Reshit ha-Hityashvut ve-ad Kum ha-Medinah* (1972) covering the period from
the mid-nineteenth century to 1948. 5. *Mafteah le-Shemot Ishim ve-'Inyanim
Mevo'ar u-Me'uyar.* Edited by Imanuel Be'eri (1981),1-4. The reader is
referred from each entry to the place in the Atlas where the subject is
mentioned. Volumes 1-4 contain place name indexes. Volumes 3-4 also
contain brief bibliographies.

442 *Atlas Karta le-Toldot Medinat Yisrael.* Editors: Jehudah Wallach and
Moshe Lissak. Jerusalem: Karta; Tel-Aviv: Misrad ha-bitahon, 1978-
1983. 4v.
This illustrated atlas depicts the history of the State of Israel. It consists of
the following parts: 1. *Shanim Rishonot* (1978) covering the years 1948 to
1961 2. *'Asor Sheni* (1980) covering the years 1961-1971 3. *"Asor Shelishi*
(1983) covering the years 1971-1981 4. *Mafteah le-Shemot ve-'Inyanim,* a
biographical dictionary and gazetteer which provides brief sketches about
individuals and places that were listed in volumes 1-3.

443 *Atlas of Israel: Cartography, Physical Geography, Human and Economic
Geography, History.* 3rd ed. rev. New York: Macmillan, 1985. 1v. (various pagings)
This atlas was published originally in Hebrew under the title *Atlas Yisrael*
(Jerusalem: Mahleket ha-Medidot,1956-1964). This edition is a revision of
the first English language edition (Amsterdam: Elsevier, 1970). It is bilingual and includes all the territories within Israel's 1985 boundaries. The
atlas depicts through maps and explanatory texts the history of Palestine
from Biblical times to the present. It provides information pertaining to
such subjects as physical geography, demography, economics, etc.

444 Bahat, Dan. *The Illustrated Atlas of Jerusalem.* New York: Simon &
Schuster, 1990. 144p.
This English edition is a revision and a translation of *Atlas Karta ha-Gadol
le-Toldot Yerushalayim* (Jerusalem: Karta,1989). It contains more than 400
color illustrations, maps, drawings, and isometric reconstructions. The
concise, easy-to-read text is based on the latest archaeological evidence. The
book covers the history of Jerusalem from the earliest settlement until
the present. The atlas includes a bibliography for further reading and an
index.

445 Ben-Dov, Meir. *Yerushalayim bi-Rei ha-Dorot.* Jerusalem: Karta, 1991.
200p.
This atlas depicts the history of Jerusalem from its founding until 1989. The
photographs, maps and drawings (some three dimensional) help clarify
the accompanying text. The atlas contains a bibliography and a name and
subject index.

446 Gilbert, Martin. *Jerusalem History Atlas.* New York: MacMillan, 1977.
136p.
Depicts the history of Jerusalem from Biblical times to the present. Each
map is accompanied by prints or photographs on the facing page.

C. BIOGRAPHICAL DICTIONARIES

See also entry 873.

447 Gelis, Yaakov. *Entsiklopedyah le-Toldot Hakhme Erets Yisrael.* Jerusalem: ha-Makhon le-Heker Yerushalayim / Mosad ha-Rav Kook, 1974-1978. 3v.

> This biographical dictionary covers the period from c.940-1940. It provides biographical descriptions of lives and achievements of "scholars" who served in rabbinical posts, or who were judges, teachers or emissaries to the Diaspora, etc., during this period. Individuals born in Palestine during this period, who served in similar capacities in the Diaspora, are also listed. The entries vary in length; some are feature length, e. g., the entry for Rabbi Abraham Isaak Kook, the chief Rabbi of Palestine (1921-1935) in volume 3. The dictionary is arranged by given name. The entries include sources for further reading and may include a portrait and or facsimiles from books or other materials. A comprehensive list of sources is also included in the end of volume 1. Each volume includes a name index arranged by surname. A cumulative name index (volumes 1-3) is included at the end of volume 3.

448 *Leksikon ha-Ishim shel Erets Yisrael, 1799-1948.* Compiled by Yaakov Shavit, Yaakov Goldstein, and Haim Be´er. Tel-Aviv: Am Oved, 1983. 520p.

> This *Leksikon* provides brief biographical descriptions of noted individuals in Palestine during the period from 1799-1948.

449 *Mi va-Mi bi-Yerushalayim.* Chief Editor: Eliezer Shmueli. Jerusalem: Zamir Bar-Lev, 1990. 464p.

> This lexicon is divided into three sections. The first section contains essays on Jerusalem's history, its cultural life, etc. The second section contains brief biographical sketches of c.1,000 individuals. The third section describes various enterprises and institutions in Jerusalem. The volume is enriched by the many colored illustrations.

450 *Nashim be-Yisrael: Leksikon.* Edited by Yael Rozman, et al. Tel-Aviv: Am Oved, 1991. 163p.

> In this Lexicon the editors provide brief biographical descriptions of women who achieved prominence in a variety of endeavors in Palestine / Israel during the period from 1885-1985. A list and a description of women's organizations is included in an appendix.

451 Rivlin, Gershon and Aliza Gershon. *Zar Lo Yavin.* Tel-Aviv: Misrad ha-bitahon, 1984. 561p.

> This lexicon lists the nom de guerre of individuals in the Jewish underground in Palestine. The lexicon is divided into two parts: A. Pseudonyms arranged in alphabetical order. The compilers provide for each pseudonym the name of the individual, unit affiliation, years, duties, etc. B. A listing of correct names arranged within the following three indexes: A. Index of names B. Place index C. General index.

452 Tidhar, David. *Entsiklopedyah le-Halutse ha-Yishuv u-Vonav.* Tel-Aviv: The author, 1943-1971. 19v.

This is a biographical lexicon of persons active in the cultural, social, and political life of the Jewish community in Palestine and Israel. A name index of all biographies is included at the end of Vol. 19.

D. BIBLIOGRAPHY / HANDBOOKS / FILMOGRAPHY
See also entries 130 and 535.

453 Amrami, Yaakov. *Bibliyografyah Shimushit: Nili, Berit ha-Biryonim, ha-Irgun ha-Tsevai ha-Leumi, Lohame Herut Yisrael.* Tel-Aviv: Hadar, 1975-

This partially annotated classified bibliography "is designed to serve as a reference guide to publications dealing with 'Nili, 'Brit Habiryonim', the 'Irgun Zvai Leumi' (Etsel), and 'Lohamey Herut Israel' (Lehi)," the secret underground organizations active in Palestine before the establishment of the State of Israel. The publications of the Underground organizations are also listed. The books, booklets, articles, dissertations and seminar papers included in the bibliography are written in Hebrew and various European languages. Volume one of the bibliography is divided into eleven sections, including: Background Material, which includes a list of the oral testimonies which were collected by the Hebrew University in Jerusalem's Institute for Contemporary Jewry, The Jabotinsky Institute in Israel, The History of the Hagana Archives, and The Weizmann Archives; Biographies and Memoirs which "deals with the biographical notes, monographs and memoirs of Underground activists, with outstanding personalities who influenced the direction of the Underground struggle and memoirs which include episodes dealing with the Underground organizations." The volume also includes an appendix which lists papers of secondary school student publications and writings. Volume two, covering the years 1975-1990, is divided into twenty-three sections, including: The Controversy Surrounding the Arlosoroff Affair; Aliya B ("Af Al Pi") 1931-1948; The "Altalena Affair," June 1948; The Capture of Deir Yassin, April 9, 1948; Background Material; Biographies and Portraits; Belles Lettres. Both volumes include a Hebrew name index (including titles). Volume two also has an author / title index (in English).

454 *A Bibliography of Israel.* Compiled by Yonah Alexander, Miriam Alexander, and Mordecai S. Chertoff. New York: Herzl Press, 1982. 263p.

This classified bibliography lists both recent and older works pertaining to such subjects as: history, geography, archaeology, Israel and the Arab Middle east, contemporary Israel, Israel among the nations, Israel and world Jewry. Each entry includes a brief annotation. The bibliography includes author and title indexes.

455 *Bibliyografyah le-Toldot Yisrael ba-Tekufah ha-Parsit, ha-Helenistit, veha-Romit. ... 1981-1985.* Compiled and edited by Devorah Dimant, Menahem Mor, Uriel Rappaport. Jerusalem: The Zalman Shazar Center for Jewish History, 1987. 129p.

This classified bibliography, the latest in a series compiled by Uriel Rappaport and others, lists 1,214 books and articles in English, Hebrew and other languages. This volume encompasses the entire Second Temple Period (538 B.C.E.-135 C.E.). The earlier bibliographies in the series are: " *Bibliyografyah le-Toldot Yisrael ba-Tekufah ha-Helenistit veha-Romit, 1946-1970,*" by Uriel Rappaport. *Mehkarim be-Toldot 'Am Yisra'el ve-Erets Yisrael* 2 (1972):247-321; *Bibliyografyah le-Toldot Yisrael ba-Tekufah ha-Helenistit veha-Romit, 1971-1975.* Compiled by Uriel Rappaport in collaboration with Menahem Mor. Jerusalem: Hebrew University, Institute for Advanced Studies, 977.; *Bibliyografyah le-Toldot Yisrael ba-Tekufah ha-Helenistit veha-Romit, 1976-1980,* by Menahem Mor and Uriel Rappaport. Jerusalem: Zalamn Shazar Center, 1982. These publications are limited to the Hellenistic and Roman periods. History of Palestine in the Second Temple Period, Jewish Literature in the period of the Second Temple, Jewish Hellenistic literature, Sects, e. g., Hasidim, Pharisees, Essenes are among the topics treated in the bibliographies. In addition, the latest volume includes materials pertaining to the Persian period, the Bar-Kokhba Revolt, early post-exilic literature and Diaspora communities, such as Elephantine/Yeb. The volumes for the years 1971-1975, 1976-1980, and 1981-1985 include subject and author indices.

456 Blank, Debra Reed. *Selected Books on Israel.* New York: JWB Jewish Book Council, 1984. 18p.
This work includes 200 annotated books in English. It is intended to help the synagogue or community center librarian select books on Israel. It is includes such subjects as: A. Arab-Israel relations B. Archaeology and travel C. Internal government and politics D. International politics and relations E. Israeli-American relations F. Literature and the arts G. Military history H. Modern history I. Religion; Social concerns, education, and ethnic relations J. Zionism.

457 Bourquin, David Ray. *First Century Palestinian Judaism: A Bibliography of Works in English.* San Bernandino, CA: The Borgo Press, 1990 109 p.
This bibliography lists alphabetically by main entry English language monographs and periodical literature pertaining to first century Palestinian Judaism. The material is arranged in the following three sections: A. Primary Sources, i. e., texts B. Books C. Periodicals and Serial Titles. The bibliography includes an index of books, an index of periodicals and serial articles, and an index of periodicals and serials.

458 Carpi, Judith. *Bibliyografyah shel Hevrat ha'-Ovdim.* Efal: Yad Tabenkin, 1989. 112p.
This bibliography of business enterprises and trade unions lists organizational reports, annual reports, memoirs, studies by and about an organization, etc. The bibliography is arranged by organization and includes publications, largely in Hebrew, published until 1985. Relevant articles that appeared in *Riv'on le-Kalkalah* during the years 1953-1985 are also included. Solel Boneh, Bank ha-Po'alim, ha-Sneh, Tenuvah, Egged, and Zim are among the organizations that are included in this bibliography. The book includes a brief introductory essay by Yitshak Greenberg entitled: " Hevrat ha-'Ovdim —Mivneh ve-Hitpathut Irgunit" about the history and structure of the "Hevrat ha-'Ovdim" and sketches of the member organizations.

459 Goel, Yohai. "Eretz Israel Reference Topics: A Bibliographic Survey." *Jewish Book Annual* (46): 44-116.

This guide to reference works on Israel includes alphabetically arranged lists of Hebrew and English sources.

460 Grundman, Moshe. *Bithon Yisrael, 1967-1991: Bibliyografyah Mu'eret u-Memuyenet.* Tel-Aviv: Ma'arachot, 1992. 448p.
This classified annotated bibliography lists more than 3,000 books, articles, and documents that pertain to all aspects of Israel's security for the period from 1967 to 1991. The work is divided into the following sections: Part I. National Security: Principles, Concepts and Policy Part II. Israel Defense Forces ("Zahal") Part III. Israel and the Regional Subsystem Part IV. Israel and the International System Part V. Arab-Israeli Wars Part VI. The War Against Terrorism Part VII. Biographies and Reference Works. The Bibliography includes Author and Periodical indexes.

461 *Israel: A Country Study.* Edited by Helen Chapin Metz. 3d ed. Washington, DC: The American University, 1990. 416p.
"This study is an attempt to treat in a concise and objective manner the dominant social, political, economic, and military aspects of contemporary Israeli society. Foreign words and phrases are defined the first time they appear in a chapter or are defined in a "Glossary" entry. Brief comments on some of the more valuable sources suggested as possible for further reading appear at the end of each chapter. In addition, chapter bibliographies are included at the end of the book. Appendix B, "Political Parties and Organizations," is provided to help readers identify the numerous political groups.

462 Kaufmann, Shoshana. *American Immigrants in Israel: A Selected, Annotated Bibliography, 1948-85.* New York: American Jewish Committee, 1987. 68p.
This is a selection of nearly 300 books, pamphlets, dissertations and articles dealing with the experiences of Americans who have immigrated to Israel. Entries include publications on the history of American aliyah, various categories of immigrants, difficulties of adjustment to Israeli society, and ongoing efforts to increase American aliyah.

463 *The Kibbutz: A Bibliography of Scientific and Professional Publications in English.* By Simon Shur and others. Darby, PA: Norwood Editions, 1981. 103p.
This is an up-to-date analytic bibliography focusing on scholarly and professional publications. Earlier bibliographies on the kibbutz include Albert I. Rabin's *Kibbutz Studies* (East Lansing, MI: Michigan State University Press, 1971.) and Simon Shur's *Kibbutz Bibliography,* 2nd ed. Tel-Aviv: Federation of Kibbutz Movements, 1972. 162p.)

464 Landau, Julian J. *Israel: A Selected Bibliography.* Israel: Israel Information Center, 1987. 25p.
This is a listing of 375 books divided into six categories: A. History B. War and peace C. International relations D. Land and people E. Jerusalem F. Biographies.

465 Mahler, Gregory S. *A Bibliography of Israeli Politics.* Boulder, CO: Westview Press, 1985. 133p.

This bibliography lists 1,419 books documents and articles in English published through the early part of 1984, which "focus upon the political dimensions of scholarship related to the study of Israel." In the introduction to the *Bibliography*, the author briefly discusses the study of Israeli politics and notes research topics of a "universal" nature, and those of "exceptional importance in Israel." A key-word index serves as a point of entry to the materials listed in the bibliography.

466 Marcus, Ralph. "A Selected Bibliography of the Jews in the Hellenistic-Roman World." *Proceedings of the American Academy for Jewish Research* 16 (1946-47): 97-181.
This classified bibliography encompasses the period of c.300 B.C.E.-200 C.E. Books and articles published from 1920-1945 are listed within the following broad subject areas: A. General works B. Jews of Palestine: a. History b. Religion and literature C. Jews of the Diaspora: a. History b.Religion and literature.

467 Meshorer, Rachel. *ha-Moshav: Bibliyografyah*. 2d ed. Rehovot: ha-Merkaz le-Heker Hityashvut Kafrit ve-'Ironit,1986. 142, 36 p.
This bibliography lists books and articles in Hebrew and English pertaining to Israeli cooperative villages. The bibliography is divided into two sections: A. Hebrew B. English. 1,390 items are listed in the Hebrew section. 371 items are listed in the English section. Both sections include a subject index. An earlier edition under the same title was published in 1979.

468 Neuberg, Assia. *Medinat Yisrael: Bibliyografyah Mu'eret*. Jerusalem: Graduate Library School of Hebrew University, 1970- .
This comprehensive, topically arranged, multilingual annotated bibliography lists books, pamphlets, collective works, and articles in Hebrew, Yiddish, English, and some European languages pertaining to the State of Israel and its history. The bibliography is divided into two major sections: A. Road to Statehood B. The State of Israel. The latter is subdivided into the following sections: A. General works B. Israel and the nations of the world C.Structure of the government and the internal affairs of the state D.Reference books. Each of the major sections is further subdivided. Volume 1, covers the years 1948-1968; Volume 2, 1969-1975; Volume 3, by Hadassah and Jacob Rothschild, 1976-1988. See also references are helpful in finding the information that is sought. Volume 2 has an "Index to Ph. D. and M. A. Dissertations." All volumes include author indexes. A cumulative index for volumes 1-2 is included at the end of volume 2.

469 Purvis, James D. *Jerusalem, The Holy City: A Bibliography*. Metuchen, NJ: Scarecrow Press, 1988-1991. 2v.
This classified bibliography lists books and articles written in English and other Western European languages about Jerusalem, from ancient to modern times. The bibliography is organized under eight major chapter headings: General studies on Jerusalem; Jerusalem during the Biblical period to 587 B.C.; Jerusalem during the Second Temple period; Roman Jerusalem; Jerusalem in Judaism; Christian Jerusalem; Jerusalem as a Muslim city; Jerusalem in modern times. Each general heading is further subdivided.

The second volume is organized in the same manner as the first volume. Materials published since 1986, earlier works not included in the first volume, as well as titles which appeared in volume one for which additional information is provided, are listed in this volume. Notices of reviews are listed in a separate section in each chapter. At the conclusion of each chapter subsection there is a listing of entry-numbers of titles in volume one which relate to that category. Volumes 1 and 2 include an author / subject index. Volume 2 also includes an index of references to volume one and an index of reviewers in volume one. Author and subject indexes are included.

470 Smooha, Sammy. *Social Research on Arabs in Israel, 1948-1977: Trends and an Annotated Bibliography.* Ramat Gan: Turtledove Publishing, 1978. 148p.

471 —. *Social Research on Arabs in Israel, 1977-1982.* Haifa: University of Haifa, 1984. 100p.
Each of the aforementioned books includes separate English and Hebrew language bibliographies. Each bibliography is divided into three parts: A. Research publications cites "social scientific publications on the Arab citizens of Israel in its pre-1967 borders." B. Other publications "includes a selection of sources on Arabs in Israel which do not qualify as research publications or whose reference to Arabs is relatively limited." C. Publications on Palestinians. Each bibliography includes a name / subject index.

472 —. *Social Research on Jewish Ethnicity in Israel, 1948-1986.* Haifa: Haifa University Press, 1987. 277p.
Smooha has compiled "a reference book on the ethnic divisions between Oriental Jews (mainly Jews from the Middle East and North Africa) and Ashkenazim (by and large Jews from Eastern and Central Europe) in Israel." The book is divided into three sections: A. A list of 614 books, chapters from books, and journal articles of "scientific merit" in English or Hebrew which focus on ethnic relations and differences. The materials included in the bibliography were written after 1948. They are listed in the bibliography alphabetically by author. More than 200 abstracts are incorporated in the bibliography. B. A classified core list of 100 publications. C. Directory of active researchers, consisting of a list of more than 60 specialists and other researchers who are active in the field. The institutional affiliation and mailing address of each individual are given. The bibliography includes a subject index.

473 Snyder, Esther Mann. *Israel.* Santa Barbara, CA: ABC-Clio Press, 1985. 272p.
This is a classified, annotated bibliography of books and articles in English that deal with Israel, "its history, geography, economy and politics; and with its people, their culture, customs, religion and social organization." The work includes an author, title, and subject index.

474 Tsabag, Shemuel. *Mediniyut ha-Huts shel Erets Yisrael: Bibliyografyah Nivheret.* Tel-Aviv: Open University, 1990. 191p.
Tsabag's bibliography lists books and articles in Hebrew and English that pertain to all aspects of Israeli foreign policy. The bibliography covers the period from 1948-1989. It is divided into thirteen main sections including such topics as Israel and the superpowers, Israeli relations with Western Europe, Israeli relations with the Third World; Israel and the Diaspora, Israel, Jordan and the Palestinians. Each section is subdivided into Hebrew

and English. These subsections are each further subdivided into books and articles. The author includes a list of periodicals and annuals that contain articles pertaining to Israeli foreign policy, as well as a list of Israeli archives that house primary source material pertaining to this topic.

475 Wallach, Jehuda Lothar. *Israeli Military History: A Guide to Sources.* New York: Garland, 1984. 291p.
This is a bibliography of books published largely in the 20th century, in Hebrew or Western languages, pertaining to the military history of the Jewish people from antiquity to the present. Each chapter includes an essay on the historical period under discussion, as well as a description of the major sources in the accompanying detailed bibliography. Relevant archives, libraries, and museums in Israel, as well as selected journals, are listed in an appendix. The work is indexed by author.

476 Wolffsohn, Michael. *Israel, Polity, Society, Economy, 1882-1986.* Translated by Douglas Bokovoy. Atlantic Highlands, NJ: Humanities Press International 1987. 302p.
This handbook is an enlarged and updated translation of the German edition: *Israel. Grundwissen Länderkunde, Politik, Gesellschaft, Wirtschaft* (Opladen: Leske & Budrich, 1984). It presents in condensed format basic information on "key aspects of the polity, society and economy of Israel ... for the period from 1882 ... to 1988." The following are the topics included in the handbook: A. Politics: System of government, the Parties, the Military, the Media, Foreign policy B. Society: Population, Religion,Interest groups, Education and recreation, Israel and world Jewry C. The Economy: Basic framework, Social and political ramifications of economic policy, selected economic data, sectors of the economy, Budget and taxes, Foreign trade, Economic dependence on foreign suppliers. The "West-Bank" territories are dealt with "only insofar as they are of relevance to Israel within the borders of 4 June 1967." A selected list of suggested reading is supplied for each major section. In addition, the work contains references within the text and an extensive "References and Sources" list. It also includes a chronological table in which the "chief dates in Israel's history" are noted.

477 *Yerushalayim le-Doroteha: Reshimah Bibliyografit.* Prepared by Mikhael Grintsvaig, et al. Jerusalem: Misrad ha-Hinukh veha-Tarbut: Yad Yitshak Ben Tsevi, 1992 or 1993. 54p.
This classified bibliography was prepared to be used in conjunction with the curriculum for "Israel Studies." Some chapters contain materials pertaining to different periods of the history of Jerusalem throughout the ages, e.g. until the destruction of the First Temple, the Second Temple, Roman period, etc. Other chapters contain materials pertaining to subjects that are related to Jerusalem, e.g. religious laws, customs and ceremonies, etc. Each item is coded to indicate its intended level, i.e. for students, for teachers, primary source etc.

E. BOOK REVIEWS

478 *Books on Israel.* Edited by Ian S. Lustick. Albany, NY: State University of New York Press, 1988- .

This series, published by the Israel Studies Association, contains review essays of recent scholarship by American and Israeli scholars pertaining to Israeli history and politics, Israeli society, culture and religion, and Israeli foreign relations "Although structuring their contributions as evaluations of new books ... the authors present their own perspectives on the issues in question, as well as overviews of developments in their fields of specialization ... Taken together these items constitute a survey of the current state of Israel studies, a presentation of the main questions being investigated and a resource guide to further reading." Volume 2, the last volume published to-date in the series, is entitled: *Critical Essays on Israeli Society, Politics, and Culture* (1991).

F. Chronologies

479 Rosenthal, Yemima. *Kronologyah le-Toldot ha-Yishuv ha-Yehudi be-Erets Yisrael*. Jerusalem: Yad Yitshak Ben-Tsevi, 1979. 331p.
Events that occurred from 1917-1935 and were deemed to be important in the history of the Yishuv (Jewish settlement in Palestine), are listed in this chronology. The events are listed chronologically within each of the following periods: A. 1917-1920, the transitional years B. 1920-1929, the establishment of the British Mandate and a Jewish national home in Palestine C. 1925-1935, Political problems and internal confrontations. Each section is preceded by a brief introduction. The data for the book was drawn largely from the press. A general index enables the user to find materials that are cited in the chronology.

480 Stern, Eliyahu. *Kronologyah le-Toldot ha-Yishuv ha-Yehudi he-Hadash be-Erets Yisrael*. Jerusalem: Yad Yitshak Ben-Tsevi, 1974. 280p.
Stern lists important events in the history of the Yishuv that occurred from 1936 through November 29, 1947. The materials were gathered largely from the press.

G. Demography

481 McCarthy, Justin. *The Population of Palestine*. New York: Columbia University Press, 1990. 242p.
This work contains a detailed collection of demographic statistics that show population changes in Palestine during the late Ottoman and Mandate periods (1878-1946). Additional statistical tables are included in the appendices, e.g. Ottoman statistics; European statistics of the Ottoman period; Mandate statistics including population, age distribution, birth and fertility, death and mortality statistics; Zionist statistics, including estimates of Jewish population at various periods (1170-1929), Jewish immigration (1919-1945), and citizenship of Jewish immigrants.

H. Directories

482 Beck, Mordechai. *Learning to Learn: A Guide to the New Yeshivot in Israel*. Jerusalem: Israel Economist, 1977. 62p.

This is a guide to yeshivot in Israel that were "created for the Jewish man or woman who was searching for his/her Jewishness ... ."

483 *Directory of Research Institutes in Israel.* Edited by Geula Gilat and Dan Bry. Tel-Aviv: National Scientific and Technological Information, 1982. 114p.
The research institutes are grouped under such categories as humanities, social sciences, sciences. The following information is provided about each institute: name and address, the name of the director and governing body, the fields of research undertaken and a list of publications.

484 *Doing Business in Israel.* Jerusalem: Somekh Chaikin, 1991. 250p.
This guide has been prepared by accountants for parties interested in doing business in Israel. Investment climate, doing business, audit and accounting, and taxation are among the topics discussed.

485 *Index of Outreach Programs in Israel.* New York: Avi Chai, 1989. 98p.
The index contains "detailed information about the myriad of programs designed to bring Jews in Israel closer to their heritage." It is "designed to assist those who are interested in referencing a particular organization or specific type of outreach program."

486 *The Israel Business Directory.* Jerusalem: Jerusalem Marketing Group (P.O. Box 23854, Jerusalem), 1989. 47p.
This directory lists associations and organizations, business research libraries; leading service companies, leading industrial companies, and government contacts (national and local, plus foreign embassies). Each entry provides names and addresses, as well as tele-facsimile and phone numbers. The directory includes an English-Hebrew business dictionary and key economic statistics.

487 *The Israeli Education System.* Jerusalem: Association of Americans & Canadians in Israel, 1985. 83p.
The purpose of this paperback is to acquaint the current and future oleh (immigrant) with the Israeli system of education by providing basic information and citing sources of information. The book is divided into 51 chapters (i.e. cities). Within each city, the arrangement is by type of school: elementary, high school, vocational (secular and religious), and higher education. For each institution, the directory gives the name of the school address, telephone number, and name of principal. While there is no index, the detailed table of contents is adequate for locating a city.

488 Jaffe, Eliezer D. *Giving Wisely: The Israel Guide to Non-profit and Volunteer Social Services.* Jerusalem: Koren Publishers, 1982. 656p.
This is an alphabetical guide to some 300 non-profit volunteer organizations in Israel active in the fields of health, education and welfare. For each organization, detailed and objective information is provided about its history, goals, services and activities, officers, finances, membership, and funding needs. It includes a bibliography and an alphabetical index of organizations.

489 *Muze'onim be-Yisra'el.* Edited by Yehudit Inbar and Ely Schiller. Jerusalem: Ministry of Education and Culture, 1990. 271p. (*Ariel* nos. 72-74, May, 1990).

This is a comprehensive guide written in Hebrew to the Museums in Israel. The following information is given for each entry: A. Address B. Telephone number C. Name of the director D. Hours the museum is open to the public. The guide includes a short bibliography of articles in Hebrew about museums in Israel. The many color and black and white photographs of the museums and artifacts from their respective collections enhance this guide.

490 Rosovsky, Nitza and Joy Ungerleider-Mayerson. *The Museums of Israel.* New York: Abrams, 1989. 256p.

Information is provided for 120 large and small museums, many of which are not frequented even by Israelis and are unknown to visitors. Each entry gives hours, telephone number, admission fee, and special strengths of each museum. More than a guide, the book encompasses the history of the country and recent archaeological discoveries. This handy, pocket-size, soft-cover book is beautifully illustrated in color, and is divided into eight geographic regions, with maps for each area. The directory includes a chronology, as well as indexes of names, subjects, and locations.

I. Dictionaries and Encyclopedias

491 *Political Dictionary of the State of Israel.* Susan Hattis Rolef, Editor. New York: MacMillan, 1987. 351p.

The *Dictionary* contains some 450 articles and is arranged alphabetically by topic. It provides the reader with basic, reliable information on all aspects of Israeli politics, including prominent personalities past and present; political figures; parties; outstanding events; the Knesset; coalition agreements; media; Israel's economic and foreign policy; its relations with Great Powers and other nations, and with the Diaspora. Historical background is provided in entries such as Mandatory Palestine, Zionism, and the Arab-Israeli conflict. The text of the Proclamation of Independence and the Law of Return are included in appendices. The *Dictionary* also includes a glossary.

492 *Leksikon Koah ha-Magen ha-"Haganah."* Chief Editor: Mordechai Naor. Tel-Aviv: Misrad ha-Bitahon: ha-Irgun ha-Artsi shel Havre ha-"Haganah", 1992. 528p.

The central theme of this illustrated lexicon is the history of the Haganah. The alphabetically arranged entries include biographical sketches of key figures, depiction of events and operations, descriptions of the units within the Haganah and discussions about the relationship between the Haganah and other groups. The entries were written by noted scholars, as well as by individuals affiliated with the Haganah. The materials in the appendices shed additional light on various facets of the Haganah, its senior command staff, and graduates of special courses. The *Lexicon* includes a classified bibliography pertaining to the history of the Haganah, its activities and its leaders. Cross references enable the user to broaden or narrow an information search. An extensive general index (name/subject) helps readers find a particular person, event, etc., even if it is covered in an entry on another subject.

493 Reich, Bernard. *Historical Dictionary of Israel.* Metuchen, NJ: Scarecrow Press, 1992. 351p.

This dictionary provides the user with concise information pertaining to persons, places, and events that are most central for an understanding of Israel. In addition the dictionary includes a chronology of events covering the period from c. the 17th century B.C.E. to the beginning of 1992, tables, and a bibliography of basic books. The tables list Israeli presidents, ministers, and immigration and population statistics. The bibliography lists books under the following subjects: A. General B. Biography and autobiography C. Culture D. Defense and security E. Economy F. Geography G. Government and politics G. History I. International relations J. Society K. Zionism and anti-Zionism.

494 Sirof, Harriet. *The Junior Encyclopedia of Israel.* New York: J. David, 1980. 480p.

The first of its kind for young readers, this illustrated volume offers a concise survey of the people, places, history, geography, culture, and institutions of Israel.

J. INDEXES

495 *Palestine and Zionism.* New York: Zionist Archives and Library, 1946-1956. 10v.

This remains a useful retrospective author, title, and subject index to periodicals and books and pamphlets pertaining to all aspects of Jewish history and culture. Emphasis is placed on such subjects as Israel, Palestine, and Zionism. The index covers the years 1946-1956.

K. YEARBOOKS

496 *The Israel Yearbook.* Tel-Aviv: Israel Yearbook Publications, 1951- .

This annual includes a summary of events for the preceding year, vital statistics and feature articles by Israeli government officials and scholars in various fields. The articles deal with current events or aspects of Israeli political, economic, social, cultural and religious life. 1991/1992 is the latest edition published.

497 *Shenaton ha-Memshalah.* Tel-Aviv, 1949- .

The yearbook includes the annual report of the various Israeli ministries. It provides information about the structure, personnel, and functions of each Ministry of the Israeli government. An English language edition entitled *Government Yearbook* is no longer published.—1990 is the latest edition published.

498 *Statistical Abstract of Israel=Shenaton Statisti le-Yisrael.* Jerusalem: Central Bureau of Statistics, 1949 / 1950- .

This annual bilingual compilation of official statistics contains basic quantitative data on such subjects as: the country's climate and environment, vital statistics, foreign trade, immigration and absorption, culture and entertainment, Judea, Samaria and the Gaza region, etc. 1993 (43) is the latest edition published.

499 *Who's Who in Israel and Jewish Personalities From All Over the World.* Tel-Aviv: Bronfman, 1985- .

This biennial publication is divided into two parts: A. Personalia B. Public and Private Bodies. The first part contains brief biographical and professional information about individuals who are prominent in various fields of pursuit in Israel and elsewhere. The second part consists of a directory of national and Zionist organizations, municipal, cultural and educational institutions, etc. Each entry includes the address and phone number of the organization, the names of its executive personnel, and a description of the organization. This publication continues *Who's Who in Israel and in the Work for Israel Abroad* (1969-1980), *Who's Who in Israel* (1952-1968) and its predecessors. The Hebrew edition, published in alternate years, is entitled *Mi va-Mi be-Yisrael* (1971 / 72-). The latest English edition is 22 (1992 / 93). The latest Hebrew edition is 7 (1988).

CHAPTER 17

ZIONISM

See also Chapters 15-16.

A. BIBLIOGRAPHY

500 Klausner, Israel. *Toldot ha-Tsiyonut.* Jerusalem: Merkaz Zalaman Shazar, 1975. 448p.
This classified bibliography lists more than 3,000 books, articles, and chapters from books pertaining to all aspects of Zionism written in Hebrew and English and published to mid-1975. Basic books in other languages, with the exception of Russian, are also included. The bibliography is divided into the following 12 subject areas: A. Bibliographies B.Encyclopedias and lexicons C. General books and articles on the history of Zionism D. Anthologies, collections of documents and periodicals E. The period of the forerunners of the movement until 1880) F. The period of Hibbat Zion (1881-1896) G. The period of political Zionism, until World War I (1897-1914) H. The period of World War I I. The period of the British Rule in Eretz Yisrael (1920-1947) J. Personalities K. The Zionist movement after the establishment of the State. Each section is further subdivided. The bibliography includes name indexes in Hebrew and English.

501 "Zionism: A Bibliography." In *Studies In Zionism* (formerly *Zionism*) 1-1980- .
This selective classified bibliography, written by various scholars, is published annually. It lists studies, research and primary source materials published worldwide (generally in the year stipulated in the annual cumulation) pertaining to all aspects of Zionism and the early years of the State of Israel (i.e. the period from 1882-1967). It includes, however, works on earlier, pre-Zionist or proto-Zionist thinkers in the seventies and eighties of the nineteenth century.

B. ENCYCLOPEDIAS

502 *Encyclopedia of Zionism and Israel.* Edited by Raphael Patai. New York: Herzl Press, 1971. 2v.
This illustrated work contains about 3,000 articles, some signed, pertaining primarily to the history and development of the Zionist movement and its constituent organizations in Palestine, Israel, and elsewhere in the world, beginning with the latter half of the 19th century and going to the present, biographies of Zionist leaders and Israeli public figures, and information about places in Israel. There is a selective bibliography at the end of volume 2.

503 Raphael, Yitzhak. *Entsiklopedyah shel ha-Tsiyonut ha-Datit.* Jerusalem: Mosad ha-Rav Kook, 1958- .

This dictionary contains signed articles by acknowledged authorities, about deceased individuals who played a role in the religious Zionist movement. Some of the biographical sketches are article length essays, e. g., the article about Rabbi Abraham Isaac Kook (1865-1913), the first chief rabbi of Palestine (in volume 5:89-442). The articles document the individual's contribution to the religious Zionist movement. They include birth and death dates and often also include a portrait of the individual, bibliographical data documenting the individual's publications, and bibliographic sources for further reading. Five volumes covering the letters aleph-tav (Tarshish) have been published to-date. A supplementary volume is planned.

CHAPTER 18

HOLOCAUST

See also Chapter 15 and entries 89-98.

A. ARCHIVAL RESOURCES

504 *Guide to Unpublished Materials of the Holocaust.* Edited by Jacob
Robinson and Yehuda Bauer. Jerusalem: Hebrew University, Institute
of Contemporary Jewry, 1970- .
This multi-volume series contains guides to archival collections in Israel
and elsewhere pertaining to the Holocaust. The following information is
provided, when available, for each collection that is surveyed: A. Name of
archives B. Name of institution and unit symbol C. Period D. Character,
purpose and activities of the institution E. Quantity of material F. Internal
division of the unit G. Files of special interest H. Method of registration of
material I. Bibliography (relating to the use of the unit's material); lists of
prominent interviewees in oral documentation projects. Each volume is
fully indexed. The following are some of the institutions whose collections
are listed in the *Guide:* The Oral History Division-Institute of Contemporary Jewry (Jerusalem), The Israel State Archives, The Jewish National and
University Library (Jerusalem), Yad Vashem, Beit Lohame ha-Getaot-The
Ghetto Fighters' House in Memory of Yitzhak Katznelson, and Moreshet-
The Anielewicz Museum in Memory of the Commander of the Warsaw
Ghetto Uprising.

505 *ha-Yahadut ha-Datit ba-Shoah, 1939-1945; Madrikh shel Mosadot ve-
Irgunim Datiyim be-Yisrael.* Editor in Chief: Meir Edelstein; Assitant
Editor: Penina Meizlish. Ramat Gan: Institute of Holocaust Research,
Bar-Ilan University, 1986. 140p.
This guide lists primary source material in Israel pertaining to the "reac-
tions, activities and philosophical attitudes of religious organizations and
personages ..." to the Holocaust. It is limited to the years 1939-1945. The
materials are housed in the following nine archives: A. Agudath Israel
Center in Eretz Yisrael B. Agudath Israel —the World Center C. Beit Meir
-Protocols D. Chief Rabbi Herzog Archives E. Archives of the Chief
Rabbinate F.The World Center of Mizrachi, the Poel Hamizrachi G. Archives of the Poel Hamizrachi H. Archives of Religious Zionism (in Mosad
Harav Kook) I. Archives of the Kibbutz Hadati (The Religious Kibbutz
Movement). The guide is arranged alphabetically. Subjects, names of
organizations and people, and place names are interfiled. Each entry may
be further subdivided by related activity, events etc. The archive that holds
materials pertaining to the entry is noted. The date of an event that is cited
is provided in parentheses. The archive's file number is also given.

B. Atlases and Gazetteers

506 Gilbert, Martin. *Atlas of the Holocaust*. Rev. ed. New York: Pergamon Press, 1988. 256p.

This new edition contains over 300 maps drawn by Martin Gilbert, each fully annotated and based on documentary evidence. Presented in chronological order, the maps provide a comprehensive record of the Holocaust. The Atlas also documents 200 acts of resistance and revolt, Jewish partisan activities, and avenues of escape and rescue. It includes a bibliography and an index.

507 Mokotoff, Gary, and Sallyann Amdur Sack. *Where Once We Walked: A Guide to the Jewish Communities Destroyed in the Holocaust*. Teaneck, NJ: Avotaynu, 1991. 514p.

The authors list 22,000 Central and East European communities where Jews lived before the Holocaust. The following information is given for each community: name and alternate name, name of country, distance / direction from a major city, latitude and longitude, Jewish population before the Holocaust, source code (i.e. reference to sources that provide information about Jewish communities). See references direct the reader to the official contemporary name of the community. A listing of town names grouped phonetically according to the Deutch-Mokotoff soundex system is provided to assist readers solve problems with misspelled or hard to spell town names. A select bibliography of atlases, gazetteers, maps and other sources is included.

508 Szajkowski, Zosa. *An Analytical Franco-Jewish Gazetteer, 1939-1945*. New York: The American Academy for Jewish Research, 1966. 349p.

Szajkowski describes the places in France of importance to Jews during the Holocaust. The places, arranged according to the 90 departments of France, include camps and other places of forced residence, places of legal and underground activity, etc. In the extensive introduction, Szajkowski presents some of the problems that would have to be investigated in order to prepare a history of French Jews during the Holocaust. The *Gazetteer* includes a map of France, an index of places, and an index of authors and titles, names of persons, organizations and subjects.

C. Bibliography

509 Bloomberg, Marty. *The Jewish Holocaust: An Annotated Guide to Books in English*. San Bernardino, CA.: The Borgo Press, 1991. 248p.

This is a selective annotated bibliography of books in English pertaining to the historical development of European anti-Semitism, the pre-war background of European Jewish Civilization, the Holocaust years, war crime trials, art and literature, and the meaning of the Holocaust. The author includes lists of core title recommendations for college and university libraries, public libraries, and high school libraries. Author / Title index.

510 Carges, Harry James. *The Holocaust: An Annotated Bibliography*. 2nd ed. Chicago: American Library Association, 1985. 196p.

This is an expanded and revised edition of a bibliography originally published in 1977 that lists close to 500 English language books published in the United States. The materials chosen for inclusion have been selected for "college and university libraries, for public libraries, and for more sophisticated high school collections." The bibliography includes secondary source materials pertaining to such topics as: anti-Semitism and the rise of Nazism, histories of the Third Reich and the Holocaust, the concentration camps, Jewish resistance, reflections on the holocaust, and survivors and the second generation. In addition the author lists collections of a general nature which contain primary source material. The regional indexes and the author-title index enhance the value of this work.

511 Edelheit, Abraham J. and Hershel Edelheit. *Bibliography on Holocaust Literature.* Boulder, CO: Westview Press, 1986. 842p.
This classified partially annotated bibliography contains 9,014 entries for English language materials published from 1930 to 1985. The monographs, scholarly articles, theses, newspapers reports, eyewitness testimonies and memoirs listed pertain to various aspects of the Holocaust, its background and aftermath, as well as to Jewish life in pre-war Europe. The authors do not list articles in Festschriften and works of fiction. The preface to each major section provides a guide for further reading. The work includes an author index. The usefulness of the bibliography would have been enhanced by the provision of internal cross references and a subject index.

512 —. *Bibliography on Holocaust Literature: Supplement.* Boulder, CO: Westview Press, 1990. 684p.
The supplement lists 6,500 additional items. A brief introductory essay places the citations into context. It includes new sections, e. g., The Holocaust — Related Novels and Short Stories, Reviews of Holocaust Literature, The Bitburg Controversy. Cross references, a glossary, author, title, and subject indexes are provided to facilitate usage.

513 —. *Bibliography on Holocaust Literature: Supplement,* Volume 2. Boulder, CO: Westview Press, 1993. 564p.
An additional 3,870 items are listed in this supplement. A brief introductory essay places the citations into context. The second supplement includes a new section on Soviet anti-Semitism and an expanded section on neo-Nazism and neo-fascism. Cross references, a glossary, author, title, and subject indexes are provided to facilitate usage.

514 Eitinger, Leo and Robert Krell. *The Psychological and Medical Effects of Concentration Camps and Related Persecutions on Survivors of the Holocaust: A Research Bibliography.* Vancouver: University of British Columbia Press, 1985. 168p.
This multi-lingual bibliography lists "studies of the medical and psychological sequelae of concentration camp incarceration and related persecutions." The bibliography includes all that has been written in medical, psychological, psychiatric, and social work literature to 1984. It includes a subject index.

515 *Facing History and Ourselves: Holocaust and Human Behavior Annotated Bibliography.* Edited by Margaret A. Drew. New York: Walker and Company, 1988. 124 p.
This bibliography is one in a series of publications published by Facing History and Ourselves, "a non-profit organization providing educators

with services and resources for examining the history of the Holocaust, genocide, racism, anti-Semitism, and issues related to adolescent and adult development." Both the children's books and the adult books included in this classified annotated bibliography "represent an effort to explore the range of human responses to the Holocaust, as well as to provide the historical background necessary to place those responses in context." A basic reading list and a supplementary reading list pertaining to the "Legacy of the Holocaust" are included in appendices.

516 Fortunoff Video Archive for Holocaust Testimonies. *Guide to Yale University Library Holocaust Video Testimonies.* New York: Garland Publishing, 1990. 130p.
> This guide consists of three sections: A. Summaries of some 225 videotape testimonies of Holocaust survivors, liberators, and bystanders that are housed in the Fortunoff Video Archive. The summaries are in English, and they are listed in the guide by HVT (Holocaust Video Testimony) number. B. An index by first name and last initial of witnesses C. An index "comprising geographic locations, subject terms, and historical figures."

517 *Genocide: A Critical Bibliographic Review.* Edited by Israel W. Charny. New York: Facts on File, 1988- .
> Each chapter "presents an authoritative, encyclopedia-like statement of the knowledge base in a given field or area of study of genocide, and an annotated critical bibliography which represents, in the judgment of the Contributing Editor, a significant compilation of definitive and meaning-ful literature in the area of study." Volume 1 is "designed to organize the state-of-the art knowledge in various fields of genocide and its preven-tion." It includes an introductory essay "The Holocaust: The Ultimate and Archetypal Genocide," by Alan L. Berger, and " The Literature, Art, and Film of the Holocaust," By Samuel Totten. Volume two includes the following essays relating to the Holocaust: "The Psychology of Denial of Known Genocides," by Israel W. Charny; "Denial of the Holocaust," by Erich Kulka; "Educating about the Holocaust: A Case Study in the Teach-ing of Genocide,"by Dan Darsa; " The Memorialization of the Holocaust: Museums, Memorials and Centers, by Sybil Milton; and "Righteous People in the Holocaust," by Pearl M. Oliner and Samuel P. Oliner. Both volumes are indexed.

518 *Genocide In Our Time: An Annotated Bibliography with Analytical Intro-ductions.* Edited by Michael N. Dobkowski and Isidor Walliman. Ann Arbor, MI: The Pierian Press, 1993. 200p.
> In this work, subject specialists address diverse aspects of genocide, e. g., ethnocide, the Holocaust, the issue of the Holocaust as a unique event, the victims who survived. They provide selective, extensively annotated bib-liographies of the major books, articles, studies, and government publica-tions related to their topics. The work includes a chronology of genocide and indexes.

519 *The Holocaust: An Annotated Bibliography and Resource Guide.* Edited by David Szonyi. New York: National Jewish Resource Center; Ktav, 1985. 396p.
> This is a comprehensive bibliography of English-language materials per-taining to all aspects of the Holocaust. It includes annotated lists of non-

fiction and fiction books, books for young readers, a filmography, a guide to musical resources, a listing of mobile and traveling exhibits, a list of Holocaust memorials in the United States and Canada, a list of survivor's groups, examples of Yom ha-Shoah and Day of Remembrance services, a guide to doing oral history, sample Holocaust curricula, and information on obtaining speakers and funding. An author, title and subject index would have enhanced the value of this bibliography.

520 *The Holocaust in Books and Films: A Selected Annotated List.* Edited by Judith Herschlag Muffs and Dennis B. Klein. 3rd ed. New York: International Center for Holocaust Studies, Anti-Defamation League / Hippocrene Books, 1986. 156p.
This is a selected annotated bibliography of some 475 English-language books and films. This much expanded revised edition is divided into the following 12 categories: European Jewry before the Holocaust; the Third Reich; Holocaust overview; Camps, ghettos, in hiding; Collaboration and indifference; Resistance and rescue; War criminals; Survivors and the generation after; After the Holocaust; Reflections and literary analyses; Nature of human behavior; The Jews; Prejudice and anti-Semitism; The Controlled society. The compilers assign reading levels to each item. The bibliography also includes lists of major Holocaust education and resource centers, libraries, archives, and audio-visual distributors in the United States. It is indexed.

521 Knoller, Rivka. *Denial of the Holocaust: A Bibliography of Literature Denying or Distorting the Holocaust, and of Literature About This Phenomenon.* Ramat Gan: Abraham and Edita Spiegel Chair in Holocaust Research, Faculty of Jewish Studies, Bar-Ilan University, 1989. 36p.
This work is divided into two parts: A. Articles, Books, and Pamphlets Denying or Distorting the Holocaust. The materials listed in this section were published in West Germany, Austria, Belgium, Sweden (1959-1989); France 1961-1962); The United States, Canada, Australia, South Africa, and Great Britain (1973-1989) and Italy (1966-1987). B. Articles, Books, and Pamphlets About Denial and Distortion of the Holocaust and About the Attempt at "Historical Revision." The materials listed in this section are written in Hebrew, Yiddish, English, French, German and Dutch.

522 Laska, Vera. *Nazism, Resistance and Holocaust in World War II: A Bibliography.* Metuchen, NJ: Scarecrow Press, 1985. 183p.
This is a partially annotated classified bibliography pertaining to the Holocaust. The work is divided into the following sections: A. Jews and anti-Semitism B. Nazism C. Resistance D. Resistance—women E. Jewish resistance; F. Holocaust G. Holocaust—women H. Women in hiding I. Pre-1945 knowledge of the Holocaust J. War crimes H. Art and photographs I. Philosophy and interpretation J. Literature. There is an author index.

523 Libowitz, Richard. "Holocaust Studies." *Modern Judaism* 10 (1990): 271-281.
Libowitz notes the increased interest in the Holocaust in the decade of the 80's as evidenced by the expansion of Holocaust Studies on college and University campuses in the United States, various public events, and the increased production and showing of films pertaining to the Holocaust. He

also reviews the major studies that were written in the 1980's pertaining to the Holocaust.

524 *Persecution and Resistance Under the Nazis.* 2nd rev. ed. London: Vallentine & Mitchell, 1960.
This is a volume in the *Catalogue Series* published by the Wiener Library (London), in which its holdings pertaining to the Nazi period and German Jewish history are listed. 1,943 items pertaining to persecution and resistance in Germany, German occupied countries, as well as the persecution of Jews and their resistance to Nazi terror are listed. The bibliography includes a list of periodicals published by Germans in exile, and a listing of illegal pamphlets and periodicals. It is indexed.

525 Piekarz, Mendel. *ha-Shoah u-Sefiheha be-Aspaklaryat Kitve 'Et 'Ivriyim.* Jerusalem: Yad-Vashem, 1978. 493p.
This is a continuation of the author's earlier work in the Joint Documentary Projects Bibliographical Series (above). This classified bibliography contains references to all aspects of the Holocaust in the daily press and weeklies in Hebrew from 1951-1975. Indexed.

526 Robinson, Jacob. *The Holocaust: The Nuremberg Evidence. Part I: Documents, Digest, Index and Chronological Tables.* Jerusalem: Yad Vashem, 1976.
This digest of documents is based largely on Columbia University Law Library's collection of Nuremberg Trial documents. Each document is listed and fully described. The volume includes a chronological table of documents listed in the digest, a glossary and a detailed index (name, place, subject) to the documents.

527 Sable, Martin. *Holocaust Studies: A Directory and Bibliography of Bibliographies.* Greenwood, FL: Penkevill Publishing Co., 1987. 115p.
This is a bibliography of 55 bibliographies published through 1986, grouped by language, which "treat the Holocaust, in toto or in some aspect(s)." Included also is a directory which provides addresses for associations and foundations, survivor organizations, archives, libraries, school and university teaching programs, monuments, plaques, etc. Each section is indexed.

528 Strom, Margot Stern. *Facing History and Ourselves: Holocaust and Human Behavior.* [s. l.]: Strom & Parsons, 1978. 232 p.
This resource book includes a "Bibliography and Filmography," by Margaret A. Drew. The address of Facing History and Ourselves National Foundation is: 16 Hurd Road, Brookline, MA 02146. Telephone: (617) 232-1595

529 Yad Vashem Martyr's and Heroes Memorial Authority and YIVO Institute for Jewish Research. *Joint Documentary Projects Bibliographical Series.* Jerusalem: Yad Vashem Martyr's and Heroes Memorial Authority; New York: YIVO Institute for Jewish Research, 1960-1977. 14v.
This series of bibliographies provides the user with references to scholarly and popular literature in Hebrew, Yiddish and English on all aspects of the Holocaust. All the volumes in the series are well indexed. The following

volumes were published in this series: 1. Robinson, Jacob. *Guide to Jewish History Under Nazi Impact, 1933-1945.* 2. Friedman, Philip. *Bibliyografyah shel ha-Sefarim ha-'Ivriyim 'al ha-Shoah.* 3. Gar, Joseph and Philip Friedman. *Bibliografye fun Yidishe Bikher Vegn Hurbn un Gvure.* 4. Braham, Randolph L. *Hungarian Jewish Catastrophe.* 5-8. Piekarz, Mendel. *ha-Shoah veha-Gevurah ba-Aspaklaryah shel ha-'Itonut ha-'Ivrit.* 9. Gar, Joseph. *Bibliografye fun Artiklen Vegn Hurbn.* 10. Gar, Joseph. *Bibliografyah shel Ma-Mamarim 'al ha-Shoah ve-'al ha-Gevurah.* 11. Bass, David. *Bibliografye fun Yidishe Bikher Vegn Hurbn un Gvure.* 12. Robinson, Jacob. *The Holocaust and After; Sources and Literature in English.* 13-14. Piekarz, Mendel. *ha-Shoah u-Sefiheha ba-Sefarim ha-'Ivriyim she-Yatsu la-'or ba-Shanim 1933-1972.*

D. DIRECTORIES

530 *Association of Holocaust Organizations: Directory.* Edited by William L. Shulman. Bayside, NY: Holocaust Resource Center and Archives, Queensborough Community College, 1990- .
This annual directory lists institutions and organizations that provide services, assemble resources, and conduct programs related to the Holocaust. The directory is arranged alphabetically by name of institution, with a geographical index by state.

531 *Directory of Holocaust Institutions.* Edited by Isaiah Kuperstein. 2nd ed. Washington, DC: U.S. Holocaust Memorial Council, 1988. 56p.
This is a useful guide to 98 Holocaust institutions in the United States, including museums, resource centers, archival facilities, memorials, research institutions and libraries. The guide describes the purpose, activities, services, collections and publications of each institution and provides the address and telephone number and the name(s) of key staff members.

532 *National Registry of Holocaust Survivors.* Washington, DC: American Gathering of Jewish Holocaust Survivors in Cooperation with the United States Holocaust Memorial Council, 1993. various pagings.
This is a listing of more than 80,000 Holocaust survivors and their families living in the United States and Canada. The list is based on the files of the National Registry. The directory is divided into three sections: A. An alphabetical listing of survivors. The names of survivors before and during the Holocaust, as well as the maiden names of women are given B. An index of names arranged by place of birth or town of residence before the Holocaust C. An index of names arranged according to places during the Holocaust.

E. ENCYCLOPEDIAS

533 *Encyclopedia of the Holocaust.* Editor-in-chief: Israel Gutman. New York: MacMillan, 1990. 4v.
This four-volume encyclopedia containins almost 1,000 articles by noted scholars pertaining to the manifold aspects of the Holocaust, its antecedents, and its postwar consequences. Each article is accompanied by a short bibliography. Related articles are linked by cross references. Includes many black-and-white photographs, illustrations and maps. It is indexed.

534 *Pictorial History of the Holocaust.* Edited by Yitshak Arad. New York: Macmillan, 1990. 396p.

The photographs, maps and accompanying text are arranged in the following major sections: A. Nazism and its origins B. Persecution of the Jews in Germany, 1933-1939 C. European Jews under Nazi rule and terror, 1939-1941 D. The ghettos E. Mass murder F. Deportation to death camps G. The death camps H. Jewish armed resistance in occupied Europe I. Partisans J. End of the war-en route to Israel.

F. FILMOGRAPHY

535 *A Catalogue of Audio and Visual Collections of Holocaust Testimony.* 2nd ed. Compiled by Joan Ringelheim. New York: Greenwood, 1992. 209 pages

This catalog describes the video and audio collections of interviews with holocaust survivors that are housed in 43 repositories in the United States. The catalog is arranged by state. Each entry includes information pertaining to the location of the collection and access to it, a summary of the content of each collection, and information on additional Holocaust material in each repository. The compiler has also included "several appendices to enable the user to find those collections containing interviews with particular groups of survivors (e.g. survivors born in France; survivors of Auschwitz ...)."

536 Gellert, Charles Lawrence. *The Holocaust, Israel, and the Jews.* Washington, DC: Published for the National Archives and Records Administration by the National Archives Trust Fund Board, 1989. 117p.

This is a classified select list of films held at the National Archives pertaining largely to the Holocaust and the birth and early history of modern Israel. Included in the listing is the film record of the evidence submitted at the European war crime trials after World War II and much of the motion picture journalism of developing events through 1961. The films are arranged according to the dates of the events within each of the topics. Each entry includes the following information: title, film number for retrieval, a story caption, technical data, copyright, release or production date. A complete listing of the titles is included in an appendix. The work is indexed.

537 Skirball, Sheba F. *Films of the Holocaust: An Annotated Filmography of Collections in Israel.* New York: Garland, 1990. 273p.

This is an annotated listing of films on the Holocaust available in Israel, regardless of where they were originally produced. The core of the bibliography is based on the holdings of Beit Lohame ha-Geta'ot-The Ghetto Fighters' House in Memory of Yitzhak Katznelson, and Yad Vashem. Part one contains an alphabetical listing of films with the following information: title, language, running time, color or B &W, a brief description of the film, and the holding institution. Part two features a listing of untitled footage taken from German and Israeli newsreels, as well as survivors' memoirs. This work includes an index of film titles by language and a subject index.

CHAPTER 19

BIBLICAL STUDIES, APOCRYPHA AND PSEUDEPIGRAPHA AND DEAD SEA SCROLLS

A. BIBLICAL STUDIES

HISTORY OF BIBLICAL TIMES

538 Albright, William Foxwell. *From Stone Age to Christianity.* 2d ed. New York: Harper & Row, 1963. 432p.

> A theological-historical study in which the author traces the development of the idea of God from prehistoric antiquity to the time of Christ. The new edition is augmented by an introduction, in which Albright surveys recent developments in this field.

539 *Ancient Israel: A Short History from Abraham to the Roman Destruction.* Edited by Hershel Shanks. Englewood Cliffs, NJ: Prentice Hall, 1988. 267p.

> This is an illustrated history of the people of Israel from their patriarchal beginnings to 70 C.E. Each chapter, covering an historical period, is written by a noted scholar, and reflects the most recent developments and latest archaeological discoveries. The bibliographic endnotes enable the student to explore subjects of interest in greater depth. The work is enhanced by the inclusion of maps and charts.

540 Bright, John. *A History of Israel.* 3d ed. Philadelphia: PA: Westminster Press, 1981. 511p.

> Following a sketch Ancient Near Eastern History, Bright presents a history of the people of Israel spanning the centuries from Antiquity to the end of the Old Testament period. Much attention is given to a discussion of religion in this period. The footnotes provide guidance for further reading. The work is enhanced by the inclusion of chronological charts, and historical maps. It includes a subject index and Scripture References.

541 Hayes, John H and James Maxwell Miller. *Israelite and Judean History.* Philadelphia, PA: Westminster, 1977. 736p.

> This is a comprehensive authoritative history of the people of Israel from the age of the Patriarchs to the Roman period (132 C.E.). Each chapter is written by a noted scholar. The work is enhanced by the inclusion of full bibliographies at the beginning of each section, a general bibliography, maps, a chronology of the Israelite and Judean kings, index of names and subjects, an index of authors and an index of biblical passages.

Introductory Works

542 Eissfeldt, Otto. *The Old Testament: An Introduction.* New York: Harper & Row, 1965. 861p.
> This work is divided into five parts: A. The pre-literary stage B. The literary pre-history of the books of the Old Testament C. An analysis of the books of the Old Testament D. The Canon E. The Text. It includes bibliographical references and indexes of passages quoted, and of names.

543 *Mikra: Text, Translation, Reading and Interpretation of the Hebrew Bible in Ancient Judaism and Early Christianity.* Editor: Martin Jan Mulder. Philadelphia: Fortress Press, 1988. 929p.
> This is a collection of essays by noted scholars, pertaining to the text of the Hebrew Bible and how it became an authoritative collection of religious writings, the translations of the Bible through the ages, and the interpretation of the Bible in Rabbinic literature. Access to the scholarly literature is provided by footnotes, by the annotated bibliography at the end of each article and by the complete bibliographical list at the end of the volume. The work includes a survey of "Some Printed (Complete) Hebrew Bibles" (appended to Chapter 3), a list of scholarly editions of the Aramaic Targumim in the selective bibliography of Chapter 7, and an index of sources.

544 Sellin, Ernst. *Introduction to the Old Testament.* Completely Revised and Rewritten by Georg Fohrer. Translated by David Green. London: SPCK, 1976. 540p.
> This work deals with the formation of the historical and legal books, the poetic books, the Wisdom books, the prophetical and apocalyptic books of the Bible. It also discusses the compilation and transmission of the Old Testament.

Atlases

545 Aharoni, Yohanan and Michael Avi-Yonah. *Macmillan Bible Atlas.* Rev. ed. New York: Macmillan, 1977. 184p.
> This comprehensive atlas consists of 264 maps and accompanying explanatory text. The editors, drawing on Egyptian, Biblical, Greek and Roman sources, depict through maps the religious, political, military and economic events in Palestine through the Early Church period.

546 *Atlas of Israel: Cartography, Physical Geography, Human and Economic Geography, History.* 2nd ed. Jerusalem: Survey of Israel, Ministry of Labour; Amsterdam: Elsevier, 1970. 1v.
> The primary focus of this Atlas is modern Israel. It, however, contains a section of ancient maps that are pertinent to the Old Testament period and are of great value to the biblical scholar.

547 *Harper Atlas of the Bible.* Edited by James Bennett Pritchard. New York: Harper & Row, 1987. 254p.
> The atlas, through 134 color maps and over 400 illustrations, graphically

depicts the history, economic pursuits, and customs and beliefs of the peoples of Palestine. Its coverage spans the eras from the Old Testament to Byzantine Palestine. It includes an "Index of Place Names," a gazetteer that lists the alternative names by which a place is known, the location of the ancient site on the modern map of the land and the grid reference.

BIBLIOGRAPHY

See also entry 690.

548 *The Book List.* London: Society For Old Testament Study, 1946- .
This annual lists, describes and evaluates current books on the Old Testament and related fields. The following cumulative volumes have been published: *Eleven Years of Bible Bibliography: The Booklists of the Society for Old Testament Study of 1946-56.* Edited by H. H. Rowley (Indian Hills, Co: Falcon's Wing, 1957.); *A Decade of Bible Bibliography.* Edited by G. W. Anderson (Oxford: Basil Blackwell, 1967.); *Bible Bibliography 1967-1973: Old Testament.* Edited by Peter R. Ackroyd (Oxford: Basil Blackwell, 1974.)

549 *A Classified Bibliography of the Septuagint.* Compiled by Sebastian P. Brock, Charles T. Fritsch, and Sidney Jellicoe. Leiden: E. J. Brill, 1973. 217p.
This is a bibliography of the texts and the literature about the Septuagint that were published to 1969.

550 Dirksen, P. B. *An Annotated Bibliography of the Peshitta of the Old Testament.* Leiden, Brill 1989. 119 p.
This is a bibliography of 532 books, articles and significant reviews. The bibliography is divided into the following categories: A. General B. Surveys and Catalogues of Mss. C. Individual Mss. D. Text Editions E. Publications Concerning Printed Editions F. Collections of Variant Readings G. Concordances and Word Lists H. Studies About Separate Books H. Specific Subjects.

551 Fitzmyer, Joseph A. *An Introductory Bibliography for the Study of Scripture.* Rome: Editrice Pontificio Biblico, 1990. 216p.
This is an annotated introductory classified bibliography of 706 basic titles "with which the student who is beginning the study of theology or of Scripture ... might do well to familiarize himself or herself." Asterisks identify the titles which the author considers to be the most important.

552 Grossfeld, Bernard. *A Bibliography of Targum Literature.* New York: Ktav, 1972-90. 3v.
This is a classified bibliography of books, articles, theses, dissertations and book reviews divided according to the following subjects: A. General Targum, i. e., works dealing with more than one Targum or with the Targum as a genre B. Targum Onqelos C. The Jerusalem (Palestinian) Targum D. Targum Jonathan to the Prophets E. Targum To The Hagiographa F. Targum and the New Testament G. Translations, Editions, Grammars and Concordances, Theses and Dissertations, and Book Reviews H. Concordances and Grammars for the Study of the Targums I. Reviews of Books and Targumic Literature. An additional chapter, "Samaritan Targum," was added in volume three. The author has extracted many items listed in

Section Two: Subject Reference | 141

the bibliography, from the *Newsletter for Targumic and Cognate Studies*. The volumes are indexed.

553 Kalimi, Isaac. *Sefer Divre ha-Yamim: Bibliyografyah Memuyenet.* Jerusalem: Simor, 1990. 230p.

This is a classified multilingual bibliography of books, articles, and dissertations about the Book of Chronicles or about chapters and/or verses thereof. Chronicles as a historical source, linguistic aspects and literary aspects, are among the topics that are covered in the bibliography. It includes an author index.

554 Powell, Mark Allan. *The Bible and Modern Literary Criticism: A Critical Assessment and Annotated Bibliography.* New York: Greenwood Press, 1992. 469p.

This annotated bibliography is organized into six major sections. The largest and most comprehensive section of the bibliography focuses on criticism, i.e. works that draw on modern literary criticism for a scholarly study of the Bible. The studies listed in this section pertaining to a particular book of the Bible are listed according to the order in which the book appears in the English Bible. Included are an Index of Authors, Editors and Compilers and an Index of Titles and Subjects.

555 Thompson, Henry O. *The Book of Daniel: An Annotated Bibliography.* New York: Garland Publishing, 1993. 547p.

Thompson, in the introduction to the bibliography, outlines the biblical material and some of the interpretive issues involved in the study of Daniel. The annotated bibliography describes 1,851 books and articles written primarily in English and published in the last fifty years. It is arranged alphabetically by author. The bibliography includes a list of journal citations to Daniel, a list of dissertations on Daniel, and author (not in main text), scripture, and subject indexes.

556 Wal, Adri van der. *Amos: A Classified Bibliography.* 2d. ed. enl. Amsterdam: Free University Press, 1983. 186p.

This is a listing of c.1,100 books and articles, published between 1800-1983, which deal with different aspects of"both text and meaning" of the Book of Amos. The Bibliography is divided into two sections: A. Literature which refers to Amos in general B. Literature referring to special verses or parts of the book of Amos.

557 —. *Nahum, Habakkuk: A Classified Bibliography.* Amsterdam: Free University Press, 1988. 208p.

This is a multilingual classified bibliography of 1,250 books and articles. The materials are arranged in four sections: A.The Book of Nahum B. The Book of Habakkuk C. The Qumran Nahum Commentary D. The Qumran Habakkuk Commentary. Each section is further subdivided by subject, e.g., stylistic features, and by chapter and verse. This useful bibliography includes an author index.

DICTIONARIES

558 Brown, Francis. *The New Brown-Driver-Briggs-Gesenius Hebrew and English Lexicon, with an Appendix Containing the Biblical Aramaic.* Edited by Francis Brown, S. R. Driver, and C. A. Briggs. Peabody, MA: Hendrickson, 1979. 1,118p.

Known as BDB, this widely used lexicon of the Old Testament is based on Wilhelm G. Gesenius' *Hebräisches und Aramäisches Handwörterbuch über das Alte Testament.* Words are listed according to their root. Aramaic words are listed in a separate section. In this edition, the Hebrew and Aramaic words have been coded to J. Strong's *The Exhaustive Concordance of the Bible* numbering system. The Addenda and Corrigenda corrections are printed on the bottom margin of the page of the word to which they refer. A complete numerical index of Strong's system has been added.

559 Einspahr, Bruce. *Index to Brown, Driver and Briggs' Hebrew Lexicon.* Chicago: Moody Press, 1977. 456p.

560 Holladay, William Lee. *A Concise Hebrew and Aramaic Lexicon of the Old Testament, Based upon the Lexical Work of Ludwig Köhler & Walter Baumgartner.* Grand Rapids, MI: Eerdmans, 1991. 425p.

This lexicon is intended primarily for students beginning to study Biblical Hebrew and Aramaic.

561 Köhler, Ludwig and Walter Baumgartner. *Hebräisches und Aramäisches Lexikon zum Alten Testament.* Leiden: Brill, 1967- .

This ia a Hebrew lexicon for the study of the Old Testament. To-date four volumes (Aleph through Tesh'a) have been published, completing the Hebrew portion of the dictionary. A fifth volume covering the biblical Aramaic vocabulary is scheduled to appear in the next few years.

562 —. *Lexicon in Veteris Testamenti Libros.* 2d ed. Leiden: E. J. Brill, 1953. 1,138p.

563 —. *Supplementum ad Lexicon in Veteris Testamenti Libros.* Leiden: E. J. Brill, 1958. 227p.

This is a dictionary of the Hebrew Old Testament in English and German by Ludwig Köhler, and a dictionary of the Aramaic parts of the Old Testament in English and German by Walter Baumgartner. The Hebrew and Aramaic words are listed alphabetically. The meanings and discussions of words are given in both German and English. The supplement includes a German-Hebrew and German-Aramaic index of words, and additions and corrections.

CONCORDANCES

564 Even-Shoshan, Avraham. *Konkorkdantsyah Hadashah le-Torah, Neviim u-Khetuvim.* 3rd ed. Jerusalem: Kiryat Sefer, 1985. 1,242p.

This concordance and dictionary, first published in 1977, lists Aramaic and Hebrew words and concepts by the form in which they appear in a modern dictionary rather than by their root. Each entry is followed by lists in Hebrew of basic meanings, related meanings, and combined forms in which the word appears, along with the standard listing of each appearance of the word in canonical order. The biblical citations are pointed. An illustrated introduction on the history of biblical concordances precedes the main body of the concordance. An "Introduction to a New Concordance of the Old Testament," by John H. Sailhammer is included in this edition.

565 Katz, Eliezer. *A Classified Concordance to the Bible=Konkordantsyah 'Inyanit.* Jerusalem: E. Katz, 1967-80.
This Hebrew-English concordance is arranged in parallel columns, compiled according to subject. A key subject index in English and Hebrew is included.

566 Kasowski, Chaim Joshua. *Otsar Leshon Targum Onkelos.* Rev. ed. by Moshe Kosovsky. Jerusalem: Magnes Press, 1986. 2v.
This is a revised edition of the concordance first published in 1933-1940 based on the version of the Targum in the 1557 Sabioneta edition of the Pentateuch. The present edition incorporates in the text the corrigenda to the previous edition, as well as the corrections found by the editor in the author's personal copy of the original edition.

567 Mandelkern, Salomon. *Kondordantsyah la-TaNaKh.* Edited by F. Margolin and Moshe Henry Goshen-Gottstein. Jerusalem: Schocken, 1977. 2v.
This standard Hebrew concordance to the Bible is arranged by root. This edition includes additions and corrections, and an index of hard to find words. The "Shulsinger Edition" (New York: Shulsinger, 1955) includes a bibliography on Hebrew lexicography entitled *Otsar ha-Leksikografyah,* by E. R. Malachi.

568 Wachsman, Hayyim. *Konkordantsyah ha-Shelemah veha-Peshutah la-TaNaKH.* Jerusalem: Feldheim, 1989. 2v.
Wachsman has entered the words of the Biblical text in his concordance in the same form in which it appears in the text. The user, therefore, need not be familiar with Hebrew grammatical rules in order to find the word that he or she seeks. The citations are to the A. Dotan edition of the Bible (Tel-Aviv: 'Adi, 1973).

ENCYCLOPEDIAS

569 *Anchor Bible Dictionary.* David Noel Freedman, Editor in Chief. New York: Doubleday, 1992. 6v.
This illustrated scholarly encyclopedic dictionary contains articles pertaining to the books of the Bible and non-canonical texts that antedate the 4th century C.E., major words, proper names and places mentioned in the Bible, historical and archaeological subjects that antedate the 4th century C.E., social and cultural institutions in the ancient world of the Bible, major literary genres and motifs, etc. The major sources relevant to the discussion in each entry are listed in the accompanying bibliography.

570 *Entsiklopedyah Mikrai t=Encyclopaedia Biblica.* Jerusalem: Mosad Bialik, 1950-1988. 9v.

This scholarly illustrated encyclopedia in Hebrew contains articles on all aspects of the Bible and the biblical period. The contributors for the most part are Israeli scholars and are authorities in their field. Each article is usually accompanied by a bibliography. The encyclopedia is indexed.

571 *Entsiklopedyah shel ha-TaNaKH.* Raphael Posner, Editor. Tel-Aviv: Yediot Aharonot, 1987. 4v.

This topically arranged illustrated encyclopedia contains short unsigned articles by Israeli scholars. Each entry includes the Biblical source for the topic under discussion.

572 *Harper's Bible Dictionary.* Paul J. Achtemeier, General Editor. San Francisco, CA: Harper & Row, 1985. 1,178p.

This is a one volume dictionary containing scholarly articles written by the members of the Society of Biblical Literature. Its articles provide information about the books of the Bible, the biblical world, the Bible's influence on Western civilization, etc. It includes photographs, maps, drawings, charts, tables, and a pronunciation guide.

573 *The Interpreter's Dictionary of the Bible.* Edited by G. A. Buttrick. Nashville, TN: Abingdon, 1962. 4v.

574 —. *Supplementary Volume.* Edited by Keith Crim. Nashville, TN: Abingdon, 1976. 998p.

This illustrated encyclopedic dictionary of the Bible contains articles, usually accompanied by bibliographies, pertaining to the books of the Bible, terms and names appearing in the Biblical text, the biblical world, etc. The "supplementary Volume" updates the articles in the *Dictionary*, and also includes new material.

GRAMMAR (HEBREW)

575 Gesenius, Friedrich Wilhelm. *Gesenius' Hebrew Grammar.* Edited and enlarged by E. Kautzsch. 2nd English ed. Oxford: Clarendon Press, 1988. 616p.

This standard Biblical Hebrew reference grammar is a translation of the author's *Hebräische Grammatik.* This edition includes a subject index, an index of Hebrew words, and a revised index of cited passages, by John B. Job.

576 Greenberg, Moshe. *Introduction to Hebrew.* Englewood Cliffs, NJ: Prentice-Hall, 1965. 226p.

"The aim of this book is to teach the fundamentals of Biblical Hebrew grammar and to enable one to acquire a mastery over a basic vocabulary of Biblical Hebrew."

577 Joüon, Paul. *A Grammar of Biblical Hebrew.* Rome: Editrice Pontificio Instituto Biblica, 1991. 3 parts in 2 v.

Takamitsu Muraoka translated, and substantially revised, the author's Grammaire de l'Hebreu Biblique published originally in 1923. The original text of this reference grammar was expanded in light of subsequent advances in the fields of Hebrew, both biblical and post-biblical, and the cognate languages, especially the Northwest Semitic languages and dialects. This work includes bibliographical references and indexes.

578 Lambdin, Thomas O. *Introduction to Biblical Hebrew*. New York: Scribner, 1971. 345p.
This textbook is "designed for a full year's course in elementary Biblical Hebrew at a college level."

579 Waltke, Bruce K. and M. O'Connor. *An Introduction to Biblical Hebrew Syntax*. Winnona Lake, IN: Eisenbrauns, 1990. 345p.
This is an up-to-date linguistic study of Biblical Hebrew syntax and a reference grammar of Biblical Hebrew in English. The bibliography which accompanies this work is divided into the following sections: A. Biblical Hebrew B. Post-Biblical Hebrew C. Other Semitic Languages D. General Linguistic and Literary Studies; Studies of Non-Semitic Languages. It includes an Index of Topics, an Index of Authorities, an Index of Hebrew Words, and an Index of Scriptural References.

GRAMMAR (ARAMAIC)

580 Bauer, Hans and Pontus Leander. *Grammatik des Biblisch-Aramäischen*. Hildesheim: Olms, 1962. 380p.
This comprehensive study of Biblical Aramaic was first published in 1927.

581 Rosenthal, Franz. *A Grammar of Biblical Aramaic*. Wiesbaden: O. Harrassowitz, 1974. 99p.
This is a grammar of Biblical Aramaic for the beginner.

PERIODICAL LITERATURE INDEXES

582 *Elenchus Bibliographicus Biblicus*. Rome: Pontifical Biblical Institute, 1968- .
This index to biblical literature and its secondary material was published originally as part of *Biblica*. It does not contain summaries or abstracts but does list the reviews of books in many languages. *Elenchus* includes Author, Word (Greek, Hebrew), and Scriptural Passages indices.

583 *Internationale Zeitschriftenschau für Bibelwissenschaft und Grenzgebiete*. Düsseldorf: Patmos, 1951- .
This annual survey of periodical articles on the Bible and related areas includes abstracts and an author index.

584 *Old Testament Abstracts*. Washington, DC: Catholic Biblical Association, 1978- .
Issued thrice-yearly, *OTA* abstracts articles that have been written about the books of the Old Testament and aspects of the biblical world. It also

publishes brief notices about major books published in the area of Old Testament studies. It includes the following indexes: A. Authors B. Scriptural Passages C. Semitic and Other Related Words.

LIBRARY CATALOGS

585 Ecole Biblique et Archeologique Française, Jerusalem. Bibliothèque. *Catalogue de la Bibliothèque de l'Ecole Biblique de Jerusalem*. Paris: Editions Gabalda, 1986. 12 v.
This dictionary catalogue, first published in 1975 (Boston: G. K. Hall), provides access to the extensive collection of materials housed in the Ecole Biblique's library pertaining to such subjects as Bible, Biblical archaeology, and Ancient Near East history, language and literature. It also serves as an index to articles pertaining to various aspects of Biblical studies. These articles are cataloged and are listed by author, as well as by chapter and verse under each book of the Bible. The subject headings are in French.

TEXTS (CRITICAL EDITIONS)

586 Bible. O. T. English. Aramaic. *The Aramaic Bible: The Targums*. Martin McNamara, Project Director. Wilmington, DE: Glazier, 1987- .
This multi-volume series, by noted scholars, aims to provide the reader with a critical modern English translation of the Targumim. The introductions to each volume in the series and the notes that accompany the text shed light on such issues as the Targum's function in early Judaism, its relationship to Jewish exegesis, the theology of the Targum, the Targum and its relationship to the Hebrew text, its importance for the study of early Judaism and of the New Testament, etc. Each volume in the series includes a bibliography. The following volumes have been published to-date: 1a. Targum Neofiti 1: Genesis (1992) 1b. Targum Pseudo-Jonathan: Genesis (1992) 6-9. Targum Onkelos to the Torah (1988) 10. Targum Jonathan of the Former Prophets (1987) 11. The Isaiah Targum (1987) 12. The Targum of Jeremiah (1987) 13. The Targum of Ezekiel (1987) 14. The Targum of the Minor Prophets (1989) 15. The Targums Of Job, Proverbs and Qohelet (1991) 18. The Two Targums of Esther (1991).

587 Bible. O. T. Hebrew. 1976. *Biblia Hebraica Stuttgartensia*. Stuttgart: Deutsche Bibelstiftung, 1976-77. 1,574p.
This text edition based on the *Leningrad Codex B19* contains a critical apparatus with variants from various versions and from the Dead Sea scrolls, and conjectural emendations.

588 Bible. O. T. Hebrew. 1954. *Biblia Hebraica*. Edited by Rudolph Kittel. 9th rev. ed. Stuttgart: Württembergische Bibelanstalt, 1954. 1,434p.

589 Scott, William R. *A Simplified Guide to BHS*. Berkeley, CA: Bibal Press, 1990. 85 p.
This work includes "An English Key to the Latin Words and Abbreviations and Symbols of *Biblia Hebraica Stuttgartensia*, by H. P. Rüger."

TEXTS (ENGLISH TRANSLATIONS)

590 Bible. O. T. English. JPS. *Tanakh: A New Translation of the Holy Scriptures According to the Traditional Hebrew Text.* Philadelphia: Jewish Publication Society, 1985.

This is an entirely new translation of the Old Testament according to the tenth century Hebrew Masoretic text. This new English version is based on contemporary Jewish, biblical, and Semitic studies.

TEXTS (CRITICAL COMMENTARIES)

591 *Anchor Bible.* Garden City: NY: Doubleday, 1964- .

This is a multi-volume commentary begun under the general editorship of William Foxwell Albright and David Noel Freedman. Each volume includes an introductory essay, a translation of the text, textual notes, extensive annotations and a commentary. The biblical text is placed in its Near Eastern context, by emphasizing archaeological discoveries and comparative Semitic linguistics.

592 *Hermeneia—A Critical and Historical Commentary on the Bible.* Philadelphia: Fortress, 1972- .

This multi-volume commentary provides the Biblical scholar with philological and historical material for critical discussion of the primary data of the biblical work in question. Many of the volumes in the series are English translations of German commentaries by renowed Protestant scholars. The English version is often revised and updated. The Old Testament series is under the editorship of Frank Moore Cross. The following volumes have been published to date: Jeremiah, Ezekiel, Hosea, Joel-Amos, Micah and Song of Songs.

593 *The JPS Torah Commentary.* Philadelphia: Jewish Publication Society, 1989- .

Each volume in the series utilizes the traditional Hebrew text and the JPS English translation. The accompanying commentary integrates classical and modern sources. The following volumes have been published to date: Genesis, by Nahum M. Sarna (1989), Exodus, by Nahum M. Sarna (1991), Leviticus, by Baruch A. Levine (1989), and Numbers, by Jacob Milgrom.

594 *Mikra le-Yisrael.* Edited by Moshe Greenberg and Shmuel Ahituv. Tel-Aviv: Am Oved; Jerusalem: Magnes Press, 1990- .

This scholarly commentary in Hebrew incorporates classical and recent scholarship in such fields as Semitic linguistics and Biblical archaeology. The following volumes have been published to-date: Rut with an introduction and commentary by Yair Zakovitch (1990); Shir ha-Shirim with an introduction and commentary by Yair Zakovitch (1992); Ovadyah with an introduction and commenatry by Uriel Simon (1992).

595 *Old Testament Library.* Philadelphia, PA: Westminster Press, 1962- .

A collection of commentaries on the books of the Old Testament, as well as, monographs pertaining to aspects of Old Testament interpretation, history, and theology.

Commentaries (Rabbinic)

596 *Art Scroll Tanach Series.* Translated and compiled by Meir Zlotowitz; overview by Nosson Scherman and others. Brooklyn, NY: Mesorah Publications, 1975- .

The volumes in this series include the Hebrew text of the Bible with a "flowing" English translation, a commentary anthologized from Talmudic, Midrashic, and Rabbinic sources, a biographical sketch of each commentator cited, and a bibliography of sources. An overview provides the historical and philosophic background for the text.

597 Kaplan, Aryeh. *The Living Torah: The Five Books of Moses.* New York: Maznaim, 1981. 647 p.

598 Kasher, Menahem Mendel. *Torah Shelemah.* New York: American Biblical Encyclopedia Society, 1949- .

This multi-volume work includes the standard Hebrew Bible text and an anthology of commentaries of a strictly exegetical character that were written from the earliest times up to the Geonic period. To-date 42 volumes (Parashat Balak, Numbers 42) have been published. An English translation by Harry Freedman entitled: *The Encyclopedia of Biblical Interpretation* (New York: American Biblical Encyclopedia Society 1953- .) is available. To-date volumes 1-9 (to Exodus Chapter 20) have been published.

599 *Mikraot Gedolot.* Jerusalem: Schocken, 1958-59. 5v.

This emended reprint of the Netter edition (Vienna, 1859) is but one of the variant editions of Mikraot Gedolot and contains numerous classical rabbinic commentaries, e.g. Rashi, Ibn Ezra.

600 *Mikraot Gedolot ha-Keter.* Edited with an introduction by Menachem Cohen. Ramat Gan: Bar-Ilan University, 1992- .

This edition is a revised scientific edition of 'Mikraot Gedolot' based on the Aleppo Codex. The biblical text is accompanied by a commentary to the Masorah— 'Eyn ha-Masorah, Targum based on Yemenite manuscripts, and medieval Biblical commentaries based on early medieval manuscripts. A general introduction by the editor is included in the first volume Joshua / Judges, the only volume published to-date.

601 *The Soncino Books of the Bible.* Abraham Cohen, General Editor. London: Soncino Press, 1945-51. 14v.

This multi-volume work includes the standard Hebrew text of the Bible, a verse-by-verse English translation, and an illuminating commentary based on the works of classical biblical scholars. There are extensive introductions to each book and an overall index in the back of each volume.

602 *The Torah: A Modern Commentary.* Edited by W. Gunther Plaut and Bernard J. Bamberger. New York: Union of American Hebrew Congregations, 1981. 1,787p.

This one volume work consists of the Hebrew text of the Pentateuch and Haftarot (weekly readings from the Prophetic books), and the Jewish Publication Society translation into English. Each of the five books of the

Pentateuch is preceded by an introductory essay. The book of Leviticus also includes an essay by William W. Hallo entitled:" Leviticus and Ancient Near Eastern Literature." A commentary by W. Gunther Plaut (Genesis, Exodus, Numbers, and Deuteronomy) and Bernard J. Bamberger (Leviticus) accompanies the text. The commentary includes explanatory notes to each of the verses, essays on sections of the text that offer insight into their meaning, and "gleanings" from the Midrash and from other literatures. The footnotes and cross references along with notes describe the sources used by the editors, and offer further explanation. The work also includes a bibliography at the end of the volume.

B. APOCRYPHA AND PSEUDEPIGRAPHA

INTRODUCTORY WORKS

603 *Jewish Writings of the Second Temple Period.* Edited by Michael E. Stone. Philadelphia: Fortress Press, 1984. 698p.
This is a collection of essays by noted scholars on topics pertaining to the Apocrypha and Pseudepigrapha. Access to the scholarly literature is provided by footnotes, by the annotated bibliography at the end of each article and by the complete bibliographical list at the end of the volume.

604 Schürer, Emil. *History of the Jewish People in the Age of Jesus Christ (175 B.C.-A.D. 135).* Edinburgh: T & T Clark, 1973-1987. 3v.
This is a new English version of the author's *Geschichte des Jüdischen Volkes in Zeitalter Jesu Christi* revised and edited by Geza Vermes and Fergus Miller. It contains a detailed discussion of the literature of the period. The extensive bibliographies have been updated to 1972.

BIBLIOGRAPHY
See also entry 455.

605 Charlesworth, James H. Assisted by P. Dykers. *The Pseudepigrapha and Modern Research with a Supplement.* Chico, CA: Scholars Press, 1981. 329 p.
This is a classified bibliography of works, published largely from 1960-1979, which deal directly or indirectly with the Pseudepigrapha. In the short introduction, the editors note the standard text editions and translations, as well as known work in progress. This bibliography complements Delling's bibliography (below).

606 Delling, G. *Bibliographie zur Jüdisch-Hellenistischen und Intertestamentarischen Literatur: 1900-1970.* 2d ed. Berlin: Akademie Verlag, 1975. 201p.
This classified bibliography, first published in 1969, has been expanded to include publications to 1970. 3,650 items are listed under 45 subject headings. This survey is continued by Charlesworth's bibliography (above). It includes an author index.

607 Bible. O. T. Apocrypha and Apocryphal Books. English. 1913. *The Apocrypha and Pseudepigrapha of the Old Testament in English.* Edited by R. H. Charles. Oxford: Clarendon Press, 1973. 2v.
> This work contains English translations of the apocryphal/deutero-canonical and pseudepigraphical literature related to the Old Testament. The translations of the individual texts by various scholars include critical and explanatory notes, and are accompanied by an introduction. The detailed topical index is of great value.

608 Bible. O. T. Apocrypha and Apocryphal Books. English. 1983. *The Old Testament Pseudepigrapha.* Edited by James H. Charlesworth. Garden City, NY: Doubleday, 1983. 2v.
> This is a modern English translation by an international team of scholars, of 65 pseudepigraphical texts related to the Old Testament. Each text is accompanied by an introduction, a list of the most important publications on the document, and critical notes. Volume 1: Apocalyptic Literature and Testaments; Volume 2: Expansions of the "Old Testament" and Legends, Wisdom and Philosophical Literature, Prayers, Psalms, and Odes, Fragments of Lost Judeo-Hellenistic Works.

609 Bible. O. T. Apocrypha and Apocryphal Books. Hebrew. 1970. *ha-Sefarim ha-Hitsonim.* Edited by Abraham Kahana. Jerusalem: Mekorot, 1970. 2v.
> This is a Hebrew translation of the Apocrypha. Each book is preceded by an introduction, and the text is accompanied by an extensive commentary.

610 Bible. O. T. Apocrypha and Apocryphal Books. English. 1984. *The Apocryphal Old Testament.* Oxford: Clarendon Press, 1984. Edited by Hedley Frederick Davis Sparks.
> This is a translation of twenty five pseudepigraphical writings. Each text is preceded by an introduction. A bibliography listing the editions of the text, other translations and general studies is included.

C. DEAD SEA SCROLLS

BIBLIOGRAPHY

611 Fitzmyer, Joseph A. *The Dead Sea Scrolls: Major Publications and Tools for Study.* Atlanta, GA: Scholars Press, 1990. 246p.
> In this book, Fitzmyer seeks to "explain the various sigla used for [the Dead Sea Scroll material], to indicate the places of publication of the Dead Sea Scroll materials made available to date, to explain the contents of the texts, and to introduce the student to various tools of study." The book is divided into the following chapters: A. The System of Abbreviation Used for the Dead Sea Scrolls B. The Dead Sea Scrolls: Major Publications C. Bibliographies of the Dead Sea Scrolls D. Survey Articles and Preliminary Reports on Unpublished materials E. Lists of the Dead Sea Scrolls and Fragments F. Concordances, Dictionaries, and Grammars for the Study of the Dead

Sea Scrolls G. Secondary Collections of Qumran Texts H. Translations of the Dead Sea Scrolls in the Collections I. Outlines of the Dead Sea Scrolls (with Select Bibliography) J. Select Bibliography on Some Topics of Dead Sea Scroll Study, e.g. Paleography, Archaeology, Theology, the Qumran Srolls and New Testament, etc. K. The Copper Plaque Mentioning Buried Treasures. Included are: I. Index of Modern Authors II. Index of Biblical Passages III. Index of Extra-Biblical Passages IV. Index of the Dead Sea Scrolls according to Sigla A V. Index of the Dead Sea Scrolls according to Sigla B.

CONCORDANCES

612 Charlesworth, James H. *Graphic Concordance to the Dead Sea Scrolls.* Tübingen: J. C. B. Mohr; Louisville: Westminster/John Knox Press, 1991. 529p.

This work, containing more than 59,000 entries, is a concordance to editions of all Qumran sectarian texts and fragments published before 1990. It is designed primarily to assist specialists who focus their research on the Dead Sea Scrolls to find word forms, phrases and concepts in the Qumran texts. The words are listed exactly as they appear in the text. Linguists who specialize in late Biblical Hebrew or Mishnaic Hebrew, historians of the period, as well as theologians will find this work most useful for their research.

INVENTORIES

613 Reed, Stephen A. *Dead Sea Scroll Inventory Project: Lists of Documents, Photographs & Museum Plates.* Claremont, CA: Ancient Biblical Manuscript Center, 1991-92. 14 v.

This is a preliminary listing of materials in the following Dead Sea Scroll collections: A. Qumran Cave 1 B. Qumran Minor Caves C. Murabba'at D. Qumran Cave 4Q128-4Q186 E. Qumran Cave 4Q482-4Q520 F. 11Q G. Qumran Cave 4 (4Q1-127 Biblical H. Qumran Cave 4 (4Q521-4Q575) Starcky I. Qumran Cave 4 (4Q364-4Q481) Strugnell J. Qumran Cave 4 (4Q196-4Q363) Milik K. Khirbet Mird L. Wadi Ed Daliyeh M. Wadi Seiyal/Nahal Hever N. Masada. Information on how to acquire copies of the texts is included.

D. ANCILLARY MATERIALS

BIBLICAL ARCHAEOLOGY

614 *The New Encyclopedia of Archaeological Excavations in the Holy Land.* Ephraim Stern, Editor. Jerusalem: Israel Exploration Society and Carta; New York: Simon and Schuster, 1993. 4v.

This english edition of the *Encyclopedia,* updates to 1991 the *Encyclopedia of Archaeological Excavations in the Holy Land,* edited by Michael Avi-Yonah (Englewood Cliffs: Prentice-Hall, 1975-1978). It contains more than 365 articles contributed by 205 archaeologists or other experts which describe the sites which were excavated within "the traditional boundaries of the

Holy Land on both sides of the Jordan River from Sinai and Elath in the south to the sources of Jordan in the North" over the last 100 years or so. Articles on collective subjects, e. g., marine archaeology, synagogues, are also included. The articles include brief bibliographies. Map grid references are given for sites in Israel and Sinai, but not always for those in Jordan. The *Encyclopedia* is amply illustrated and includes a glossary, an index to persons, an index to places, and an index to Biblical references.

615 Negev, Avraham. *The Archaeological Encyclopedia of the Holy Land*. Rev. ed. New York: Thomas Nelson, 1986. 419p.
This is an updated edition of a work first published in 1972, which "lists the majority of the geographical names mentioned in the Bible ... identifying them as far as possible, describing the excavations that have been carried out ... and analyzing the importance of the finds they have yielded." The encyclopedia traces the history of each location from Biblical times up to the Arab conquest. The work is richly illustrated and includes chronological tables.

616 Vogel, Eleanor K. *Bibliography of Holy Land Sites*. Cincinnati: Hebrew Union College, 1982-88. 3v.
This is a bibliography of books and articles pertaining to Holy Land sites, arranged alphabetically by site. The bibliography includes works published through 1987. The Bibliography was published originally in *Hebrew Union College Annual*, Volume 42 (1971), Volume 52 (1981) and Volume 58 (1987).

ANCIENT NEAR EASTERN TEXTS AND PICTURES

617 Pritchard, James Bennett. *The Ancient Near East in Pictures Relating to the Old Testament*. 3d ed. Princeton, NJ: Princeton University Press, 1969.
ANEP is a companion volume to ANET. The book is divided into two parts: A. A collection of over 750 photographs and drawings from various texts. These materials are arranged according to such topics as gods and their emblems, daily life, etc. B. An explanatory text, which provides the reader with background information about the illustrative materials. This section also includes a bibliography.

618 —. *Ancient Near Eastern Texts Relating to the Old Testament*. 3d ed. Princeton, NJ: Princeton University Press, 1969.
ANET, first published in 1950, contains a selection of Egyptian, Sumerian, Akkadian, Hittite, Ugaritic, South Arabic, Canaanite, and Aramaic documents, translated into English by noted scholars. The texts are arranged according to literary form: A. Myths, epics, legends B. Legal texts C. Historical texts D. Rituals, incantations, and descriptions of festivals E. Hymns and prayers F. Didactic and wisdom literature G. Lamentations H. Secular songs and poems I. Letters J. Miscellaneous txts. Additional documents are included in a supplementary section. When they do not fit into the text, additions to the translations and notes are included in the Addenda. Included are an index of Biblical references and an Index of names.

Computer Software Programs (Biblical Studies)

See also entry 72.

619 *Torah Scholar.* Edison, NJ: Kabbalah Software (8 Price Drive, Edison, NJ 08817.)

"Torah Scholar is a unique hypertext-based study tool that finally makes it easier to learn from a computer than from a printed page." It includes: "the full text of the Pentateuch in both Hebrew and English, the linear translation of Hebrew and English text; 'Go To' by chapter/verse or by weekly portion ... fully integrated note taking capabilities, with the ability to copy text into notes and to export notes into other word processors, ability to create hypertext links between any note or picture and any letter of the Hebrew or English text ..."

Chapter 20

Rabbinic Literature, Jewish Law and Judaism

A. Rabbinic Literature

Introductions

620 *The Literature of the Sages.* Editor: Shmuel Safrai. Philadelphia: Fortress Press, 1987- .

This, the first of two volumes, contains a collection of introductory essays by noted scholars. It is part of the series *Compendia Rerum Iudaicarum ad Novum Testamentum.* The work opens with an historical survey of the "Rabbinic Period"; a discussion of the major historical and literary problems relating to the concept "Oral Torah"; and a discussion of the characteristics, origins, and sources of Halakha, as well as the stages in the history of Tannaic Halakha. The remaining essays deal with the Mishnah, the Tractate Avot, the Tosefta, the Palestinian Talmud, the Babylonian Talmud, and the External Tractates. These chapters include sections on textual criticism. In addition to individual chapter bibliographies, the collection features a cumulative bibliography. A list of extant manuscript editions follows the chapters on the Mishna, Tosefta, and Talmud. The book also includes an index of personal names (appearing in the literature up to and including the Gaonic period), as well as an index of sources. The second volume (forthcoming) will deal with Midrash, Aggada, Midrash Collections, Targum and Prayer.

621 Mielziner, Moses. *Introduction to the Talmud.* 4th ed. New York: Bloch, 1968. 415p.

This introduction, first published in 1894, is "intended for readers who desire to acquaint themselves with the 'sea of the Talmud'". It is divided into four parts: A. Historical and literary introduction B. Legal hermeneutics of the Talmud C. Talmudical terminology and methodology D. Appendices and indices. The latter section includes: "Outlines of Talmudical ethics, " by the author, additional notes, corrections, etc., index to subjects and names, special Biblical, Mishnaic and Talmudic references, "Talmud and Midrash; A Selected Bibliography:1925-67," by Alexander Guttmann, index to technical terms and phrases, and a key to abbreviations used in the Talmud and commentaries.

622 Strack, Herman L. and G. Stemberger. *Introduction to the Talmud and Midrash.* Newly trans. by Markus Bockmuehl. Edinburgh: T & T Clark, 1991. 472p.

This concise scholarly introduction to the whole of Rabbinic literature is based on the author's *Einleitung in Talmud und Midrash* (1887). The text and the bibliography have been revised and expanded by G.Stemberger and includes new materials that have come to light and current scholarship. The works is divided into three parts: A. General introduction B. Rabbinic Literature (Mishnah; Tosefta; Palestinian Talmud; Babylonian Talmud) C.

Midrashim. Each section includes a bibliography of relevant materials. The sections that deal with texts contain discussions pertaining to contents and structure, their origin according to tradition, redaction, etc. Manuscripts and text editions are noted. The *Introduction* includes an index of subjects, an index of passages, and an index of names.

623 *The Study of Ancient Judaism.* Edited by Jacob Neusner. New York: Ktav, 1981. 2v.

"These introductions to the literary evidence of earlier Rabbinic Judaism deal with ... Mishnah, the Midrashic compilations, the liturgy," (in Volume 1) "and (in Volume 2) the two great Talmuds. The purpose is to explain the state of scholarship, with special interest in methods used for framing and answering the principal questions of systematic critical learning in our own day: What do we know? How do we know? Why is it important?" Volume 1 includes a " Bibliography on the Mishnah," by Baruch M. Bokser, and a " Bibliography on Midrash," by Lee Haas. Volume 2 consists of "An Annotated Bibliographical Guide to the Study of the Palestinian Talmud," by Baruch M. Bokser, and a classified bibliography, " The Babylonian Talmud," by David Goodblatt.

GAZETTEERS

624 Eshel, Ben Zion. *Yishuve ha-Yehudim be-Bavel bi-Tekufat ha-Talmud.* Jerusalem: Magnes Press, 1979. 276p.

625 Oppenheimer, Aharon. *Babylonia Judaica in the Talmudic Period.* Wiesbaden: L. Reichert, 1983. 548p.

This gazetteer is part of the *Tübinger Atlas des Vorderen Orients Beihefte* series. It identifies, lists and describes places of Jewish settlement in Babylonia during the Talmudic period. The work is based on Rabbinic literature (primarily the Babylonian Talmud), as well as Greco-Roman and Arabic sources. The following information is given for each entry: A. ources in the original language and in English translation B. Location C. Historical data D. Summary of earlier research E. Bibliography. Maps of "Talmudic Babylonia" and "Babylonia and its Environs," a "Chronological Table of Amoraitic Generations in Babylonia", a bibliography, an index of sources and a general index are included.

626 Reeg, Gottfried. *Die Ortsnamen Israels nach der Rabbinischen Literatur.* Weisbaden: L. Reichert,1989. 696p.

"This study presents the material upon which the map 'Israel According to Rabbinic Literature' of the *Tübinger Atlas des Vorderen Orients* is based. Approximately 400 of the 674 place names mentioned in the book appear on the map." The other names were omitted because the form of the name or their localization was too doubtful. The gazetteer is arranged alphabetically by the Hebrew name. Each entry includes: A Name and coordinates of the map. B. Variant reading C.Texts which contain important information about the site (in German translation) D. References in Rabbinic sources E. Bibliographical data F. Identification with other historical names G. Proposals of localization mentioned in the literature H. Name forms in other languages I. Correct form of a rabbinic name. The work includes in an appendix texts in translation that were not cited in the gazetteer. Indices of names (i. e., Rabbinic names, transliterated names, Hebrew place names,

Greek place names) that contain cross references enable the user to find the place name in the gazetteer.

BIBLIOGRAPHY

627 Diamond, Eliezer. "The World of the Talmud." In *The Schocken Guide to Jewish Books*, 47-69. New York: Schocken Books, 1992.
This bibliographic essay cites and describes historical surveys, summaries and analyses of Rabbinic thought, introductions to translations of the literature of the period, and works on the relationship between Second Temple and Rabbinic Judaism and early Christianity. All the materials are in English.

628 Kohn, Phinehas Jacob. *Otsar ha-Beurim veha-Perushim*. London: ha-Madpis, 1952. 625p.
This bibliography lists commentaries and novellae on all genres of Talmudic and Halakhic literature. The compiler includes materials written in the period beginning with the sixteenth century to the mid-twentieth century. The bibliography is arranged by genre of literature, e. g., Mishnah, Tosefta, etc. The materials are listed alphabetically by title under each genre. Author, title, and place of publication indexes are included at the end of the volume.

629 *Sare ha-Elef*. Edited by Menahem M. Kasher and Jacob B. Mandelbaum. 2d ed. Jerusalem: Beit Torah Shelemah, 1978 2v.
This bibliography lists and describes Hebrew books written during the period beginning with 500 until 1500. The bibliography is divided into the following seven divisions, each further subdivided: A. Post-Biblical literature B. Commentaries on the Pentateuch C. Commentaries on the Prophets and Writings D. Commentaries on the Talmud E. Responsa F. Codes G. Miscellaneous, including: grammar, philosophy, ethics, etc. The materials are listed alphabetically by title. The entries include a full bibliographic description of each title. Other editions and manuscripts of the same work are noted, The authors also cite secondary literature pertaining to the book. The work includes various indices including an author index, a title index, and a subject index to the miscellaneous section.

630 Townsend, John T. "Rabbinic Sources." In *The Study of Judaism: Bibliographical Essays*, 35-80. New York: Anti-Defamation League, 1972.
Following a brief introduction, Townsend lists Rabbinic works that "come from the sixth century or earlier. Added to these are certain later works that tend to be cited by writers on Christian origins. In most cases the bibliography contains some indication of the date for each listing ... The bibliography includes the best editions and concordances of the various sources along with some of the more important commentaries, lexicons, and other aids." It also includes "the best English translations where they exist as well as many other European language translations, particularly where English translations are lacking. Wherever there are duplicate listings of editions, translations, etc. for a given work, the order indicates the author's preference. The bibliography includes an introduction and selected secondary works."

631 —. "Minor Midrashim." In *Bibliographical Essays in Medieval Jewish Studies*, 331-392. New York: Anti-Defamation League/Ktav, 1976.
Following a brief introduction, Townsend lists the midrashim that have been published in collections by Jellinek, Horowitz, Ginzberg, Wertheimer, Eisenstein, and others. The index is arranged in order of the Hebrew alphabet by the first significant Hebrew word in the title. The Hebrew titles are transcribed in Roman characters. "Each entry lists all places in the various collections where a work appears along with various notations about texts and recensions. Important editions and translations of a work are also mentioned. Wherever possible the listings give some indication of when a work was written. ... The source of a Midrash appears whenever the midrash is part of a well known larger work other than a midrashic anthology, such as *Yalqut Shim'oni.*"

Manuscript Catalogs

See also entries 206-210.

632 *A Tentative Catalogue of Manuscripts of the Rashi Commentary to the Talmud.* Compiled and edited by Shlomo H. Pick and Sarah Munitz. Ramat Gan: Bar-Ilan University, Rashi Project, Department of Talmud, 1988. 54, 10p.
This tentative catalog consists of a dual listing of all extant manuscripts of the Rashi commentary to the Talmud. The first list arranges the manuscripts according to the libraries in which they are found. References are made to: A. Previous catalogs B. Citations in *Les Glosses Francaises Dans Les Commentaires Talmudiques De Raschi*, by A. Darmesteter and D. S. Blondheim (Paris, 1929) C. Microfilm or photostat number of the Institute of Microfilmed Hebrew Manuscripts, where applicable. The second list is arranged in the order of the tractates of the Talmud. The compilers view this publication as a first step towards the publication of a scholarly edition of the Rashi commentary to the Talmud.

Concordances

633 Kasowski, Chaim Josua. *Otsar Leshon ha-Mishnah.* Jerusalem: Massadah, 1969. 4v.
The words in this concordance to the Mishnah are arranged by root.

634 —. *Otsar Leshon ha-Talmud.* Jerusalem: Ministry of Education and Culture; Jewish Theological Seminary of America, 1954-1982. 41v.
This multi-volume concordance to the Babylonian Talmud, arranged by root, includes a five volume supplement, *Otsar ha-Shemot le-Talmud Bavli*, by Binyamin Kosovsky. (Jerusalem: Ministry of Education and Culture; Jewish Theological Seminary of America, 1976-1983). The supplement lists the names of all persons, places, etc., in the Talmud Bavli. It provides citations to places in the Talmud Bavli where the name appears.

635 —. *Otsar Leshon ha-Tosefta.* Jerusalem, 1932-1961. 6v.
This is a complete concordance to the Tosefta. The words are arranged by root.

636 Kosovsky, Binyamin. *Otsar Leshon ha-Tanaim*. Jerusalem, Jewish Theological Seminary of America, 1965-1966. 4v.

This is a concordance to the Mekhilta d'Rabi Ishmael. The words are arranged by root.

637 —. *Otsar Leshon ha-Tanaim*. Jerusalem, Jewish Theological Seminary of America, 1967-1969. 4v.

This is a concordance to the Sifra. The words are arranged by root.

638 —. *Otsar Leshon ha-Tanaim*. Jerusalem, Jewish Theological Seminary of America, 1970-1974. 5v.

This is a concordance to the Sifre. The worda are arranged by root.

639 Kosovsky, Moshe. *Otsar Leshon Talmud Yerushalmi*. Jerusalem: The Israel Academy of Sciences and Humanities and the Jewish Theological Seminary of America, 1979- .

This concordance is based on the Venice 1524 edition of the Talmud Yerushalmi. The wors are arranged by root. The completed set will include an onomasticon comprising names of all persons, places, etc., occurring in the Talmud Yerushalmi and a thesaurus of biblical Midrashim. Four volumes of the concordance, covering the letters Alef to Khaf, have been published to-date. In addition, the name onamasticon (one volume) has been published.

DICTIONARIES

See also entry 754.

640 Catane, Moche. *Otsar ha-Lo'azim=Recueil des Glosses*. Tel-Aviv: Gittler, 1984. 230p.

In this dictionary, Moche Catane provides the Hebrew meaning for Old French words (Lo'azim) which appear in Rashi's commentary on the Talmud. The dictionary is arranged according to the tractates of the Talmud. The words are listed under each tractate in order of their appearance. A detailed explanation is given following the first occurrence. Words that occur more than once are recorded. The user is referred back to the first occurrence for the meaning. The dictionary includes indices of Old French words in both Hebrew and Latin characters.

641 Frank, Yitshak. *The Practical Talmud Dictionary*. Jerusalem: Ariel United Israel Institutes, 1991. 303p.

This dictionary, designed for English speakers, is based in part on Ezra Zion Melamed's Hebrew Talmudic dictionary, *Eshnav ha-Talmud* (Jerusalem: Kiryat Sefer, 1976). Over 3,500 Aramaic words from the Babylonian Talmud are translated into both Hebrew and English. Hebrew words and phrases are also translated into English. The words and phrases are vocalized. They are entered as they are spelled in the Talmud. The entries include, in addition to the translation, some, if not all, of the following elements: an etymology of the term, an explanation of the function of this term in a Talmudic context, a Talmudic quotation illustrating the use of the term, the source of the Talmudic quotation, and cross references to other entries. The *Dictionary* includes a comprehensive list of the Hebrew and

Aramaic acronyms that appear in the standard editions of the Babylonian Talmud (Appendix I) and tables of measures, weights, coins and numbers (Appendix II).

642 Gukovitzki, Israel. *Sefer Targum ha-La'az ....* London: The Author, 1985. 144p.

In this dictionary, Israel Gukovitzki provides the meaning for the Old French words which appear in Rashi's commentary on the Talmud in Hebrew, English and Modern French. The words are arranged alphabetically. The dictionary includes an index of Old French words in Latin characters and an index of lo'azim in Hebrew characters arranged according to the tractates of the Talmud.

643 Jastrow, Marcus. *A Dictionary of the Targumim, the Talmud Babli and Yerushalmi, and the Midrashic Literature.* New York: Judaica Press, 1971. 2v. in 1.

The definitions in this dictionary are in English. Extensive quotations from the literature are included to exemplify usage. The dictionary includes an index of Scriptural quotations.

644 Melamed, Ezra Zion. *Milon Arami-'Ivri le-Talmud Bavli.* Jerusalem: Foundation Samuel et Odette Levy, 1992. 573 p.

The entries in this Aramaic-Hebrew dictionary to the Babylonian Talmud are arranged according to the way the word appears in the Talmud. A word that begins with a prepositional prefix, however, is entered under the letter following the prefix.

645 Segal, Chaim S. *Munahe Rashi.* Jerusalem: Harry Fischel Institute, 1989. 170p.

This dictionay is "an annotated lexicon of standard terminological definitions, exegetical norms and grammatical rules as formulated by Rashi in his Biblical and Talmudic commentaries." The main body of the work is complemented by the authors commentary "Or la-yesharim" in which he discusses the use of the definition in other occurrences of the term in Rashi's commentaries.

646 Sokoloff, Michael. *A Dictionary of Jewish Palestinian Aramaic of the Byzantine Period.* Ramat Gan: Bar-Ilan University Press, 1990. 832p.

This comprehensive Aramaic-English dictionary provides the user with a tool for an accurate understanding of the Aramaic dialect of the Jewish Palestinian literature of the Byzantine period. Therefore, it is an invaluable tool for scholars working in the fields of Rabbinic literature.

647 Sperber, Daniel. *A Dictionary of Greek and Latin Legal Terms in Rabbinic Literature.* Ramat-Gan: Bar-Ilan University Press, 1984. 230p.

This is a specialized dictionary consisting of almost 200 Greek and Latin legal terms in Rabbinic literature. The author provides the user with the following types of information for each term: definition in English; illustrative texts in translation; parallels; related references; variant readings; comparative material from Hellenistic, Roman and juristic papyrological sources; and full bibliographic references. The work includes Greek, Latin, Pehlevi, and general indices.

See also entry 598.

648 *The Babylonian Talmud: Index Volume.* Compiled by Judah J. Slotki. London: Soncino Press, 1990, 416p.

The *Index Volume*, originally designed for the all-English edition of the Soncino Talmud, includes a general subject index, an index of scriptural references, and a "Rabbinical" index. The latter enables the user to identify the sages and find their sayings in the Talmudic text. The Index volume to the Hebrew-English edition Talmud includes a *"Key to the Talmud"* to complement the general index. This key cites the Hebrew daf (page) number of the original Talmudic text in one column and the number of the corresponding page in the Soncino English-only editon in the other. This enables the reader to use the General Index as a key to the standard Hebrew text.

649 Copperman, Hillel. *Bi-Netivot ha-Midrash.* Jerusalem: The Author, 1984 or 1985. 1,165p.

Copperman has prepared "a comprehensive and exhaustive lexicon of all the subjects dealt with in the Midrash rabbah, on the Chumash, and Five Megillot." The lexicon includes a Biblical citation index.

650 Epstein, Baruch ha-Levi. *Torah Temimah.* [n.p., n.d.] 5v.

The author has collected many statements, commentaries, decisions, etc.found throughout the entire range of Talmudic literature. He has arranged this material alongside its referent in the Pentateuch and the Five Scrolls, indicated the source of the citation, and provided a commentary to elucidate the teachings of the halakhot that the sages have deduced from the language and content of the verse. An English translation by Shraga Silverstein is available under the title: *The Essential Torah Temimah* (Jerusalem; New York: Feldheim, 1989. 5v.).

651 Goldschmidt, Lazarus. *Oznayim la-Torah.* Edited by Rafael Edelmann. Copenhagen: E. Munksgaard, 1959. 607p.

This index to the Talmud Bavli is arranged according to subjects. A keyword precedes the sentence in parenthesis. Each sentence is quoted with a reference to all places where it is found in the Talmud. The citations refer the user to the standard Hebrew text, as well as to volume and page in Goldschmidt's German translation of the Talmud.

652 Hyman, Aaron. *Torah ha-Ketuvah veha-Mesurah.* 2nd rev. and enl. ed. Tel-Aviv: Dvir, 1979. 3v.

This index, arranged by Scriptural passages, enables the user to find the places in the Talmud Bavli, Talmud, Yerushalmi, the Midrashim, etc. where a particular verse is cited.

653 Midrash Rabbah. *Midrash Rabbah.* Translated into English ... under the editorship of Harry Freedman and Maurice Simon. London: Soncino Press, 1961. 10v.

This complete and unabridged English translation of the Midrash Rabbah includes an *Index Volume,* compiled by Judah J. Slotki. It is comprised of three parts: A. General Index, i.e. an index to the subject matter in the

Midrashim as well as geographical and personal (other than Rabbinical) names. B. A complete list of scriptural references C. A list of Talmudic references, i.e. a list of citations from the Talmud which shed light on Midrashic passages. Contains a glossary and a list of abbreviations.

654 Mishnah. *Mishnayot.* Translated by Philip Blackman. New York: Judaica Press, 1964. 7v.

Volume 7, *"Supplement and Index"* includes: a Biblical index to Taharoth (Volume VI), a general index to Taharoth (Volume VI), a Biblical index to Volumes I-VII, a general index to volumes I-VII. The indexes can be used as a key to the materials in the standard Hebrew editions of the Mishnah.

HANDBOOKS AND MANUALS

655 Carmell, Aryeh. *Aiding Talmud Study.* 5th ed., newly rev. and expanded with many new key words and new features. Jerusalem: Feldheim, 1986, 88p.

This guide includes key words and phrases from the Talmud in vocalized Aramaic with English translation; commonly used abbreviations explained and translated into English; a concise survey of Aramaic (Talmudic) grammar; chronological charts of Tannaim and Amoraim; an English translation of Shmuel ha-Nagid's Introduction to the Talmud; Tables of Talmudic weights and measures; chronological charts of Talmudic sages; and a map of Torah centers in the time of the Mishna and Talmud; previously published as: *Aids to Talmud Study.*

656 Rakover, Nahum. *Moreh Derekh bi-Mekorot ha-Mishpat ha-'Ivri.* Jerusalem: Sifriyat ha-Mishpat ha-'Ivri, 1983. 89p.

This guide was written to direct individuals in the use of the basic texts in Jewish law. It is divided into three chapters: A. Sources: Bible, Mishnah and Talmud, Geonic literature, Halakhic literature including codes and responsa B. Introductory works C. Reference works. The author uses the laws of the watchman to show the user how to use these basic sources. He also makes use of facsimiles of pages from texts, as well as charts to explain the construction of texts and their use. A list of abbreviations and a chronological listing of Halakhists, arranged by country, are included in the appendix. The chronology covers the period from the 11th century to the first half of the twentieth century. The guide also includes an index to the chronology and a name, title and subject index.

657 Steinsaltz, Adin. *A Reference Guide.* New York: Random House, 1989. 323p.

The *Guide*, a companion volume to *Talmud: The Steinsaltz Edition* (New York: Random House, 1989-), was conceived primarily as a tool to facilitate the study of the Babylonian Talmud, both for the beginner and the more advanced student. The Guide is also a useful tool for students who wish to study the Jerusalem Talmud, as well as Halakhic or Aggadic Midrashim. It contains, for example, an explanation of the structure and content of the traditional Talmudic page. Chapters on Aramaic and Rashi script enable the student to learn the rudiments of both. Glossaries explain the terminology of Talmudic discourse, terms and concepts of Halakhah, and provide information on weights and measures that are cited in the Talmudic text. The *Guide* includes a general index.

QUOTATIONS

See also Chapter 12.

658 Gross, Moshe David. *Otsar ha-Agadah*. Jerusalem: Mosad Harav Kook, 1954-1955. 3v.
This is a topically arranged index to Aggadic literature in the Mishnah, Tosefta, the Talmudim, the Midrash, and the Zohar.

659 Hasidah, Yisrael Yitshak. *Otsar Maamare Halakhah*. Jerusalem: R. Mass, 1977 or 1978. 3v.
This is an alphabetically arranged listing of approximately 65,000 Halakhic sayings culled from the Talmudim, Midrash and Zohar. It includes a detailed subject index.

660 Rakover, Nahum. *Nive Talmud*. Jerusalem: Sifriyat ha-Mishpat ha-'Ivri, 1990. 442p.
This alphabetical dictionary contains idioms, sayings, and idiomatic phrases used in the area of Jewish law. They were gathered largely from the Mishnah and Talmud. Rakover provides the meaning for each phrase and shows how each is used. He also provides a source citation. See references direct the user to related entries. The Dictionary includes a subject index.

B. JEWISH LAW

INTRODUCTIONS

661 Elon, Menahem. *ha-Mishpat ha-'Ivri*. 2nd enl. ed. Jerusalem: Magnes Press, 1978 2v.
This work contains a detailed discussion pertaining to the "history of Jewish law and its basic principles, the legal sources through which Jewish law continued to grow and develop through the ages." It includes an extensive two part bibliography (A. Hebrew B. Other languages) and a list of "Sources", and is indexed.

662 Urbach, Ephraim Elimelech. *The Halakhah: Its Sources and Development*. Ramat Gan: Massada; Jerusalem?: Yad la-Talmud, 1986. 519p.
"The purpose of this book is to describe and explain the fundamentals of the Halakhah and the principles and methodology involved in the development as they are reflected in the literature of the Oral Law." The following are among the topics that Urbach discusses: A. Regulations and ordinances B. The place of custom in Halakhah C. The Courts D. Sages of the Halakhah—their personality, methods and authority E. The Babylonian Talmud—the book and its authority. The study includes bibliographic notes, a list of sources, a bibliography and a general index.

ENCYCLOPEDIAS

663 Elon, Menahem. *The Principles of Jewish Law*. Jerusalem: Keter, 1975. 566 columns.

This collection of articles, published originally in the *Encyclopaedia Judaica*, provides a "methodical description of the principles and institutions of Jewish law."

664 *Entsiklopedyah Talmudit le-'Inyane Halakhah.* Jerusalem: Talmudic Encyclopedia Publishers, 1951-.
This is a comprehensive presentation, arranged alphabetically, of all Halakhic subjects dealt with in the Talmud and in post-Talmudic Rabbinic literature, from the Geonic period down to the present day. To-date, 20 volumes have been published covering the letters Alef to Halitsah. A revised edition is also in progress. An English translation entitled *Encyclopedia Talmudica* (Jerusalem: 1969-.) is also available. The entries follow the Hebrew alphabetical order and include explanatory notes and abridged sources. Four volumes (to brerah) have been published to-date.

665 Steinberg, Avraham. *Entsiklopedyah Hilkhatit Refuit.* Jerusalem: Makhon Shlesinger la-Heker ha-Refui Sha'are Tsedek, 1988-
This encyclopedia includes articles on the following broad topics: A. Halakhic topics that are of concern to the doctor and / or patient, e.g. laws of mourning, Sabbath B. Topics that have halakhic and ethical implications, e.g. suicide, contraception C. General topics that are related to medicine, halakhah, and ethics, e.g. freedom of choice, visiting the sick, life and death D. Medical problems that have halakhic implications, e.g. paternity, infertility E. Halakhic topics that are related to the various parts of the body. Each entry includes: a definition of the concept (topic), a summary of its treatment in the Bible and Talmud, and a summation of all relevant halakhic decisions to-date. The Encyclopedia is illustrated and includes an index of sources, and a bibliography pertaining to Halakha and medicine. To-date, two volumes, alef-mem (milah), have been published.

Note: Original articles, abstracts and reports pertaining to Halakhah and medicine may be found in the journal *Assia* (Jerusalem, 1976- .) See also in this journal"s "ha-Mador ha-Bibliyografi" for a listing of related articles that have been published in other sources.

BIBLIOGRAPHY

666 Eisenstadt, Samuel. *'En Mishpat.* Jerusalem: ha-Mishpat, 1931. 464p.
This multi-lingual classified bibliography of Jewish law lists materials published until 1930.

667 *Jewish Law: Bibliography of Sources and Scholarship in English.* Compiled by Phyllis Holman Weisbard and David Schonberg. Littleton, CO: Fred B. Rothman, 1990. 558p.
This is a comprehensive classified bibliography of research materials in English pertaining to various aspects of Jewish law. The bibliography begins with three general sections: General works on Jewish law, Literary sources on Jewish law in English translation, and Bibliographies of Jewish law. The body of the work is divided into 38 legal categories, e.g. the status of women in Jewish law, medical-legal issues, and Jewish law in the State of Israel. The introductory essay to each legal category provides the reader with an understanding of how that area of law is regarded within the system of Jewish law. The three appendices — (a) Jewish history, (b)

community studies, and (c) biographical studies — provide useful historical background. The bibliography is indexed.

668 Rakover, Nahum. *The Multi-language Bibliography of Jewish Law.* Jerusalem: The Library of Jewish Law, 1990. 871p.

669 —. *Otsar ha-Mishpat.* Jerusalem: Harry Fischel Institute, 1975-1990. 2v. Both bibliographies list books, doctoral dissertations and articles published under the following 17 general headings: A. The Foundations and Nature of Halakha B. Sources C. Jewish Law in General D. Jewish Law in the State of Israel E. Comparative Law F. Society and Government G. Courts and Procedure H. Evidence I. Contracts (Collections, Terminology) J. Penal Law K. Status of the Individual L. Family / Inheritance M. Torts N. Acquisition and Contract O. Various Concepts P. Reference Works Q. Biographies of Sages. Each of the general categories is further sub-divided. The former bibliography lists materials in all languages except Hebrew. The latter lists only materials in Hebrew. Access to the materials is facilitated by a detailed table of contents and multiple indexes: subjects, place names (for the section entitled "Communities-Organizations and Administration") rabbinical scholars (for the section entitled "Biographies of the Sages"), authors, list of periodicals, collections and their abbreviations. The last index is not in the first of the two volumes of the *Otsar.*

Responsa Literature (Indexes)

670 Cohen, Boaz. *Kuntres ha-Teshuvot.* Jerusalem: Makor, 1970. 226p. This bibliography, originally published in 1930, lists c.2,000 works of responsa. The materials are arranged by title in five chapters: A. Books and articles that deal with responsa B. Books and articles that deal with Geonic responsa C. Responsa of the Geonim D. Responsa after the Geonim with no distinguishing title (listed by author) E. Responsa after the Geonim listed alphabetically by title. The bibliography includes an index of countries arranged by century (up to the 19th century). The index is an aid to the user who is interested in the history of the Jews and their literature in a specific periods, who will be able to find related material in the works of responsa. E. Index of authors (including authors whose responsa are in other works). An addenda by Solomon Freehof entitled: "Hosafot le-kuntres ha-teshuvot le-Bo'az Kohen," (*Studies in Bibliography and Booklore* 6:30-41) lists responsa published after 1930. The Cohen number is given for added editions and reprints of works listed in Cohen's bibliography.

671 Eidensohn, Daniel. *Yad Moshe: Mafteah Kelali le-Sh"uT Igrot Moshe shel Mosheh Fainshtain.* 3rd corr. and enl. ed. Brooklyn, N. Y.: The Author, 1989. 218p. This edition includes topical indexes in Hebrew and English to *Igrot Mosheh,* the responsa of Rabbi Moshe Feinstein. The citation directs the user to the section and page number in the *Igrot.* A *Shulhan 'Arukh* conversion table, which lists every section in the *Shulhan 'Arukh* and the corresponding Hebrew index term in *Yad Moshe,* is included.

672 Elon, Menahem. *Mafteah ha-Sheelot veha-Teshuvot shel Hakhme Sefarad u-Tsefon Afrikah.* Jerusalem: Makhon le-Heker ha-Mishpat ha-'Ivri, 1981-

Section Two: Subject Reference | *165*

This series of indexes encompasses the responsa of the rabbis who resided in North Africa and Spain until the expulsion in 1492. It will include the following indexes upon completion: A. *Mafteah ha-Mishapati (Legal Digest)* 2v. B. *Mafteah ha-Histori (Historical Digest)* 3v. C. *Mafteah ha-Mekorot (Source index)* 2v. The *Legal Digest*, arranged by subject, enables the user to find responsa that deal with aspects of civil, criminal, public, administrative and personal status law. The *Historical Digest* is ordered by respondent, e.g. Isaac Alfasi, Joseph ben Meir ha-Levi Ibn Migash, etc. A topically arranged index, under each respondent, enables the user to find materials of historical importance in the responsa of the respondent. The following are some of the broad topics included in the *Historical Digest*: Political, legal and social status of the Jews (including relations with non-Jews); Community institutions and leadership; Settlement and emigration; Economy; Realia; Beliefs and opinions. These broad topics are further subdivided. The *Source Index* is arranged in the following order: Bible, Mishnah, Midrashe Halakha, Tosefta, Talmud Bavli, Midrashe Agadah, Minor Tractates. It refers the user from a particular verse or passage to responsa in which that verse or passage had been cited. (The second volume will include the works of the Geonim and Rishonim.) The following volumes have been published to-date: *Mafteah ha-Mishpati*. Jerusalem, 1986. 2v.; *Mafteah ha-Histori*. Jerusalem, 1981- . 2v.; *Mafteah ha-Mekorot*. Jerusalem, 1981- . 1v.

673   Golinkin, David. *An Index of Conservative Responsa and Halakhic Studies: 1917-1990*. New York: The Rabbinical Assembly, 1992. 80p.
      The formal responsa written by various Conservative Rabbinic bodies such as the Committee on Jewish Law and its successor, the Committee on Jewish Laws and Standards, are indexed by Golinkin under such headings as kashrut, mourning, medical ethics, women, and marriage. He has also indexed the responsa of individual Conservative rabbis, e.g. Isaac Klein, Aaron Blumenthal, as well as the practical halakhic studies of individual Conservative rabbis and laymen which have appeared in the pages of such publications as *Conservative Judaism, Judaism* and the *Proceedings* of the Rabbinical Assembly. Within a given topic citations are arranged either chronologically or alphabetically. The major topics have been sub-divided. Topics have been cross-referenced to assist the user.

674   *Otsar ha-Poskim 'al Shulhan 'Arukh Even ha-'Ezer*. 2d ed. Jerusalem, 1955-
      The *Otsar* contains a digest of all extant rabbinic responsa bearing upon Jewish law and ritual. The digest is arranged in the order of the *Shulhan 'Arukh* and accompanies the text. Eighteen volumes have been published to-date covering siman (chapter) 1-69.

675   *Otsar ha-Poskim: Mafteah ha-Sh"uT Hoshen Mishapat*. Jerusalem, 1992- .
      This detailed index to responsa literature is arranged by subject and is classified in the order of the *Shulhan 'Arukh*. The work includes the text of the *Shulhan 'Arukh*, and a list of books and authors that have been cited. A subject index facilitates the retrieval of information. One volume covering hilkkot dayanim, the laws of judges (1-17), has been published.

CODES (INDEXES)

676   Assaf, David. *Otsar Leshon ha-Rambam*. Haifa: The Author, 1960-.
      This is a concordance to the Mishneh Torah by Maimonides. To-date ten volumes have been published, covering the letters Alef to Mem.

677 Avraham, Avraham. *La-ruts Orah.* Mahadurah Hadashah u-Murhevet. Jerusalem [1988] 403p.
This Hebrew index to Joseph Caro's *Shulhan 'Arukh Orah Hayim* is divided into the following six sections: A. Simanim (Chapters) 1-127 B. Simanim 128-241 C. Simanim 242-344 D. Simanim 345-428 E. Simanim 429-529 F. Simanim 530-697. Each section contains an alphabetically arranged subject index. An overall general subject index is located at the beginning of the volume.

678 —. *Yaruts Devaro.* Jerusalem [1991?]. 239 p.
This work is a detailed Hebrew subject index to Joseph Caro's *Shulhan 'Arukh Yoreh Deah.*

679 Eisenbach, Moshe. *Mafteah ha-Shulhan ha-Shalem.* Jerusalem: Va´ad le-Hotsaat Sifre Masa Halakkhah, 1991. 403p.
This alphabetical Hebrew subject index enables the user to find the halakhot (laws) that are cited in Joseph Caro's *Shulhan 'Arukh Orah Hayim,* the emendations of Moses Isserles, the commentary *Beer Hetev,* by Judah Titkin, and the *Mishnah Berurah,* by Israel Meir Kagan (Hafets Hayim).

680 *Mafteah le-Firushim 'al Mishneh Torah leha-RaMBaM.* Edited by Barukh Kahana, Eliyah Shelomoh Ra'anan, Ya'akov Blum. Jerusalem: Makhon Halakhah Berurah u-Verur Halakhah, 1991. 838, 31p.
This work is arranged according to the order of laws in Maimonides' code, the *Mishneh Torah.* Under each law, the compilers cite Halakhic works that either discuss that particular law in Maimonides's code or the same topic. Therefore, in essence this work serves as a general index for halakhic subjects arranged in accordance with the Maimonidean code. A bibliography of sources is included at the end of the index.

681 Maimonides, Moses. *Mishneh Torah.* Edited by Zvi H. Preisler. Jerusalem: Ketuvim, 1985. 870p.
This one volume edition of the *Mishneh Torah* is based on the Warsaw-Vilna printing. It is partially pointed and includes an index to Biblical citations cited in the Code. It also includes a detailed subject index. Citations are grouped under broad terms. Cross references refer the user from specific terms to these headings. Although some headings are unwieldy the index remains useful. This edition is a useful "reference edition"' because of its size and indexes.

682 Platnick, Abraham Joseph. *Jewish Law-Index to Code.* Miami: A. J. Platnick, 1989. 246p.
This work contains a detailed subject index in English to the Hyman Goldin edition of Solomon Ganzfried's *Kitsur Shulhan Arukh (Code of Jewish Law).* This editon contains an English translation of Ganzfried's work.

683 Slotky, Eliahu David. *Entsiklopedyah Hilkhatit Hasde David.* Jerusalem: Bitachon Printing, 1973 or 74. 430 p.
This alphabetically arranged topical index enables the user to find the halakhot (laws) in Maimonides' *Mishneh Torah* and Caro's *Shulhan 'Arukh.*

C. Computer Software (Rabbinic Literature and Jewish Law)

684 *CD-ROM Judaic Classics Library.* Chicago, IL: Davka Corporation (7074 N. Western Ave., Chicago, IL 60645)
The Judaic Classics Library CD-Rom is avaliable for PC (DOS) and Macs. It includes a speedy search program that enables the user to search for words and phrases, with prefixes and suffixes, and / or logic and restrictions to specific books and sections. Retrieval is rapid. The *Limited Edition* includes the complete text of the Tanakh (Hebrew Bible) with the Rashi commentary on the Pentateuch, and the Talmud Bavli (Babylonian Talmud) with the Rashi commentary. The *Second Edition* includes all of the books of the *Limited Edition* and Aggadic Midrashim, Maimonides' Mishneh Torah, the Talmud Yerushalmi (Jerusalemite Talmud), the Zohar, the Torah commentaries (Ramban, Or ha-Hayim, Ba´al ha-Turim), Onkelos, and books of Musar (Sha´are Teshuvah, Orkhot Tsadikim, and Mesilat Yesharim). The *Third Edition* includes in addition to the above the Shulhan ´Arukh Orah Hayim with the Mishnah Berurah, the Be´ur Halakhah, Sha´´ar ha-Tsiyun, the Shulhan ´Arukh Hoshen Mishpat with Ketsot ha-Hoshen, Mekhilta, Sifre, Sifra, the Tosefta, Masektot Ketanot, and the writings of the Maharal (excluding Gur Aryeh).

685 *Global Jewish Database.* Ramat-Gan: Bar-Ilan University (U.S.A.: Ofrer Inc., 1 Executive Dr., Fort Lee, NJ 07024).
The database is now available on CD-ROM with an advanced text information retrieval system. Two versions are available: A. *Taklit Torah* contains the Tanach (Hebrew Bible), Midrashim, Talmud Bavli (Babylonian Talmud) with Rashi's commentary, Talmud Yerushalmi (Jerusalemite Talmud), and Rambam's Mishneh Torah B. *Taklit Sh"ut* contains Tanach, Mishnah, Midrashim, Talmud Bavli with Rashi's commentary, Talmud Yerushalmi (Jerusalemite Talmud), Rambam's Mishneh Torah, Jacob Tur's Turim, and 253 books of Responsa covering a period from the 8th century to the present. The text information retrieval system enables the user to browse through texts, search texts by keyword or expressions, store parts of the texts in files, modify these saved texts with a text editor and print parts of the text. An IBM PC / AT (or clone) with RAM memory of at least 2 MB is required to run the program.

686 Saul Lieberman Institute of Talmudic Research of the Jewish Theological Seminary of America. *Computer Programs and Databanks.*
The Institute disseminates the following computerized research tools: A. *The Sol and Evelyn Henkind Talmud Text Databank.* " This databank presents the user with the full manuscript texts of the Babylonian Talmud." It "allows the user to view any specific page of Talmud in manuscript text, or to search for specific words and combination of words, within the entire corpus. The second function allows one to perform the tasks traditionally associated with the concordance, and *Dikdukei Sofrim* (variant readings of Talmud composed by N. N. Rabinowitz ...), with great speed." The database can be acquired in one of two forms: a. the text with search capability b. The database in text-only form. Scholars can export extended passages of text for ASCII use, e.g. incorporate quotations in articles. B. *Index of References Dealing with Talmudic Literature.* "This databank provides bibliographical references to discussions on Talmudic literature. The references

are given in terms of a specific page, or pages, within 300 works [indexed]. These works comprise modern Talmud scholarship, medieval Talmud study (Rishonim), and parallel references within the Talmudic Midrashic literature." C. *Classified List of Genizah Fragments in the Elkan Nathan Adler Collection*. This computerized classified list enables the user to retrieve the following information about each fragment: physical dimensions, language of the fragment, names mentioned, bibliographic or literary connections, etc. The Databanks are designed to run on the IBM PC / XT / AT or IBM PS / 2 and all close compatibles.

687 *Talmud Scholar with Dictionary.* Kabbalah Software (8 Price Drive, Edison, NJ 08817.)

This software package includes the complete Babylonian Talmud with an on-line instant English translation dictionary, as well as biographies of Talmudic sages. Hypertext capabilities and graphics are included. The package is available in both Mac and PC versions.

D. Judaism

Bibliography

688 Bavier, Richard. "Judaism in New Testament Times," In *The Study of Judaism: Bibliographical Essays*, 7-34. New York: Anti-Defamation League, 1972.

The author, in a brief introduction, describes anthologies, theologies, histories, etc. that have been written about Judaism in New Testament times. This is followed by a bibliography which contains both primary and secondary sources in English.

689 Oppenheim, Micha F. *The Study and Practice of Judaism: A Selected, Annotated List.* Brooklyn: Torah Resources, 1979. 78p.

This is a bibliography of traditional Torah literature in English, divided into 13 subjects. Over 500 books and pamphlet are included. There are author and title indexes.

690 Starkey, Edward D. *Judaism and Christianity: A Guide to the Reference Literature.* Littleton, CO: Libraries Unlimited, 1991. 256p.

"This bibliography identifies, describes, evaluates, and compares" 763 "reference books dealing with Judaism and Christianity, and the Bibles of these two religious traditions, published in English through 1988." The bibliography is divided into two sections: A. The reference literature on Christianity and Judaism B. The reference literature on the Bibles of Judaism and Christianity. Each section is further subdivided by type of reference work. Author / Title and Subject indexes are included.

Encyclopedias / Dictionaries / Handbooks

691 Birnbaum, Philip. *Encyclopedia of Jewish Concepts.* New York: Sanhedrin Press, 1979. 722p.

More than 1,600 concepts and terms related to the essential teachings of Judaism are defined in English in this one volume compendium. The terms are arranged alphabetically by the transliterated Hebrew term. The topical index enables the reader to find the concept or term that he is looking for. This index is divided into twenty major categories, e.g. Bible, Torah, feasts and festivals. In addition the work includes an index of concepts in Hebrew and English.

692 Bulka, Reuven P. *What You Thought You Knew About Judaism: 341 Misconceptions About Jewish life.* Northvale, NJ: J. Aronson, 1989. 436p.
The author has gathered over 300 commonly held misconceptions about Judaism that circulate widely among Jews and non-Jews, and arranged them in six broad categories: A. Special events and special days B.Taking care: physical and spiritual C. Eros and thanatos (marriage, divorce, illness, death, etc.) D. People E. Food for thought — thought for food F. Past and present. Bulka debunks these myths and misconceptions about Judaism. The book includes sources, a glossary, a bibliography, and an index.

693 Cahn-Lipman, David E. *The Book of Jewish Knowledge: 613 Basic Facts About Judaism.* Northvale, NJ: J. Aronson, 1991. 457p.
"The purpose of this book is to help the reader become familiar with all those once common names, objects, rituals, events, and Jewish concepts." The book is divided into three sections: A. *Facts* containing 613 one sentence building blocks pertaining to the Jewish holidays, ritual objects, etc. B. *Data* relating to the topics covered in section A.. III. *Self-tests.* Indexed.

694 Cohen, Arthur A. and Paul R. Mendes-Flohr. *Contemporary Jewish Religious Thought: Original Essays on Critical Concepts, Movements and Beliefs.* New York: Scribner, 1987. 1,163p.
This is a collection of 140 commissioned essays defining various aspects of Jewish thought and belief, among them: "Conservative Judaism" by Gerson Cohen; "Orthodox Judaism" by Emanuel Rackman, "Reform Judaism" by Michael Meyer; and "Judaism" by Gershom Scholem. Each essay is accompanied by a brief bibliography which directs the reader to the literature for further inquiry. A glossary provides basic information for terms, authors, historical movements, and events mentioned at least twice in the essays. Author and subject indexes are included.

695 Cohn-Sherbok, Dan. *A Dictionary of Judaism and Christianity.* Philadelphia: Trinity Press International, 1991. 181p.
In this dictionary the author defines and compares the key concepts, beliefs and practices of Judaism and Christianity. He notes the similarities, as well as the differences, between the two religions.

696 *The Encyclopedia of Judaism.* Editor, Geoffrey Wigoder. New York: Macmillan, 1989. 768p.
The *Encyclopedia* focuses on "Jewish religious life and development, excluding secular concerns." The biographical articles highlight the lives of outstanding individuals who have contributed to the development of Judaism. The articles were written by well-known scholars in different fields and of differing ideological backgrounds. The many illustrations enrich this work. The Hebrew translation or transliteration of the term is

often given. Terms are also defined in a Glossary. Cross references and a detailed subject index help the user to find materials in the *Encyclopedia*.

697 Glustrom, Simon. *The Language of Judaism*. Northvale, NJ: J. Aronson, 1988. 433p.
This work presents a basic vocabulary of 186 Hebrew words and phrases that are unique and central to Judaism. Each term is given in Hebrew, transliteration and English translation, and the deeper meaning and significance of the concept are discussed. The terms are grouped into 15 categories. The work concludes with a 16-page subject index.

698 *Judaism: A People and its History*. Edited by Robert M. Seltzer. New York: Macmillan, 1989. 338p.
This work, intended for college students and the general reader, contains twenty-six essays from the *Encyclopedia of Religion* pertaining to the history, religion, and culture of the Jewish people. The book is divided into five sections: A. Roots of Tradition, an overview of the Jewish concept of "Jewish Peoplehood" B. Post Biblical Judaism and Classic rabbinic texts C. Jewish people and its identity. The articles in this section "indicate "the variety of ways in which Judaism accommodated to Islamic, Greek Orthodox, Roman Catholic and Protestant milieux in the Middle East, North Africa, Europe and America during periods of ferment, chaos, stability and stagnation." D. Articles that together outline much of the Jewish religious observance E. The issue of modernization. Each article includes a bibliography. A "Synoptic Outline" at the end of the volume lists the articles under the headings Judaism, Biographies, and Israelite Religion.

699 Telushkin, Joseph. *Jewish Literacy: The Most Important Things to Know About the Jewish Religion, Its People, and Its History*. New York: Morrow, 1991. 687p.
This work, intended in part as a study guide, enables the student to acquire an overview of Judaism and Jewish history. The material is arranged topically under the following categories: A. The Bible B. The Second Commonwealth: The Mishnah and the Talmud C. Early medieval period under Islam and Christianity D. Late medieval period E. Modern period — Western and Eastern Europe F. Zionism and Israel G. The Holocaust I. American Jewish life J. Soviet Jewry K. Antisemitism L. Jewish texts M. Jewish ethics and basic beliefs N. The Hebrew calendar and Jewish holidays O. Life cycle P. Synagogue and prayers. Each article includes "Sources and Further Readings." The author provides a general index to enable the reader to access the materials in the discussions.

700 Unterman, Alan. *Dictionary of Jewish Lore and Legend*. London: Thames and Hudson, 1991. 216p.
This dictionary contains brief descriptions of terms and names related to Jewish folklore and legend, the Jewish festivals, customs and ceremonies, historical events, the framework of Jewish law, etc. It also includes biographical sketches of Biblical personalities and of Jewish notables throughout the ages. See references direct the user to the term that is being used. A brief list of books for further reading is included at the end of the *Dictionary*.

701 Kolatch, Alfred J. *The Jewish Home Advisor.* Middle Village, NY: Jonathan David, 1990. 362p.

The book offers information and guidance for anyone wishing to carry out the practices of Judaism. The varied practices of Orthodox, Conservative, Reform, Reconstructionist, Hasidic, Ashkenazic and Sephardic Jews are presented. The guide covers all aspects of Jewish life, and is designed to serve as a handbook for those who are experienced in carrying out the rituals of Judaism, as well as those whose familiarity with Jewish religious practices is limited. The first part of the book discusses Jewish practices that relate to home and family; the second concerns itself with synagogue practice and holiday celebrations. The manual includes a list of "selected books for the home library" and an index. This how-to book complements the author's previous works, *The Jewish Book of Why* and *The Second Jewish Book of Why,* which focus on the reasons behind particular laws and observances.

702 —. *The Second Jewish Book of Why.* Middle Village, NY: Jonathan David, 1985. 423p.

Designed to explain the reasoning behind contemporary Jewish observance and practice, this volume deals in Question and Answer form with complex controversial topics such as, abortion, conversion, birth control, sex, homosexuality, artificial insemination, organ transplants, smoking, intermarriage, who is a Jew, Jewish-Christian relations, theology, and laws and customs of Jewish women. The previous volume, *The Jewish Book of Why* (1981) deals with fundamental questions about Sabbath and holidays, dietary laws, synagogue practice, and the Jewish life cycle. *The Second Jewish Book of Why* includes a 46-page index to both books and a bibliography.

703 Latner, Helen. *The Book of Modern Jewish Etiquette: A Guide for All Occasions.* New York: Schocken, 1981. 373p.

This book is an attempt to present in one reference volume a guide to the Jewish way to celebrate a marriage, the birth of a child, a bar or bat mitzvah, to cope with difficult times in life brought on by old age, illness, death, or divorce. There are chapters on: Everyday good manners; Jewish practice, the basics of observance; Happy occasions; Difficult times; Travel. The work is indexed.

704 Trepp, Leo. *The Complete Book of Jewish Observance.* New York: Behrman House, 1980. 370p.

This is a concise encyclopedic guide to Jewish rituals and observances presenting Orthodox, Conservative, and Reform practices. What is done, when it is to be done, and the reasons why are offered. Included are a bibliography and index.

CHAPTER 21

JEWISH THOUGHT

A. PHILSOPHY
See also entries 89-98.

OVERVIEWS

705 Guttmann, Julius. *Philosophies of Judaism.* Philadelphia: Jewish Publication Society of America, 1964. 464p.

> Guttmann in this history of Jewish religious thought summarizes the thought of Jewish philosophers from Philo to Rosenzweig. This study contains an extensive bibliography.

706 *Jewish Philosophers.* Edited by Steven J. Katz. Jerusalem: Keter, 1975. 299p.

> The articles in this book, with the exception of two essays written by the editor, are taken from the *Encylopaedia Judaica.* Together, these articles introduce the reader to Jewish thought throughout the ages. The compendium includes a glossary of religious and philosophical terms, a biographical index and a bibliography.

707 Samuelson, Norbert. *An Introduction to Modern Jewish Philosophy.* Albany, NY: State University of New York Press, 1989. 320p.

> "The book is divided into three sections. The first provides a general historical overview for the Jewish thought that follows. The second summarizes the variety of basic kinds of popular, positive Jewish commitment in the twentieth century. The third and major section summarizes the basic thought of those modern Jewish philosophers whose thought is technically the best and/or the most influential in jewish intellectual circles. The Jewish philosophers covered include Spinoza, Mendelssohn, Hermann Cohen, Martin Buber, Franz Rosenzweig, Mordecai Kaplan and Emil Fackenheim. The text includes summaries and a selected bibliography of primary and secondary sources."

708 Sirat, Colette. *A History of Jewish Philosophy in The Middle Ages.* Cambridge: Cambridge University Press, 1985. 476p.

> In this introductory work, Sirat surveys Jewish philosophic creativity, primarily in the period from the mid-9th century to the 16th century. Excerpts from basic philosophic texts are presented and analyzed in an attempt to elucidate their meaning and to situate them in their historical context. The *History* includes a 46 page classified bibliography keyed to the chapters in the book. The bibliography includes a listing of works by the philosophers of the period and works about them and their thought.

BIBLIOGRAPHY

709 Frank, Daniel. "Recent Scholarship on Maimonides and Medieval Jewish Philosophy." *Journal of Jewish Studies* 43 (1992): 332-37.
Frank surveys recent scholarship on Maimonides and medieval Jewish philosophy.

710 "Jewish Philosophy: Medieval and Modern," by Michael Paley and Jacob J. Staub. In *The Schocken Guide to Jewish Books*, 203-227. New York: Schocken, 1992.
The authors provide the layman and student with a suggested list of basic books written in English pertaining to medieval and modern Jewish philosophy.

711 "Medieval Jewish Religious Philosophy," by Lawrence V. Berman. In *Bibliographical Essays in Medieval Jewish Studies*, 233-265. New York: Anti-Defamation League of B'nai Brith, 1976.
This survey provides bibliographic information on works on medieval Jewish religious philosophy. It is intended primarily for beginners. Therefore, the author limited the bibliography largely to English language material. The essay is divided into four sections: A. Histories, anthologies, encyclopedias, and thematic monographs B. Themes (a. Kalam b. Neoplatonism. Aristotelian and later trends) C. Individual thinkers in chronological order e. g., Saadia ben Joseph, Solomon ibn Gabirol, Bahya ben Joseph ibn Paquda, Abraham ibn Ezra, etc. D. Bibliography, including primary sources.

712 "Modern Jewish Thought," by Fritz Rothschild and Seymour Siegel. In *The Study of Judaism; Bibliographical Essays*, 113-184. New York: Anti Defamation League of B'nai Brith, 1972.
This survey provides bibliographical information on works on modern Jewish thought. The survey is divided into six sections: A. Introduction B. Surveys, anthologies and histories of Jewish thought C. Handbooks on Jewish religion D. Movements in Judaism: Reform, Conservative, Orthodox (including Hasidic and Musar), Zionist, Jewish Socialist E. Jewish thinkers from Mendelssohn to the present F. Bibliographic listing.

713 Novak, David. "Jewish Theology." *Modern Judaism* 10 (1990): 311-323.
Novak discusses the major manifestations of Jewish theology in the decade of the 1980's and examines the covenant theology of Eugene Borowitz and David Hartman. He also indicates the apparent direction of Jewish theology in the decade of the 90's. The essay includes bibliographic notes.

714 Seeskin, Kenneth. "Jewish Philosophy in the 1980's." *Modern Judaism* 11 (1991): 157-172.
This essay describes the trends and themes that have dominated Jewish philosophic studies during the eighties. It includes bibliographic notes.

715 Vajda, Georges. *Jüdische Philosophie*. Bern: A. Francke, 1950. 40p.
This comprehensive bibliography includes materials published to 1950. Hebrew publications are not included.

716 —. "Les Études de Philosophie Juive du Moyen Âge depuis la Synthése de Julius Guttmann." *Hebrew Union College Annual* 43 (1972) : 125-47; 45 (1974): 205-42.
This annotated bibliography supplements and updates the bibliography in Guttmann's *Philosophies of Judaism*.

DICTIONARIES

717 Klatzkin, Jacob. *Otsar ha-Munahim ha-Pilosoifyim...* New York: Feldheim, 1968. 2v.
Klatzkin provides explanations in Hebrew and German for philosophic terms found in medieval Jewish philosophic texts. He makes extensive use of quotations from the literature to illustrate meanings and usage.

B. MYSTICISM
OVERVIEWS

718 Scholem, Gershom. *Kabbalah.* New York: Quadrangle, 1974. 492p.
This volume is comprised of reedited and revised articles, originally written for the *Encyclopaedia Judaica*, which summarize the history, ideas, and impact of Kabbalah. The inclusion of chapter bibliographies makes this volume extremely useful as a reference tool. A general index and an index of titles are included.

BIBLIOGRAPHY

719 Scholem, Gershom. *Bibliographia Kabbalistica.* Leipzig: W. Druglin, 1927. 230p.
Scholem lists books and articles pertaining to Gnosis, Kabbalah, Sabbateanism, the Frankist movement, and Hasidism. The materials are arranged alphabetically by author. A listing of editions of the Zohar and commentaries to it are listed in an appendix. The bibliography includes a subject index.

720 Spector, Sheila A. *Jewish Mysticism: An Annotated Bibliography on the Kabbalah in English.* New York: Garland, 1984. 389p.
This bibliography covers material relating to the Kabbalah and its interpretation, and includes translations of texts, books, and scholarly articles published in English from 1659 to the present. It has chapters on such topics as general reference works, introductory surveys, the history of Kabbalah, major scholars, and Hasidism. Indexed.

721 Wijnhoven, Jochanan A. "Medieval Jewish Mysticism," In *Bibliographical Essays in Medieval Jewish Studies,* 267-330. New York: Anti-Defamation League of B'nai Brith, 1976.
This survey provides bibliographic information on Jewish Mysticism with particular emphasis "on developments from late antiquity until the 19th century." The survey is divided into six parts : A. Introduction B. General studies C. Chronological treatment of periods, trends and personalities in

Jewish mysticism D. Borderline areas of mysticism (e. g., Gnosticism and mythology; Angels, demons, and magic) E. Contemporary Jewish mysticism F. Bibliography, including primary sources.

ANTHOLOGIES

722 *The Wisdom of the Zohar: An Anthology of Texts.* Systematically arranged and rendered into Hebrew by Fischel Lachower and Isaiah Tishby. English translation by David Goldstein. Cambridge: Published for the Littman Library by Oxford University Press, 1989. 3v.

> This anthology is a translation of *Mishnat ha-Zohar.* It enables the English reader to gain insight into the teachings of the Zohar and benefit from the extensive introductions and explanations by Isaiah Tishby. The English edition includes a bibliography, a select glossary, an index of references to the Zohar, an index of scriptural references, and an index to the anthology texts.

CONCORDANCES / DICTIONARIES / INDEXES

723 Jolles, Jacob Zebi. *Sefer Kehilat Ya'akov.* Jerusalem, 1971. 2v. in 1.

> This edition of the dictionary is a reprint (except for the introduction) of the Lemberg, 1870 edition. Jolles defines names and terms found in Cabalistic literature.

724 Schäfer, Peter. *Konkordantsyah le-Sifrut ha-Hekhalot=Konkordanz zur Hekhalot Literatur.* Tübingen: J. C. B. Mohr,1986-1988. 2v.

> This is a concordance to Hekhalot literature.

725 Slotky, Eliahu David. *Yad Eliyahu.* Jerusalem: Yeshivat ha-Mekubalim Sha'ar ha-Shamayim. 1962 or 63. 380p.

> This encyclopedia serves as an index to Lurianic Kabbalah. It includes articles pertaining to commandments, customs and ceremonies as well as definitions of difficult words in the Zohar.

726 —. *Aderet Eliyahu.* Jerusalem: Yeshivat ha-Mekubalim Sha'ar ha-Shamayim,1973 or 74. 415p.

> This work is an alphabetically arranged topical index to the more than 10,000 sayings, proverbs, fables, names of angels, etc. mentioned in the *Zohar, Zohar Hadash,* and *Tikune ha-Zohar.*

C. HASIDISM

See also entry 719.

BIBLIOGRAPHY

727 Faierstein, Morris M. "Gershom Sholem and Hasidism." *Journal of Jewish Studies* 38 (1987): 221-233.

> In this brief article, the author reviews recent research written on the history of Hasidism. He also tries to "chart the course of the debate since

Scholem's essay in *Major Trends in Jewish Mysticism*" (New York: Schocken,1961).

728 —. "Hasidism-The Last Decade in Research." *Modern Judaism* 11 (1991): 111-124
Faierstein discusses the major scholarly works that have been written in the 1980's pertaining to Hasidism. He also notes aspects of Hasidic history that require further research. The essay includes bibliographic notes.

729 Gries, Zeev. "Hasidism: The Present State of Research and Some Desirable Priorities." *Numen* 34/1 (1987): 97-108, 34/2: 179-213.
This survey is divided into two parts. The first part "establishes principles for the study of Hasidism. The second, surveys the lines along which research has developed with particular emphasis on major trends." The survey contains extensive bibliographic notes.

BIOGRAPHY

730 Alfasi, Yitshak. *ha-Hasidut*. Tel-Aviv: Ma'ariv, 1974. 269p.
This lexicon contains brief biographies of more than 2,500 Hasidic personalities. The biographies are grouped within dynasties. The lexicon includes a general survey on Hasidism, chapters devoted to a description of several Hasidic Courts and a discussion of such subjects as women in Hasidism, etc. It also includes many portraits and facsimiles. Name and city indices enable the user to find each figure within the dynasties.

731 —. *Sefer ha-Admorim*. Tel-Aviv: Ariel, 1961. 136p.

732 *Entsiklopedyah la-Hasidut*. Edited by Yitzhak Raphael. Jerusalem: Mosad ha-Rav Kook, 1980-.
This is an encyclopedia of Hasidism in Hebrew. The completed work will include a complete bibliography of all Hasidic works, short biographies of all Hasidic personalities, histories of Hasidic centers, a discussion of Hasidism during the Holocaust, and selections from Hasidic thought and teachings. The following volumes have been published to-date: 1. Sefarim, Alef-Tet (1980), compiled by Shalom Porush, provides a full bibliographic description of Hasidic works. 2. Ishim Alef-Tet (1986) compiled by Yitzhak Alfasi contains c.600 bio-bibliographical sketches. Bibliographical references are noted in many entries.

DICTIONARIES
See also entries 738-53.

733 Steinsaltz, Adin. *Rashe Tevot ve-Kitsurim be-Sifrut ha-Hasidut veha-Kabalah*. Tel-Aviv: Sifriyati, 1968? 47p.
This is a dictionary of abbreviations found in Hasidic and Kabalistic texts.

CHAPTER 22

LANGUAGE AND LITERATURE (GENERAL MATERIALS)

See also entries 271-74 and 345-50.

HISTORY

734 Waxman, Meyer. *A History of Jewish Literature.* New York: Yoseloff, 1960. 5v. in 6.

This is a history of Jewish literature from about 200 B.C. to the present written for the "large lay intelligent public." It includes bibliographies and index.

735 Zinberg, Israel. *A History of Jewish Literature.* New York: Ktav, 1972-1978. 12 vols.

This edition is a translation of *Di Geshikhte fun der Literatur bay Yidn* (Vilna: Tamar, 1929-1937) and *Di Bliy Tekufe fun der Haskole* (Waltham, MA: Brandeis University; New York: CYCO, 1966). The history discusses a wide range of Jewish literary creativity written in Hebrew, Yiddish, Arabic and European languages. It covers the period beginning with the tenth century in Spain to the end of the Haskalah (Enlightenement) movement in Russia in the second half of the nineteenth century. Zinberg allows the authors being discussed to speak for themselves through extensive quotations from their works. The English edition supplements Zinberg's notes to many chapters with a section of bibliographical notes listing a selection of significant books and articles useful to the reader desiring to pursue a special topic further.

BIBLIOGRAPHY

736 *Plays of Jewish Interest.* Edward M. Cohen, Editor. New York: Jewish Theater Association (Distributed by the National Foundation for Jewish Culture, 330 Seventh Ave., New York, NY 10001), 1982. 126p.

This is an annotated listing of plays of Jewish interest, including translations of works originally published in Hebrew and Yiddish. Sources, staging requirements, and synopses are given. The work is indexed.

A. HEBREW LANGUAGE
BIBLIOGRAPHY

737 Hospers, J. H. and C. H. J. de Geus. "Hebrew." In *Basic Bibliography for the Study of Semitic Languages.* Edited by J. H. Hospers, v.l, 176-283. Leiden: Brill, 1974.

This comprehensive bibliography intended for students of Semitic languages lists bibliographical, historical, philological and literary materials pertaining to the Hebrew language. This chapter is divided into the following sections: A. Biblical and Epigraphical Hebrew B. Samaritan Hebrew C. Qumran, Murabba'at, Masada, etc. D. Mishnaic and Talmudical Hebrew E. Hebrew of the Middle Ages F. New and Modern Hebrew.

DICTIONARIES

738 Alcalay, Reuben. *Milon Angli-'Ivri Shalem: Milon 'Ivri-Angli Shalem.* Ramat-Gan, Israel: Masadah, 1975. 3v.

This is an authoritative, comprehensive English-Hebrew, Hebrew-English dictionary.

739 Baltsan, Hayim. *Webster's New World Hebrew Dictionary.* New York: Prentice Hall, 1992. 827p.

The dictionary is designed to make it possible for "beginners not acquainted with the Hebrew alphabet—to ascertain the meaning, pronunciation, spelling, or usage of any Hebrew word." The author achieves this goal by " presenting each Hebrew word first in a phonetic transliteration using the Latin alphabet, followed by its proper Hebrew spelling." He then " presents the Hebrew entry words of the Hebrew-English part of the dictionary in the Latin alphabetical order." Included are a "Guide" to the dictionary and an "Introduction to Hebrew."

740 Ben-Amotz, Dan and Netivah Ben-Yehudah. *Milon 'Olami le-'Ivrit Meduberet.* Tel-Aviv: Levin Epshtain, 1972-1982. 2v.

This work, and its supplement, *Milon Ahul-Manyuki le-'Ivrit Meduberet,* provide definitions for words used in colloquial Hebrew. Examples are given to illustrate the use of the word. The many illustrations which accompany the text graphically illustrate usage and enrich the text.

741 Ben Yehuda, Eliezer. *Milon ha-Lashon ha-'Ivrit.* New York: T. Yoseloff, 1959. 8v.

This reprint is a complete, scholarly, historical dictionary of ancient, medieval, and modern Hebrew. Equivalents are given in German, French, and English, but explanations are in Hebrew. The "Mavo" (introduction) volume, includes essays on the nature of the dictionary and the sources used in its composition, as well as discussions on Semitic languages in general and the Hebrew language in particular.

742 Comay, Aryeh. *Igron le-Milim Nirdafot u-Kerovot Mashma'ut.* Tel-Aviv: Ahiasaf, 1990. 287p.

Comay has prepared an alphabetically arranged thesaurus of the Hebrew language. The synonyms follow each entry.

743 Corbeil, Jean Claude. *Milon Hazuti 'Ivri-Angli.* Nusah 'Ivri: Barukh Sarel and Rimonah Gerson. Jerusalem: Carta, 1992. 723p.

This comprehensive thematically arranged illustrated dictionary is based on the author's *Dictionnaire Thématique Visuel.* (Montreal: Québec/ Amérique, 1986. It enables the user to access more than 3,000 objects from words or find a term from a picture. It includes a detailed table of contents and index of terms in both Hebrew and English.

744 Even-Shoshan, Avraham. *ha-Milon he-Hadash.* Jerusalem: Kiryat Sefer, 1966-1970. 7v.
This is the standard Hebrew-Hebrew dictionary of modern Hebrew.

745 —. *Milon Bet-ha-Sefer: Menukad u-Metsuyar.* Jerusalem: Kiryat Sefer, 1982. 712p.
This is an illustrated Hebrew-Hebrew dictionary for the beginning elementary school student. The compiler includes those words that would be most familiar to the student.

746 Inbal, Shimshon. *Milon /'Ivri / Amerikani/ Angli /'Ivri li-Shenot ha-Alpayim=Hebrew English Dictionary.* Jerusalem: S. Zack, 1992. 513, 806p.
This English-Hebrew; Hebrew English dictionary is based on American usage.

747 Klein, Ernest. *A Comprehensive Etymological Dictionary of the Hebrew Language for Readers of English.* New York: Macmillan, 1987. 721p.
This dictionary includes detailed etymologies of some 30,000 words and word forms. Each term is identified by the part of speech or linguistic stratum from which it comes, and is defined in a concise and clear manner. The various meanings of the entry term are listed and numbered consecutively. The etymological information for each entry is set off in brackets for easy identification. The derivatives, most of which appear as separate entries in the book, then follow. The author includes transliteration charts for Hebrew, Arabic, and Greek, as well as a bibliography of references.

748 Kna'ani, Ya'akov. *Milon Hidushe Shlonski.* Tel-Aviv: Sifriat Poalim, 1989. 248p.
Kna'ani lists in this dictionary close to 6,000 words coined by the noted Hebrew author Abraham Shlonsky (1900-1973).

749 —. *Otsar ha-Lashon ha-'Ivrit.* Jerusalem: Massada, 1960-1989. 18v.
This multi-volume historical dictionary lists Hebrew, as well as Aramaic and other foreign words that are used in spoken and scientific Hebrew. Kna'ani brings short quotations from all branches of literature to illustrate the usage of words.

750 Lazar, Yisrael. *ha-Milon he-Hadash: 'Ivri-Angli Angli-'Ivri.* Jerusalem: Kiryat Sefer, 1991. 343, 419p.
This bilingual dictionary contains words and concepts which are most commonly used in Hebrew and English in daily life, in the press and media, in education, and in the realm of science and technology. The compiler uses ketiv male, the full spelling of the Hebrew words, as established by the Academy of the Hebrew Language.

751 *Leksikon Lo'azi-'Ivri Shimushi.* Ramat Gan: Prolog, 1992. 352p.
This dictionary provides a Hebrew definition for foreign words and concepts which have been incorporated into spoken Hebrew.

752 *ha-Milon ha-Histori la-Lashon ha-'Ivrit. Homarim la-Milon.* Jerusalem: Academy of the Hebrew Language, 1988. 105 microfiches.

In this compilation of sources for the *Historical Dictionary*, all semantically related items are assembled around a common root. The sources that have been made available to-date are derived from works written in Hebrew from the close of the Biblical Canon to the end of the Tannaitic era (200 B. C. E.-300 C. E.). Some of these materials will be used to illustrate the meanings and usages of words that will be included in the *Historical Dictionary* that will be published by the Academy. A guide to the microfiche is included.

753 Sivan, Reuben and Edward A. Levenston. *The New Bantam-Megiddo Hebrew and English Dictionary.* New York: Schocken Books, 1977. 294p.
This Hebrew-English and English-Hebrew dictionary is based on *The Megiddo Modern Dictionary* (Tel-Aviv: Megiddo, 1965-1966. 2v.).

ABBREVIATIONS / ACRONYMS

754 Ashkenazi, Shmuel and Dov Jarden. *Otsar Rashe Tevot.* Jerusalem: R. Mass, 1965. 600 columns.
This is a comprehensive thesaurus of abbreviations used in all branches of Hebrew literature. A supplemental listing of 4,000 abbreviations was published under the title *Mefa'neah Ne'lamim.* Jerusalem: Shiloh, 1968/69. 92 columns.

755 Chajes, Saul. *Otsar Beduye ha-Shem=Pseudonymen-Lexicon der Hebräischen und Jiddischen Literatur.* Hildesheim: G. Olms, 1967. 535, 66p.
This dictionary, first published in 1933, covers the period from the Geonim to the beginning of the twentieth century. It lists 5,145 pseudonyms used by authors of Hebrew and Yiddish literature. The dictionary is arranged alphabetically by pseudonym. The following information is provided for each entry: a notation of one or two books or articles in which the author used this pseudonym, identification of the author, the source for the pseudonym and comments. The second part of the dictionary contains an index of authors' names (in Latin characters) and an index of sources. Corrections and additions may be found in *'Alim le-Bibliyografyah* 1 (1934):1-2; *Kiryat Sefer* 11 (1934/35):297-300; *Yivo Bleter* 13 (1938):585-618.

756 Halpern, Meir. *ha-Notrikon, ha-Simanim, veha-Kinuyim.* Vilna: B. A. Kletskin, 1912. 265p.

757 Marwick, Lawrence. *Biblical and Judaic Acronyms.* New York: Ktav, 1979. 225p.
This dictionary includes acronyms, abbreviations and initialisms used in the field of Biblical and Judaic studies.

GRAMMARS

758 Barkali, Saul. *Luah ha-Pe'alim ha-Shalem.* Jerusalem: R.Mass, 1972. 92p.
This work contains charts for the declention of Hebrew verbs in all tenses and moods.

759 —. *Luah ha-Shemot ha-Shalem.* Jerusalem: R. Mass, 1969. 164p.
This work contains charts for the declention of Hebrew nouns.

760 Glinert, Lewis. *The Grammar of Modern Hebrew.* Cambridge: Cambridge University Press, 1989. 765p.
This reference grammar was written for "the advanced student of Modern (and, specifically, Israeli) Hebrew who knows next to no linguistics, and the general linguist who knows no Hebrew."

761 Goshen-Gottstein, Moshe Henry. *ha-Dikduk ha-'Ivri ha-Shimushi.* 5th ed. Jerusalem: Schocken, 1975. 246p.
This useful grammar was written for use in high schools and in teacher training seminars.

B. HEBREW LITERATURE

BIBLIOGRAPHY
See also entries 89 and 95.

762 Band, Arnold. "Literary Criticism in Israel." *Modern Judaism* 11 (1991): 1-15.
Band reviews the trends in Israeli literary criticism in the decade of the 80's. The major publications of the decade are cited in the "Notes" at the end of the article.

763 *Bibliography of Modern Hebrew Literature in Translation.* Tel-Aviv: Institute for the Translation of Hebrew Literature, 1972- .
This publication lists current translations of modern Hebrew literature into foreign languages. It supplements the bibliographies by Yohai Goell (below). The bibliography is arranged by language group. The materials are listed by genre within each language group. Full citations are given for each item. The last issue covers the years 1985-1986 and includes Arabic for the years 1980-1986.

764 Goel, Yohai. *Bibliography of Modern Hebrew Literature in English Translation.* Jerusalem: Israel Universities Press, 1968. 110p.
Goell lists c.7,500 translations of Hebrew works, the originals of which were published from about 1880 to the end of 1965. The translations appeared in book form or in periodicals. The materials are arranged alphabetically by author within each genre of literature, e.g. general anthologies, prose, poetry drama, etc. The bibliography includes an index of authors, an index of translators, a list of periodicals and an author / title index in Hebrew.

765 —. *Bibliography of Modern Hebrew Literature in Translation.* Tel-Aviv: Institute for the Translation of Hebrew Literature, 1975. 117p.
This bibliography lists translations of Hebrew works into various foreign languages other than English. Only monographic translations of Hebrew works that were published after 1917 are included. The bibliography is arranged by language and further subdivided within each language by

genre. A list of monographs on modern Hebrew literature is included in an appendix. The bibliography includes an index of Hebrew authors and an index of translators, editors, and authors of monographs.

766 Goldberg, Isaac. *Selected Hebrew Literature in Translation.* New York: JWB Jewish Book Council, 1984. 16p.
This is a selected, annotated listing of the best in modern Hebrew literature available in English. The bibliography is divided into the following categories: anthologies (general, poetry, prose), poetry, fiction, drama, literature for children and young adults, humor, history and criticism, and periodicals. Each entry has full bibliographical information. Availability in paperback is indicated.

767 *Heker ha-Shirah veha-Piyut [1948-1978]: Bibliografyah.* Compiled and edited by E. Adler, et al. Beer-Sheva: Ben-Gurion University of the Negev Press, 1990. 451, 30p.
This is a cumulative edition of the comprehensive bibliography of books and articles on Hebrew medieval poetry compiled by Prof. Jefim Schirmann. The bibliographies were published in *Kiryat Sefer*, 26-54 (1948/9-1979). This edition is arranged alphabetically and allows the researcher to retrieve data by author, title, and incipit.

768 Lahad, Ezra. *ha-Mahazeh ha-'Ivri be-Makor uve-Tirgum.* Jerusalem: Merkaz Hadrakhah le-Sifriyot, 1970-1989. 2v.
This bibliography supplements and brings up to date Abraham Yaari's *ha-Mahazeh ha-'Ivri ha-Mekori veha-Meturgam me-Reshito ve-'ad ha-Yom: Bibliyografyah* (Jerusalem, 1957). Lahad lists dramatic works written originally in Hebrew or translated into Hebrew. The work includes the following indices: A. Titles of plays B. Names of translators and adapters C. Languages from which the plays were translated D. Plays pertaining to the History of Palestine (Israel) E. Plays pertaining to life in Palestine (Israel) F. Plays for special holidays G. Persons who were the subject of a play. Volume one of the bibliography includes in an appendix a list of original plays in Israel from 1948-1970. The appendix includes an index of plays by title and an index of plays arranged by theater.

769 Yaari, Abraham. *ha-Mahazeh ha-'Ivri ha-Mekori veha-Meturgam me-Reshito ve-'ad ha-Yom: Bibliyografyah.* Jerusalem, 1957. 187p.
Yaari lists and describes 1,400 Hebrew plays written originally in Hebrew or translated into Hebrew. The bibliography covers the period beginning with the publication of the first Hebrew play in 1673 to the present. It includes the following indices: A. Title. B. Translators / Adapters C. Jewish history subdivided by topic D. Personalities about whom the plays were written E. Holidays F. Palestine and Israel G. Languages from which the plays were translated.

INDEXES

770 Davidson, Israel. *Otsar ha-Shirah veha-Piyut.* New York: Jewish Theological Seminary of America, 1924-1933. New York: Ktav, 1969. 4v.
"A bibliographical repository of all religious poetry composed from the time of the closing of the Biblical canon to our day, and secular poetry until

the time of Moses Hayyim Luzzatto (1707-1747)." The work is alphabetically arranged by the incipit of each poem and includes a list of sources and an index of poets. The reprint includes an introduction by H.J. Schirmann and a reprint of the author's supplement published in the Hebrew Union College annual (1938).

BIOGRAPHICAL DICTIONARIES

771 Kressel, Getzel. *Leksikon ha-Sifrut ha-'Ivrit.* Merhavyah: Sifriyat Po'alim, 1965-1967. 2v.
This authoritative bio-bibliographic lexicon lists about 3,000 authors of Hebrew literature who flourished from the beginning of the 18th century to the present. Entries are followed by extensive bibliographies.

772 Sokolow, Nahum. *Leksikon Shel Sofre Yisrael ba-Meah ha-Kodemet.* Tel-Aviv: Makhon Mazkeret, 1980. 208p.
This reprint edition of Sokolow's *Sepher Zykaron* (Warsaw, 1888) includes an introduction and supplementary material by Getzel Kressel. It is divided into three sections: I. Helek ha-'arakhim consists of a bio-bibliographical dictionary of "contemporary" authors who wrote in Hebrew, Yiddish and other languages. About 270 authors are listed. II. Helek hamikhtavim contains autobiographical sketches. The following are among the authors who are included in this section: Mendele Mokher Seforim, Shimon Berenfeld; Abraham Epstein. III. Hakhme Yerushalayim contains biographical sketches of noted personalities who resided in Jerusalem, e. g., Israel Frumkin, Eliezer Ben Yehudah, Eleazar Rokach. In view of the fact that the authors in the lexicon died in the intervening years, Kressel provides a list of the place and date of death for the authors.

773 Zeitlin, William. *Bibliographisches Handbuch der Neuhebräischen Literatur. (Kiryat Sefer).* 2. neu bearb. und erweiterte Aufl. Leipzig, K.F. Koehler's Antiquarium, 1891-1895. 2v. (548 p.)
This bibliographic lexicon in German provides biographical sketches of Hebrew authors who flourished in the period beginning with the Enlightenment until 1890. Each biographical sketch includes a listing of the author's publications. The lexicon includes an index of Hebrew titles.

C. ARAMAIC

BIBLIOGRAPHY

774 Drijvers, H. J. W. "Syriac and Aramaic," In *Basic Bibliography for the Study of Semitic Languages.* Edited by J.H. Hospers, v.1, 283-335. Leiden: Brill, 1974.
This comprehensive bibliography, intended for students of Semitic languages, lists bibliographical, historical, philological and literary materials pertaining to Syriac and Aramaic. This chapter is divided into the following sections: A. Syriac B. Aramaic: Old Aramaic, Official Aramaic, Palmyrene, Nabataean Aramaic of Hatra, Jewish Aramaic, Samaritan Aramaic, Syro-Palestinian Christian Aramaic, Babylonian Talmudic Aramaic, Mandaic.

775 Fitzmyer, Joseph A. and Stephen A. Kaufman. *An Aramaic Bibliography.* Baltimore: Johns Hopkins University, 1992- .
This volume, *Old, Official, and Biblical Aramaic,* is the first of a two volume bibliography of Aramaic texts that will be used as the basis for the projected *Comprehensive Aramaic Lexicon.* It consists of three sections: A. An introductory bibliography which cites materials pertaining to Aramaic studies, e.g. printed collections of texts and translations, bibliographies and surveys, Aramaic language, grammars, lexicography, onomastica, law literature, religion. B. Texts of Old and Official / Standard Aramaic (from Syria/Palestine, Mesopotamia, Egypt, Arabia, Asia Minor, Iran and the East), and Biblical Aramaic (general studies, Ezra and Daniel). Each document is briefly described and labelled with a siglum. The document's *editio princeps* is cited and a place where it may be found is noted. Authors who have discussed the text are listed C. References to books and articles on the Aramaic texts. The materials in this section are listed according to authors (cited in the second section) and arranged alphabetically and chronologically. The bibliography includes two appendices: A. A list of Aramaic *dubiousa* B. A list of texts by sigla (in alphabetical order) including references to other collections.

D. Sephardic Languages and Literature

Bibliography

776 Besso, Harry V. *Ladino Books in the Library of Congress: A Bibliography.* Washington, D.C.: Library of Congress, 1964. 44p.
Besso lists 289 titles, mostly books, held by the Library of Congress. A select list of works cited in the bibliography and a list of publications arranged by place of publication can be found in appendixes. Ladino titles held by such institutions as the New York Public Library's Jewish Division can be found in their published catalogs (listed above). Also see Abraham Yaari's bibliography below.

777 Bunis, David M. *Sephardic Studies: A Research Bibliography Incorporating Judezmo Language, Literature and Folklore, and Historical Background.* New York: Garland Publishing, 1981. 243p.
This classified bibliography lists 1,891 books, articles, and recorded materials. The author has appended a list of institutions and organizations concerned with Sephardic studies and has included author and subject indexes.

778 Gaon, Moshe David. *ha-Itonut be-Ladino.* Jerusalem: Ben-Zevi Institute, 1965. 143p.
This is a definitive bibliography of the Judeo-Spanish (Ladino) press.

779 Bet ha-Sefarim ha-Leumi veha-Universitai. *Reshimat Sifre Ladino.* Compiled by Abraham Yaari. Jerusalem: University Press, 1934. 125p.
This work is a "catalogue of Judeo-Spanish books in the Jewish National and University Library." (See Harry V. Besso above)

780 Kayserling, Meyer. *Biblioteca Española-Portugeza-Judaica.* Augmented ed. New York: Ktav, 1971. 272p.
This is a bibliography of vernacular Ibero-Jewish literature arranged alphabetically by author. The present edition includes related studies by the author, a bibliography of his publications by M. Weiz, and a prolegomenon by Y. H. Yerushalmi, which includes an up-to-date "annotated list of Ibero-Jewish bibliographies."

781 *Kitve Sofrim Yehudim Sefaradiyim u-Mizrahiyim bi-Leshonot Yehudiyot ve-Zarot.* Edited and with an introduction by Itzhak Bezalel. Tel-Aviv: Tel-Aviv University, 1982- .
This volume is the first in a series, whose purpose it is to study and document the literary creativity of Sephardi and Oriental Jewish authors who write in languages other than Hebrew. It contains an introductory essay by Itzhak Bezalel and a bibliographic survey of belles lettres in the twentieth century written by Sephardi and Oriental Jewish authors. The bibliography is divided into the following language groups: Italian and Judeo-Italian, English, Bulgarian, Georgian, Macedonian, Judeo-Spanish (Ladino), Arabic, French, Russian (by Georgian Jews). Each section is arranged alphabetically by author's name. Each entry contains a brief biographical sketch and a list of the author's works. The entries are written in Hebrew and in Latin characters in parallel columns.

782 Sala, Marius. *Le-Judeo-Espagñol.* The Hague: Mouton, 1976. 117p.
This is a bibliographic survey of studies pertaining to the history of Sephardic communities and Sephardic culture, with special emphasis on Judeo-Spanish language and literature.

783 Studemund, Michael. *Bibliographie zum Judenspanischen.* Hamburg: Helmut Buske Verlag, 1975. 148p.
This bibliography, arranged alphabetically by author, lists 1,368 items. It is not annotated and not indexed.

784 Wexler, Paul. *Judeo-Romance Linguistics: A Bibliography.* New York: Garland Publishing, 1989. 174p.
This topically arranged, comprehensive bibliography lists 1,638 books and articles published through 1987. The work cites materials pertaining to comparative Judeo-Romance linguistics, as well as publications relating to the following languages: A. Judeo-Latin B. Judeo-Italo-Romance C. Judeo-Gallo-Romance D. Judeo-Ibero-Romance E. Judeo-Rhaeto-Romance. The bibliography includes an Index of Authors and Anonymous Articles.

E. YIDDISH LANGUAGE

See also entries 829 and 881-88.

HISTORY

785 Weinreich, Max. *Geshikhte fun der Yidisher Shprakh.* New York: YIVO Institute for Jewish Research, 1973. 4v.
This comprehensive history of the Yiddish language includes extensive notes and a bibliography. The text was translated by Shlomo Noble with

the assistance of Joshua A. Fishman and published under the title *History of the Yiddish Language: Concepts, Facts, Methods*. (Chicago: University of Chicago Press, 1980. 833p.) This edition does not include the footnotes and bibliography. The index to the English edition includes the Yiddish words (in romanization) mentioned in the text. It thus can serve as a guide to romanized Yiddish.

DIALECTOLOGIES

786 *The Language and Culture Atlas of Ashkenaz Jewry*. Prepared and published under the aegis of an Editorial Collegium Vera Baviskar, Marvin Herzog, Uriel Weinreich. Tübingen: Max Niemeyer Verlag; New York: Yivo, 1992- .
This atlas will, upon completion, comprise a sophisticated Yiddish dialectology. To-date volume one, *Historical and Theoretical Foundations*, has been published. It is divided into four parts: I. Introduction to the Language and Culture of Ashkenaz Jewry II. Assembly of the Data III. The Status and Study of Yiddish Dialects IV. The Systematic Dialectology of Yiddish. The volume includes maps, an index to maps and a bibliography.

BIBLIOGRAPHY

787 Baker, Zachary M. "Yiddish Studies Pathfinder." *Judaica Librarianship* 3 (1986-1987): 125-128.
This pathfinder provides a guide to "essential resources in both Yiddish and English pertaining to all aspects of Yiddish studies."

788 Bratkowsky, Joan G. *Yiddish Linguistics: A Multilingual Bibliography*. New York: Garland, 1988. 407p.
This work is a classified bibliography of books and articles in English, Yiddish, and other languages published since 1959 pertaining to Yiddish linguistics. It is intended for scholarly use. The bibliography supplements Uriel and Beatrice Weinreich's *Yiddish Language and Folklore* (The Hague: Mouton, 1959). The author includes, in addition to general works, materials on the following topics: A. Structure of Yiddish B. History of Yiddish C. Dialectology D. Interaction of Yiddish with other languages E. Onomastics F. Stylistics G. Semiotics H. History of linguistics and biography of linguistics I. Sociolinguistics J. Psycholinguistics K. Applied linguistics. It includes a name index.

DICTIONARIES

789 Galvin, Herman and Stan Tamarkin. *The Yiddish Dictionary Source-Book: A Transliterated Guide to the Yiddish Language*. Hoboken, NJ: Ktav, 1986, 317p.
This dictionary contains over 8,500 words and proverbs in transliteration and English translation. The editors have included those words most useful for everyday conversation. In addition, the *Dictionary* contains a guide to Yiddish pronunciation and grammar and a series of topically arranged appendices containing Yiddish proverbs and popular expres-

sions. The editors in the introduction provide a brief history of the Yiddish language and Yiddish culture in the United States.

790 *Groyser Verterbukh der Yidisher Shprakh.* Judah A. Joffe and Yudel Mark, Editors in Chief. New York: Yiddish Dictionary Committee, 1961-.
This is an all inclusive, scholarly, historical Yiddish-Yiddish dictionary. To date four volumes have been published covering the letter Aleph.

791 Harkavy, Alexander. *Yidish-English-Hebreisher Verterbukh.* New York: Schocken, 1986. 583p.
This trilingual dictionary is a reprint of the 2nd exp. ed. (New York: Hebrew Publishing Co., 1928). It includes an introduction by Dovid Katz. "Harkavy provides the vocabulary (together with Hebrew equivalents) of nineteenth and early twentieth century works that reflect the real language of immigrant generations in America at the turn of the century."

792 Stutchkoff, Nahum. *Der Oytser fun der Yidisher Shprakh.* Edited by Max Weinreich. New York: Yivo, 1950. 933p.
This thesaurus of the Yiddish language contains over 150,000 synonyms, idioms, and proverbs. The words are arranged by concept. An alphabetical index is included.

793 Tsanin, Mordekhai. *Milon Yidish-'Ivri Shalem.* Tel-Aviv?: Hotsa'ah le-or a. sh. H. Leyvik, 1982. 472p.
"A complete Yiddish-Hebrew dictionary."

794 —. *Milon 'Ivri-Yidi Shalem.* Tel-Aviv?: Hotsa'ah le-or a. sh. H. Leyvik, 1983. 888p.
"A complete Hebrew-Yiddish dictionary."

795 Weinreich, Uriel. *Modern English-Yiddish, Yiddish-English Dictionary.* New York: YIVO, 1968. 789p.
This is an up-to-date English-Yiddish, Yiddish-English scholarly dictionary.

GRAMMARS (TEXT BOOKS)

796 Katz, Dovid. *Grammar of the Yiddish Language.* London: Duckworth, 1987. 290p.
This grammar is intended for students enrolled in Yiddish language courses, general readers or advanced students who require a reference grammar.

797 Rockowitz, Anna C. *201 Yiddish Verbs Fully Conjugated In All Tenses.* Woodbury, NY: Barron's Educational Series, 1979. 219p.
"This book contains complete conjugations of 201 frequently used verbs in all tenses and moods in current usage. The 201 verbs were systematically selected to present samples of every type and participle form." The text includes a "Yiddish-English Verb Index."

798 Schaechter, Mordkhe. *Yidish Tsvey.* Philadelphia: Institute for the Study of Human Issues, 1986. 497p.
This work teaches rules of standard Yiddish and is intended for intermediate courses.

799 Weinreich, Uriel. *College Yiddish: An Introduction to the Yiddish Language and to Jewish Life and Culture.* 5th rev. ed. New York: Yivo, 1971. 399p.
This basic introductory grammar is intended for introductory courses or for self-study.

F. Yiddish Literature

History

800 Liptzin, Sol. *A History of Yiddish Literature.* New York: Jonathan David, 1985. 521p.
This one volume historical survey of Yiddish literature from the 16th century to the present, includes a discussion about Yiddish literary creativity in both Israel and Latin America. The bibliography "serves primarily as a guide to further reading in English on Yiddish literary movements and Yiddish writers. Indexed.

801 Madison, Charles A. *Yiddish Literature: Its Scope and Major Writers.* New York: Schocken, 1971. 540p.
This survey includes an introductory essay entitled "Judeo-German to Modern Yiddish" and essays on fourteen noted Yiddish writers from Mendele to the Singer brothers. In each of these essays Madison presents a compact biography of the author, an extensive summary of his literary creativity, and a brief personal evaluation. The survey also includes "Yiddish Writings in English Translation" and "A Bibliography of Source Materials." Indexed.

802 Shmeruk, Chone. *Sifrut Yiddish: Perakim le-Toldoteha.* Tel-Aviv: Mifalim Universitaiyim, 1978. 339p.
Shmeruk discusses all forms of Yiddish literary creativity from the earliest times to the flowering of modern Yiddish literature in the nineteenth century. He notes the sources from which Yiddish literature drew its inspiration and shows the relationship to other literatures. The work includes bibliographic notes and a bibliography.

Bibliography

803 Abramowicz, Dina. *Yiddish Literature in English Translation: Books Published 1945-1967.* 2nd ed. New York: YIVO, 1968. 39p.
This comprehensive bibliography lists translations that were published between 1945-1967. The bibliography includes a supplementary list of translations that were published to the end of April 1968. It is arranged alphabetically by author and is not annotated. An index by literary category is included.

Section Two: Subject Reference | 189

804 *Yiddish Literature in English Translation: List of Books in Print.* New York: YIVO, 1976. 22p.

This annotated bibliography lists 126 in-print items arranged by literary categories. It is "intended as a practical aid for teachers and students of Yiddish literature who wish to base their courses on books currently available."

805 Norich, Anita. "Yiddish Literary Studies." *Modern Judaism* 10 (1990): 297-309.

Norich discusses the status of Yiddish studies, Yiddish publications and areas of research in the 1980's. She notes future needs. The essay includes bibliographic notes.

806 Zfatman, Sarah. *ha-Siporet be-Yidish me-Reshitah 'ad Shivhe ha-Besht (1504-1814).* Jerusalem: Hebrew University, 1985. 201p.

This is a chronologically arranged bibliography of manuscripts and printed works of Yiddish narrative prose from its beginnings in 1504 to 1814. The bibliography includes works written in both Yiddish and German in Hebrew characters. Annotations include some or all of the following information: a full transcription of the title page and colophon; a brief citation from the beginning or end of the story; a detailed bibliographic description of the work, with place and date of publication, size and pagination, the source from which it was translated, and/or a summary of its contents; a listing of the libraries known to have holdings; and a bibliography of secondary sources. The bibliography is accompanied by indexes of title, name and character, and place and holding library.

BIO-BIBLIOGRAPHY

807 Kagan, Berl. *Leksikon fun Yidish Shraybers.* New York: Rayah-Ilman Kagan, 1986. 812 columns.

A bio-bibliographical lexicon of modern Yiddish authors. This work supplements, corrects, and updates the *Leksikon fun der Nayer Yidisher Literatur* (New York: CYCO, 1956-1981). Close to 700 entries are new or have been fully revised. In addition, the author includes in a separate section a list of 5,800 pseudonyms which appear in Yiddish literature and press.

808 *Leksikon fun der Nayer Yidisher Literatur.* New York: World Congress for Jewish Culture, 1956-1980. 8v.

This bio-bibliographical dictionary of modern Yiddish literature covers Yiddish writers and Yiddish writing since the beginning of the 18th century.

809 Reisen, Zalman. *Leksikon fun der Yidisher Literatur, Prese un Filologie.* 2nd rev. ed. Vilno: Kletskin Verlag, 1929. 4v.

Although dated, this authoritative lexicon remains useful.

810 *Leksikon fun der Yudisher Literatur un Prese.* Warsaw: Tsentral, 1914. 768 col.

This lexicon includes pre-modern Yiddish writers and a list of contemporaneous Yiddish periodicals. This material was not incorporated in Reisen's later work.

G. YIDDISH THEATRE

BIOGRAPHICAL DICTIONARIES

811 Zylbercwaig, Zalmen. *Leksikon fun Yidishn Teater.* New York: Verlag Elisheva, 1931-1969. 6v.

This is an authoritative biographical dictionary of individuals who played a role in the Yiddish theater during the past 150 years. Vol. 5, "Kdoyshim Band," contains biographies of 320 Jewish actors who perished during the Holocaust. Vol. 6 depicts the history of the Yiddish theater. The work includes bibliographical references.

CHAPTER 23

MISCELLANEOUS SUBJECTS

A. AGING

812 Guttman, David. *Jewish Elderly in the English-Speaking Countries.* New York: Greenwood Press, 1989. 140p.
This partially annotated bibliography lists journal articles published during the last 15 years in the United States, Great Britain, and Israel. All the items cited are in the English language. The material is organized into six chapters followed by a list of additional resources on Jewish aging and aged, a bibliography on aging in the Jewish world, a list of related journals, an author index, and a comprehensive subject index.

B. ANTI-SEMITISM
See also entries 321, 377, 419 and 420.

BIBLIOGRAPHY

813 *Antisemitism: An Annotated Bibliography.* Edited by Susan Sarah Cohen. New York: Garland, 1987- .
This is a multi-lingual annotated bibliography of books, articles, doctoral dissertations and master's theses about anti-Semitism. The bibliography is divided into three sections: A. Bibliographies and reference works B. Anti-Semitism throughout the ages C. Anti-Semitism in literature and the arts. It includes author and subject indexes. To-date two volumes have been published: Volume 1. 1984-1985 Volume 2. 1986-1987.

Note: The Felix Posen Bibliographic Project of the Vidal Sassoon International Center For the Study of Antisemitism of the Hebrew University on-line database is accessible through the Israeli University Libraries Network (Aleph).

814 *Bibliographie zum Antisemitismus=A Bibliography on Antisemitism.* Edited by Herbert A. Strauss. Munich; New York: K. G. Saur, 1989-
This multi-volume work lists the holdings of the special collection housed at the Library of the Zentrum für Antisemitismusforschung, Technische Universität, Berlin. The Zentrum's library, which opened in 1983, "collects sources on and accounts of the conditions of origin, intellectual foundations, and historical manifestations of anti-Semitism throughout history, ranging from defamation to deprivation of rights, expulsion, and murder of the Jewish minority. To-date three volumes (A-Z) have been published. Volume four, the subject index has not yet been published.

815 Singerman, Robert. *Antisemitic Propaganda: An Annotated Bibliography and Research Guide.* New York: Garland Publishing, 1982. 448p.
The bibliography is divided into two parts: A. An annotated bibliography

of 1,437 anti-Semitic books, pamphlets and tracts in the English language published from 1871 to 1981. At least one holding institution is noted for each title cited. The listing is arranged chronologically by date of the original publication or date of the original work. This enables the researcher to trace the evolution of anti-Semitic thought. B. A *"Research Guide"* which lists 478 books and articles in English pertaining to the political and social aspects of organized anti-Semitism, anti-Semitism in individual countries, as well as, individual propagandists and movements. The work is indexed.

SURVEYS

816 *Antisemitism World Report 1992.* London: Institute of Jewish Affairs, 1992. 127p.
This report "is the first researched-based,investigative survey which provides a documented assessment of current levels of anti-Semitism country-by-country, throughout the world" in 1991. "Entries include the following sections: historical legacy; anti-Semitic parties, organizations and movements; manifestations of anti-Semitism; anti-Semitism in mainstream political, cultural and religious life; denial of the Holocaust; opinion polls; effects of anti-Zionism; anti-Semitic publications; legal matters; efforts to counter anti-Semitism."

C. ART AND CEREMONIAL OBJECTS

BIBLIOGRAPHY

817 Mayer, Leo A. *Bibliography of Jewish Art.* Jerusalem: Hebrew University, 1967. 374p.
This bibliography, arranged alphabetically by author, cites books and articles about works of Jewish art which were created in the period between the destruction of the Temple and the early 19th century.

818 Weinstein, Jay. *A Collector's Guide to Judaica.* London: Thames and Hudson, 1985. 240p.
This richly illustrated work is intended for buyers, sellers, institutions and dealers. It serves as a "useful guide to understanding Jewish ceremonial art in its broader art-historical context and to encourage a full enjoyment of the objects themselves by identifying some of the features" the collector should look for. The author describes a variety of Jewish ceremonial objects and discusses such topics as: styles in Judaica, textiles and rugs, paintings and prints, ceramics and glass, fakes and forgeries, and Bezalel and the modern arts. The work includes a price guide, a glossary, a list of museums with Judaica collections, a select bibliography, and an index.

D. COOKERY

BIBLIOGRAPHY

819 Kirshenblatt-Gimblett, Barbara. "Jewish Charity Cookbooks in the United States and Canada: A Bibliography of 201 Recent Publications." *Jewish Folklore and Ethnology Review*, 9, 1 (1987): 13-18.

820 Shosteck, Patti. "Bibliography." In *A Lexicon of Jewish Cooking: A Collection of Folklore, Foodlore, History, Customs and Recipes*, 221-232. Chicago IL: Contemporary Books, 1981. 240p,
This extensive bibliography lists cookbooks and books which deal with Jewish tradition and food.

E. ETHICS

BIBLIOGRAPHY

821 Breslauer, S. Daniel. *Contemporary Jewish Ethics: A Bibliographic Survey*. Westport, CT: Greenwood Press, 1985. 213p.
This is the first of a projected two-volume annotated bibliography designed to help scholars and students working in Judaic studies, religious studies, or ethics find articles and books that discuss "specific issues in Jewish moral decision making." The following are among the topics included in this volume: History of Jewish ethics; Issues in Jewish ethics; Themes in Jewish ethics; Jewish ethics and non-Jewish ethical theories. The work is prefaced by an introductory survey of contemporary Jewish ethics. Included in the bibliography are books and articles in Hebrew, English and other languages that were published, for the most part, between 1968 and 1983.

822 ——. *Modern Jewish Morality: A Bibliographical Survey*. Westport, CT: Greenwood Press, 1986. 239p.
This bibliographical survey is a companion volume to the author's *Contemporary Jewish Ethics* . The work is divided into two major sections: A. An introductory review of the major moral questions B. A bibliographical survey covering such topics as sexuality and the family, moral dilemmas associated with aging, death and mourning, aspects of political morality, etc. The critical annotations describe "both the contents of the entry and its relationship to modern Jewish moral reflection." The sources cited are generally from professional literature and theological sources, representing thinkers from differing Jewish traditions. The bibliography includes author, title, and subject indexes.

F. FAMILY

BIBLIOGRAPHY

823 Bubis, Gerald B. *Saving the Jewish Family*. Lanham: University Press of America, 1987. 216p.

In a lengthy essay, Bubis examines and evaluates the factors affecting the Jewish family in the post-emancipation period. The essay is accompanied by a selective bibliography of over 1,200 articles in English published between 1970 and 1982, intended to guide individuals "involved in developing strategies to work with Jewish families." The citations are confined primarily to social work and communal literature, and include materials on such topics as abortion, the aged and aging, conversion, divorce, Havurot, and women. Also included in the book are 13 demographic tables.

824 *Jewish Family Issues: A Resource Guide*. Edited by Benjamin Schlesinger. New York: Garland, 1987. 143p.

This guide contains essays about the "Jewish family of the past," Jewish one parent families, and the Jewish woman. It also contains a classified bibliography of English-language materials published between 1960 and September 1986, focusing primarily on Jewish family life in the United States, Canada and Israel. The 524 citations are arranged under 78 topical headings dealing with marriage, children, family and women. Some sections deal with the historical perspectives of Jewish family life throughout the ages. The bibliography includes demographic tables of Jewish populations in various parts of the world (reprinted from the *American Jewish Yearbook*, 1985) and an author index.

825 Schlesinger, Benjamin. *The Jewish Family: A Survey and Annotated Bibliography*. Toronto: University of Toronto, Press, 1971. 175p.

This work is divided into two parts. A. Survey B. Bibliography. The former section contains a retrospective study of Jewish family life from Biblical times to the Shtetl of Eastern Europe, by Benjamin Schlesinger; a study of the American Jewish family, by Jack Balswick; a review of existing studies of intermarriage among Jews, by Israel Ellman; a study of family life in Israeli Kibbutzim, by Benjamin Schlesinger. The latter section contains a bibliography of 429 items pertaining to such subjects as home, marriage, intermarriage, etc. A list of 172 fiction books which deal with Jewish family life and statistical tables which cover the world Jewish population of 1968 are included in appendices. The bibliography includes an author index.

826 Singer, David. *Focus on the American Jewish Family: A Selected Annotated Bibliography, 1970-1982*. New York: American Jewish Committee, William Petschek National Jewish Family Center, 1984. 22p.

An annotated bibliography of 1000 articles and books published during the period 1970-1982 pertaining to contemporary American Jewish family life. Topics such as intermarriage, divorce, single-parent families, and abortion are treated. The compiler has excluded works of fiction and historical studies.

G. Folklore And Legends

Bibliography

827 Ben-Amos, Dan. "Jewish Folklore Studies." *Modern Judaism* 11 (1991):17-66.
This essay describes "trends, themes, and problems that have dominated Jewish folklore studies during the eighties, particularly in Israel and the United States." It includes a list of cited references arranged by author.

828 Haboucha, Reginetta. *Types and Motifs of the Judeo-Spanish Folktales.* New York: Garland Publishing, 1992. 965p.
This work provides ready access to 619 Judeo-Spanish tales published in Latin characters. The author provides a plot summary of each tale, analyzes its thematic content, indicates type variants and motifs, characterizes distribution and identifies Jewish, as well as, international analogues. She summarizes each version separately so as to show its distinctive character. Abstracts of identical versions are also given. The tales have been grouped into the following categories: I. Animal Tales II. Tales of Magic III. Religious Tales IV. Romantic Tales V. Numskull Stories VI. Jokes and Anecdotes. The extensive bibliographic notes contain references to published Judeo-Spanish variants and other parallels, and identify Jewish, Hispanic, European, and Near Eastern analogues to facilitate comparative research. The bibliography of secondary literature includes a listing of collections not cited in the notes, and other works consulted. The following indexes provide easy access to the materials in the corpus: I. Index of Judeo-Spanish Tales by Compiler — a complete listing of the narratives studied II. Index by Type III. Index by Motif.

829 Weinreich, Uriel and Beatrice Weinreich. *Yiddish Language and Folklore: A Selective Bibliography for Research.* The Hague: Mouton, 1959. 66p.
This bibliography, consisting of 481 entries, is "intended primarily as an introduction to the study of language and folklore of Ashkenazic Jewry." Topics such as grammar of standard Yiddish, sound systems, spelling and transcription, folksongs and folk music, humor, and cookery are covered.

830 Yassif, Eli. *Jewish Folklore: An Annotated Bibliography.* New York: Garland Publishing, 1986. 341p.
This annotated bibliography lists 1,356 studies on Jewish folklore that have been published during the past one hundred years. Articles in Hebrew and Western languages are covered but Yiddish is excluded. Entries often include the compiler's evaluation of the work and details pertaining to the themes, motifs and subjects discussed in the cited work. In addition, the compiler summarizes the contents of each cited Hebrew publication. Included is an index of themes, motifs, names, etc.

Anthologies

831 Bialik, Hayyim Nahman and Joshua C. Ravnitzky. *Sefer ha-Agadah.* Tel-Aviv: Dvir, 1950. 678p.

This compendium of Rabbinic lore culled from primary sources was first published in Odessa, 1908-11. The compilers have reworked the form of the Aggadah to make the it more literary. They eliminate homiletical digressions and in some instances join and conflate separate aggadot into lengthy and more continuous narratives. The compilers, however, preserve the Rabbis' voice. The anthology is divided into six parts: A. Historical events covering the period from creation to the destruction of the Second Temple, Jerusalem and the land B. Deeds of the sages C. Israel and the nations of the world, covering such topics as the Land of Israel, exile, redemption, Torah, Sabbath D. Relations between human beings and God E. Between man and man F. The world and all that it holds. The bibliographic notes direct the reader to the original source, thus serving as an index to Aggadic literature. The anthology includes a glossary, an index of names and subjects, and an index of Biblical references. *The Book of Legends*, an English translation by William G. Braude, has recently been published (New York: Schocken Books, 1992. 895p.)

832 Bin Gorion, Micha Joseph. *Mimekor Yisrael: Classical Jewish Folktales.* Edited by Emanuel Bin-Gorion. Translated by I. M. Lask. Bloomington, IN.: Indiana University Press, 1976. 3v.

This anthology is a translation of *Mi-Mekor Yisrael* (Tel-Aviv: Dvir, 1965) and includes an introduction by Dan Ben-Amos. The materials are arranged in four books, each of which in turn has four sections. The four books are: A. National tales covering the period from Bible days to the period of the exile B. Religious tales including stories from the Talmud C. Folktales D. Oriental tales, i.e. "Jewish reworking of Indian, Persian and Arabic wisdom." The anthology includes Sources and References by Emanuel Bin Gorion and an index of persons and places.

833 Frankel, Ellen. *The Classic Tales: 4000 Years of Jewish Lore.* Northvale, NJ: J. Aronson, 1989. 659p.

This anthology contains a collection of 300 Jewish stories arranged chronologically from biblical to modern times. The tales are representative of the entire range of Jewish folk imagination. The work includes six indexes: A. Holidays B. Torah readings C. Character types D. Symbols E. Topics F. General Index of names and places. It also includes a list of sources and a glossary.

834 Ginzberg, Louis. *Legends of the Jews.* Philadelphia: Jewish Publication Society, 1961. 7v.

Ginzberg has gathered from Talmudic and Midrashic literature, the Apocryphal and Pseudepigraphic literature, Jewish Hellenistic literature, and the writings of the Church Fathers all Jewish legends in so far as they refer to Biblical personages and events. He often paraphrases and retells Rabbinic legends in his own voice. His extensive notes direct the user to the original source, thus serving as an index to Aggadic literature. The anthology includes a subject index by Boaz Cohen.

H. GENEALOGY AND ONOMASTICONS

MANUALS AND SOURCEBOOKS

835 *The Encyclopedia of Jewish Genealogy.* Edited by Arthur Kurzweil and Miriam Weiner. Northvale, NJ: J. Aronson, 1991- .

This is a projected multi-volume work that will contain in-depth articles by an international group of experts on all aspects of Jewish genealogical research. The first volume, "Sources in the United States and Canada" is organized into three sections: A. Immigration and Naturalization, which includes articles on naturalization records, federal court records, and passenger records as sources for genealogical research B. United States; Guide to Institutional Resources arranged by City C. Canada: Guide to Institutional Resources Arranged by City. Additional information is contained in the fourteen appendixes, including a list of Jewish genealogical societies throughout the world, a listing of town plans in the U. S. S. R. and Poland, genealogical resources in the New York City area, and records in the Mormon Archives in Salt Lake City, Utah. It is indexed.

836 *Genealogical Resources in the New York Metropolitan Area.* Edited by Estelle M. Guzik. New York: Jewish Genealogical Society, 1989. 404p.

This updated and expanded edition of the guide, which was first published in 1985, provides detailed information about the genealogical resources of 32 libraries, 20 archives, and 52 government agencies and courts in the metropolitan New York City area. Each entry includes the name of the institution's director, address, hours, resources, and available finding aids. The Appendixes include: A. A revised and expanded "Bibliography of Eastern European Memorial Books," compiled by Zachary M. Baker. The call number and location of each Yizkor book in the following five Judaica libraries in New York City is noted: Bund Archive of the Jewish Labor Movement, Jewish Theological Seminary Library, New York Public Library. Jewish Division, Yeshiva University Library, YIVO B. A list of the New York area Jewish cemeteries C. Soundex code systems for U. S. Archives and for Slavic names. The guide includes name, place, and subject indices.

837 *Jewish Genealogy: Beginner's Guide.* Edited: Irene Saunders Goldstein. Vienna, VA: Jewish Genealogy Society of Greater Washington, 1991. Various pagings.

This loose leaf manual serves as a guide for the beginner who is seeking to trace his / her ancestry. Information is provided about such topics as:" How to Begin; Vital Records; Jewish Names; and Shtetl Geography." In addition, the compiler describes the genealogical resources in the Washington, D. C. area in such institutions as the National Archives and Library of Congress, as well as Jewish records held by other institutions in other parts of the United States. The guide includes a bibliography.

838 Kranzler, David. *My Jewish Roots: A Practical Guide to Tracing and Recording Your Genealogy and Family History.* New York: Sepher-Hermon, 1979. 112p.

This step-by-step "how to" book with easy to follow instructions is designed to enable the novice to trace his / her ancestry. It includes historical background information, illustrations, maps, original charts and forms.

839 Kurzweil, Arthur. *From Generation to Generation: How to Trace Your Jewish Genealogy and Personal History.* New York: Schocken Book, 1982. 353p.
This detailed guide shows how to trace family history by telling the user where to find the documents and records that are needed for this purpose. It provides instructions for using these materials.

840 Rottenberg, Dan. *Finding Our Fathers: A Guidebook to Jewish Genealogy.* New York: Random House, 1977. 401p.
This comprehensive "how to" book includes a listing of 8,000 Jewish family names and their origins, and an extensive bibliography which lists works on individual family histories, Jewish names, etc.

841 Sack, Sallyann Amdur. *A Guide to Jewish Genealogical Research in Israel.* Baltimore, MD: Genealogical Publishing, 1987. 110p.
This guide provides detailed information about the genealogical resources in Israeli institutions and private collections, including: Yad Vashem; Central Archives of the Holocaust; Search Bureau for Missing Relatives; Central Archives for the History of the Jewish People. The appendices include a listing of yizkor books, landsmanschaften listed at the Yad Vashem Library, etc.

842 — and Suzan Fishl Wynne. *The Russian Records Index and Catalog.* New York: Garland Publishing, 1987. 897p.
This is an index to names in the case files from the former Czarist Consular offices in the United States and Canada. The files cover the period of 1860-1924. Much of the material pertains to Jews from Russia who emigrated to the United States and Canada during this period. The work is intended for genealogists, and is just about the only finding aid printed in English for those seeking family data on Russian ancestors. The consular materials are currently housed at the U. S. National Archives.

BIBLIOGRAPHY

843 Stern, Malcolm H. "Bibliography of Jewish Genealogy." *Avotaynu* 7:1 (1991): 22-23.
This brief annotated bibliography lists manuals and sourcebooks, periodicals, research archives and libraries, and collected genealogies.

844 Zubatsky, David A. and Irwin M. Berent. *Jewish Genealogy: A Source Book of Family Histories and Genealogies.* NY: Garland, 1984-1990. 2v.
This is a comprehensive bibliography of "published and unpublished Jewish genealogies, family histories and individual family names." Similar in format to Rottenberg's *Finding Our Fathers,*" this book has been re-searched more extensively, and refers to archives as well as articles and monographs. The body of the work is arranged alphabetically by family name. Annotations and / or biographical descriptions are provided to aid the user in identifying the cited family. Coverage is worldwide.

COMPILED GENEALOGIES

845 Rosenstein, Neil. *The Unbroken Chain: Biographical Sketches and Genealogy of Illustrious Jewish Families from the 15th-20th Century.* Rev. ed. New York: CIS Publishers, 1990. 2v.

This biographical dictionary, first published in 1976, traces the genealogy of the families which descended from R. Meir Katzenelnbogen (MaHaRaM of Padua), the noted 16th century Rabbi, to the present day. It contains genealogical charts and biographical sketches of the members of the families. An index by family name directs the user to the family that is sought.

846 Stern, Malcolm H. *First American Jewish Families: 600 Genealogies—1654-1988.* 3rd ed. updated and revised. Baltimore, MD: Ottenheimer Publishers, 1991. 442p.

The author has compiled the genealogies of Jewish families established in the United States and Canada prior to 1840 and has traced their descendants, wherever possible, to the present. It is divided into four parts: A. A Compendium of Genealogy B. Addenda et Corrigenda C. Bibliography and Sources (Manuscripts and documents, Periodicals, and Books) D. Update. An Index by family name subdivided by given name directs the user to the family chart that is sought. This edition supersedes earlier editions.

ONOMASTICONS

847 Beider, Alexander. *A Dictionary of Jewish Surnames from the Russian Empire.* Teaneck, NJ: Avoteynu, 1993. 784p.

This dictionary lists over 50,000 Jewish surnames from the Russian Pale of Settlement (excluding the Kingdom of Poland). The *Dictionary* is divided into three parts. In Part I, the author describes the origins, derivations and sources of Jewish surnames from eastern Europe. This part includes a bibliography and a glossary of technical terms. In Part II, the dictionary, Beider entered each name in accordance with his transcription of the Russian name found in voter lists. For each entry Beider notes where in Russia individuals bearing that name lived at the beginning of the 20th century. He also provides information about the type of the name, e.g. rabbinic, occupational, patronymic, geographical, etc. All known derivatives and variants of each surname are listed. In Part III the author lists the surnames according to the Daitch-Mokotoff soundex system.

848 Gorr, Shmuel. *Jewish Personal Names: Their Origin, Derivation, and Diminutive Form.* Teaneck, NJ: Avoteynu, 1992. 112p.

All names in this dictionary are arranged by root. Variants of each root are given. The author explains (in footnotes) how these variants were derived.

849 Guggenheimer, Heinrich W. and Eva H. Guggenheimer. *Jewish Family Names and Their Origins: An Etymological Dictionary.* Hoboken, NJ: Ktav, 1992. 882p.

In this dictionary, the authors provide an inventory of and etymological explanations for 65,000 names for nearly every Jewish group—Ashkenazic,

Sephardic, Oriental, and modern Israeli. The authors, in the introduction to the dictionary, discuss Jewish proper names, sobriquets, and modifications of names. The work includes a list of abbreviations and a brief bibliography.

850 Kaganoff, Benzion C. *A Dictionary of Jewish Names and Their History.* New York: Schocken, 1977. 250p.
Part 1: A history of Jewish names. Part 2: A dictionary of selected Jewish names (with an index of names mentioned in Parts 1 and 2). Personal and family names are discussed.

851 Kolatch, Alfred J. *The Complete Dictionary of English and Hebrew First Names.* Middle Village, NY: Jonathan David, 1984. 488p.
This is a thoroughly revamped and greatly enlarged version of *The Name Dictionary,* published in 1967. It contains more than four times as many names as the earlier edition. Included among the more than 11,000 entries in this dictionary are numerous Biblical names, plus practically every Hebrew first name currently in use in Israel. Talmudic and Yiddish names are also included. The correct spelling of Hebrew and Yiddish names is indicated in Hebrew script immediately following each main entry. An additional feature is a comprehensive name vocabulary of Hebrew and Yiddish names grouped according to meaning and matched to English names.

852 Laredo, Abraham Isaac. *Les Noms des Juifs du Maroc: Essai d'Onomastique Judeo-Marocaine.* Madrid: Consejo Superior de Investigaciones Cientificas, Instituto "B. Arias Montano," 1978. 1,161p.
This work is a comprehensive study of the formation of the family names of the Jews of Morocco. The study is divided into four parts. Part one provides a brief sketch of the history of the Jews of Morocco, the social structure of their community in ancient times, and of their tradition of giving names. Part two contains a historical discussion of the development of names among Moroccan Jews beginning with ancient times to the present. Part three contains a detailed classified listing of names according to characteristics, e. g., geographic origin, physical characteristics, occupations, precious metals, animals, etc. Part four consists of an alphabetic dictionary of approximately 1,500 names arranged by Hebrew spelling. Each entry consists of the name in both Hebrew and Latin characters, the meaning of the name, variant spellings, etymological, historical, geographical and folkloristic comments, as well as a chronological listing of noted individuals bearing that name accompanied by biographical and bibliographical notations. The dictionary includes a bibliography. This is an invaluable tool for the general study of Jewish names of Sephardic or Arabic origin.

853 Seror, Simon. *Les Noms des Juifs de France au Moyen Âge.* Paris: Éditions C. N. R. S., 1989. 333p.
This is an onomasticon of names used by the Jews of France during the Middle Ages. The work includes a bibliography, an index of names in Latin characters, and an index of names in Hebrew characters.

854 Singerman, Robert. *Jewish and Hebrew Onomastics: A Bibliography.* New York: Garland, 1977. 132p.

Section Two: Subject Reference | 201

This work is a classified comprehensive bibliography of scholarly and popular literature on the etymology, history and folklore of Hebrew and Jewish personal names. "Considerable attention is given to the compulsory adoption of names by Jews in France and Germany as part of the Jewish emancipation process in those countries." The bibliography is organized into twenty-two broad subject categories, e.g., reference and dictionaries, encyclopedias, periodicals; Biblical names; Rabbinical literature; names in Divorce; and names of women. Of particular importance are the sections devoted to Jewish names in Europe, North Africa, Asia, the United States and South America. To facilitate the study of Jewish names and their sources, the author has included in an appendix an "Index of Norbert Pearlroth's 'Your Name' column, *Jewish Post and Opinion*, Sept.7, 1945 to Sept. 24, 1976." The bibliography also includes an Index of Authors and Selected Subjects and an Index of Individual Names.

855 Toledano, Joseph. *La Saga des Familles: les Juifs du Maroc et Leurs Noms.* Tel-Aviv: Editions Stavit, 1983. 345p.

This onomasticon of Moroccan family names includes a brief essay on the origin of each family name. In addition, it includes short biographies of noted persons bearing the name. The onomasticon is illustrated.

I. JEWISH POLITICAL STUDIES
See also Chapter 15.

BIBLIOGRAPHY

856 Elazar, Daniel J. "Jewish Political Studies." *Modern Judaism* 11 (1991): 67-90.

This essay describes "trends, themes, and problems that have dominated Jewish political studies during the eighties, particularly in Israel and the United States. The author notes activities and projects that need to be undertaken. The essay includes bibliographic notes.

857 Tabory, Mala and Charles S. Liebman. *Jewish International Activity: An Annotated Bibliography.* Ramat Gan: Bar-Ilan University, Argov Center, 1985. 241p.

This is a selective, annotated bibliography of historical studies, published prior to 1974, pertaining to "Jewish political activity on the international arena during the 19th and early 20th centuries." It includes " studies of: a. Jewish organizations with multi-country membership or bases; b. Those activities of national Jewish organizations which extend beyond their own countries to assume an international character; and C. Inter-governmental activity (generally conferences) concerned with questions of Jewish interest." The study includes " The Nature of International Jewish Activity" by Charles S. Liebman, an essay in which the author "sets out the future direction in which the field could be expected to develop."

J. JEWISH WOMEN'S STUDIES

See also entries 93, 332 and 450.

BIBLIOGRAPHY

858 Brewer, Joan Scherer. *Sex and the Modern Jewish Woman: An Annotated Bibliography.* Essays by Lynn Davidman and Evelyn Avery. Fresh Meadows, NY: Biblio Press, 1986. 88p.
This work includes two introductory essays and a comprehensive annotated bibliography of works published between 1900 and 1985. Materials related to the topics of "Jewish women and sexuality, the sexual attitudes and behavior of American Jews, and attitudes and norms concerning sexuality within the Jewish tradition" are listed. The bibliography includes "sources of material, information and research data," a bibliography, and an index of authors cited in the bibliography.

859 Hamelsdorf, Ora and Sandra Adelsberg. *Jewish Women and Jewish Law: Bibliography.* Fresh Meadows, NY: Biblio Press, 1980. 57p.
This bibliography "is intended to introduce the user to the historical background and the ongoing discussion in recent years by Jewish women, rabbis, and Jewish communal institutions, as all consider the claims for change in Jewish practice toward women based on adherence to traditional Jewish law (Halacha)." The compilers list the literature of the four major branches of Judaism: Orthodox, Conservative, Reform, and Reconstructionist. Books, periodical articles, unpublished papers and dissetations pertaining to such subjects as the Jewish woman's role and status within the family, in Jewish courts, in the synagogue, etc. are listed. The bibliography includes a glossary, and a list of sources which appear in the citations.

860 Heschel, Susannah. "Women's Studies." *Modern Judaism* 10 (1990): 243-258.
This essay presents "some examples of the scholarship in the best-developed areas of Jewish women's studies, history (German and American) and literature (Anglo-Jewish and Israeli)." The essay includes bibliographic notes.

861 *The Jewish Woman 1900-1985: A Bibliography.* Partially annotated by Aviva Cantor with 1983-1986 citations compiled by Ora Hamelsdorf. 2nd ed. Fresh Meadows, NY: Biblio Press, 1987. 193p.
This work includes an introductory essay evaluating trends in writing about Jewish women and a bibliography. The bibliography is divided into two parts. Part I is a reprint of the first edition (1979) with supplements. Part II covers the years 1980-1986. More than 4,000 items pertaining to such subjects as Jewish women in history / herstory, Jewish women in religious life and law, Jewish women in the United States and Canada, Jewish women in Israel, Jewish women in other countries, Jewish women in the Holocaust and Resistance, and Jewish women in poetry are listed. The bibliography also lists unpublished papers, recent women's conferences, studies and surveys, and bibliographies. It includes references to part I and II and an index to authors.

862 Rudd, Inger Marie. *Women and Judaism: A Select, Annotated Bibliography*. New York: Garland, 1988. 232p.
This selective and annotated bibliography lists 842 items pertaining to "woman's life from ancient to modern times: women in religion, education and employment, marriage and family, politics and society." The majority of the material pertains to women in the United States and Israel. The bibliography is arranged by author. It includes monographs, journal articles, essays, and articles from collections largely published in this century.

DIRECTORIES

863 "Jewish Woman's Networking Directory." In *Jewish and Female: Choices and Changes in Our Lives Today*, by Susan Weidman Schneider, 515-594. New York: Simon and Schuster, 1984.
The "yellow pages" provides the name, address and telephone number of organizations that deal with issues of concern to Jewish women, e.g. affirmative action, battered women, child care, lesbian and gay, etc.

LIBRARIES

864 Posner, Marcia. *Organizing a Jewish Women's Library*. New York: Jewish Book Council, 1988. 25p.
This is a step-by-step guide to organizing a library of Jewish women's books and resource materials.

K. JEWISH-CHRISTIAN RELATIONS

BIBLIOGRAPHY

865 Fisher, Eugene J. "A New Maturity in Christian-Jewish Dialogue: An Annotated Bibliography, 1975-1989." In *Our Time: The Flowering of Jewish-Catholic Dialogue*, edited by Eugene J. Fisher and Leon Klenicki. 107-161. New York: Paulist Press, 1990.
This bibliographic essay, arranged topically, describes current books and articles in English on the Jewish-Christian dialogue. The following are some of the topics that are covered: A. The New Testament and Judaism B. The trial of Jesus C. The medieval period and the Reformation D. Jews and Christians in America E. The Holocaust and Christian Jewish relations F. Muslim-Jewish-Christian Relations.

866 Shermis, Michael. *Jewish-Christian Relations: An Annotated Bibliography and Resource Guide*. Bloomington: Indiana University Press, 1988. 291p.
This is the largest known published list of materials dealing with Christian-Jewish concerns, in many different formats, including: books, pamphlets, important articles, journals, congresses, media, and syllabi. The over 500 books cited are classified under eighteen subject categories. The guide contains a directory of organizations and speakers, as well as subject, name, title, and media indexes.

L. Music and Dance

Bibliography

867 Dion, L. "Klezmer Music in America: Revival and Beyond." *Jewish Folklore and Ethnology Newsletter*, 8, 1-2 (1986): 2-8.
This essay deals with the revival of Klezmer music in America. It is followed by a Directory (8-14).

868 Edelman, Marsha Bryan. *A Bibliography of Jewish Music: Resource Materials for Educators.* New York: Hebrew Arts School, 1986. 50p.
This is a bibliography of readily accessible teaching tools from beginning to advanced levels as well as a selected list of pieces "appropriate for a professional repertoire" and a limited discography. Liturgical and ethnic music —e. g., folk melodies —are included.

869 Goren, A. "The Ethnic Dance in Israel with Selected Filmography." *Jewish Folklore and Ethnology Newsletter*, 8, 3-4 (1986): 1-6.

870 Heskes, Irene. *The Resource Book of Jewish Music: A Bibliographical and Topical Guide to Book and Journal Literature and Program Material.* Westport, CT: Greenwood Press, 1985. 302p.
This is an annotated, classified bibliography of published English textual resources whose purpose is "to provide a bibliographical tool for the examination of Jewish music... intended to serve reference needs of musicians, scholars and the general public." The annotations include information regarding the subject covered by the cited source, the range of content, and manner of treatment. They are not critical, but rather are designed to aid the user to assess the source's value as a reference tool. Chapters are devoted to: Reference works; Books; Articles; Jewish music periodicals; Instruction and performance resources on Jewish music; Jewish music collections; Dance with Jewish music. The bibliography is enhanced by the inclusion of a Glossary of Judaica and author and subject indexes.

871 Sendrey, Alfred. *Bibliography of Jewish Music.* New York: Columbia University Press, 1951. 404p.
This classified bibliography consists of close to 10,000 entries in two parts: literature and music, including recordings. It includes separate author indexes for each section.

872 Staub, Sh. "The Jewish Dance-Current Bibliography." *Jewish Folklore and Ethnology Newsletter*, 8, 3-4 (1986): 31-32.

873 Tischler, Alice. *A Descriptive Bibliography of Art Music by Israeli Composers.* Warren, MI.: Harmonie Park, 1988. 424p.
This catalog contains biographical sketches and information about the compositional activity of sixty-three Israeli composers. Individuals who began their work after 1910 were included. The younger generation born after 1947 and Israelis living permanently in other countries are excluded.

The following information is given for each biographee when applicable and known: Biographical sketch; Sources for further information about the composer and his or her music; Titles (in English and Hebrew) chronologically ordered; Medium ; Text author; Text language; Publication information; Duration; Location of score; Performance information; Recordings; Notes. The catalog includes a classification index, an author index, a transliterated Hebrew title index, and a multilingual title index.

874   Weisser, Albert. *Bibliography of Publications and Other Resources on Jewish Music*. Rev. and enl. ed. New York: National Jewish Music Council, 1969. 117p.
This is a bibliography of 1,023 books and articles written in English through 1967. The work is based on part on The Bibliography of Books and Articles on Jewish Music prepared by Dr. Joseph Yasser and published in 1955. It includes a "list of libraries containing collections of Jewish music, books and materials on Jewish music," and is indexed by subject.

ENCYCLOPEDIAS

875   Nulman, Macy. *Concise Encyclopedia of Jewish Music*. New York: McGraw Hill, 1975. 276p.
This work includes some 500 entries covering a wide range of subjects: liturgy, folk, theater, definitions, histories, and biographies. It is illustrated, with bibliographical footnotes.

RESOURCE GUIDE

876   *Seasons of Our Lives: A Resource Guide of the Music, Books, Films, and Videos of Jewish Life Cycle Occasions*. Compiled by Bruce Ruben and Judith Clurman. New York: JWB Jewish Music Council, 1986. 49p.
This is a selective guide to music (songs and cantorial selections), books, films and videos for each life cycle function, e.g. birth, bar/bat mitzvah, confirmation, wedding, and death and mourning. It is designed to give rabbis, cantors, music educators, and other Jewish professionals the opportunity to enrich the musical tradition for these occasions. The guide unfortunately does not list available records, tapes or cassettes. A bibliography of books pertaining to the Jewish life cycle, compiled by Marcia Posner, enhances the value of this work.

BIOGRAPHY

877   Lyman, Darryl. *Great Jews in Music*. Middle Village, NY: Jonathan David, 1986. 326p.
This biographical dictionary contains about one hundred "major biographies" supplemented by an appendix of thumbnail sketches (including also Israeli music figures). "The primary aim in selecting the major biographees was to offer a representative variety of musical artists who reflect the widespread impact of Jews in Music." Entries on major composers are followed by lists of some of their representative works. Entries on singers who record pop songs are followed by lists of their representative recordings. The work is indexed.

M. THE PRESS

ENCYCLOPEDIAS

878 Gilbo´a, Menuha. *Leksikon ha-'Itonut ha-'Ivrit ba-Me'ot ha-Shemoneh 'Esreh veha-Tesha' 'Esreh.* Jerusalem: Mosad Bialik, 1992. 471p.

This study, first published in part in 1986, lists and describes Hebrew periodicals published between 1691-1856. The author provides the following information for each publication: A. Bibliographic data, i.e. title and imprint; B. Number of volumes published C. Biographical data on the editors D. A statement of the purpose of the periodical and a summary of its contents E. A list of the prominent contributors to the journal. At the end of each article, there are references to other related periodicals as well as a short bibliography. The following indexes are included to facilitate usage: A. Titles B. Editors C. Places of publication.

BIBLIOGRAPHY

879 Fuks, Marian. *Praza Zydowska w Warszaie, 1823-1939.* Warsaw: Panstwowe Wydawn Naukowe, 1979. 362p.

This history of the Jewish press in Warsaw, from its beginning in 1823 to 1939, includes a list of newspapers and periodicals that were censored in Warsaw in 1906, a list of underground newspapers that were published in the Warsaw Ghetto from 1940-1943, a list of periodicals in Polish, Hebrew, Yiddish and other European languages, and a bibliography. It includes bibliographic data relating to the Communist press that was not included in the above.

880 Glikson, Paul. *Preliminary Inventory of the Jewish Daily and Periodical Press Published in the Polish Language, 1823-1982.* Jerusalem: Hebrew University-Institute of Jewish Studies—Center for Research on Polish Jewry, 1983. 69p.

Glikson lists 521 Polish language dailies and periodicals (including weeklies, fortnightlies, almanacs, yearbooks, ephemera) published by and for the Jews which appeared between 1823-1982. The survey includes dailies and periodicals published in "the Kingdom of Poland, Western and Eastern Galicia, the Second Polish republic, the General gouvernement, the Polish People's Republic, and also periodicals published outside Poland: in Palestine, Austria, France, Great Britain, Italy, the United States of America, Sweden and Denmark." Thirty-four periodicals in the Polish language published in Israel during the years 1948-1982 are listed in an appendix. Multi-lingual publications are also included. The bibliography is arranged alphabetically by title. The following information is given for each periodical: A. Title and subtitle; subsequent changes B. Frequency of appearance C. Place(s) and date(s) of appearance of the first and the last issue known; number of issues published D. Publisher(s). The inventory includes a bibliography of books and articles on the history of the Jewish press in Eastern Europe, and in Poland in particular.

881 Kirzhnitz, A. *Di Yiddishe Prese in der Gevezener Rushisher Imperie, 1823-1916.* Moscow, 1930. 149p.

Kirzhnitz lists periodicals that were published between 1823-1916 in Polish areas under the rule of the Czar, as well as elsewhere. These publications were intended for the Jewish public in the Russian Empire.

882 Lewin, Isaac. *Otsar Kitve 'Et Toraniyim.* New York: Research Institute of Religious Jewry, 1980. 315p.

"A bibliography of Hebrew Rabbinical periodicals which appeared in Israel, and Western Europe, China (Shanghai), North Africa, and North America during the years 1691-1948." The bibliography is arranged alphabetically by title. The author notes for each title listed the date of first publication when known, the editor(s) and contributors, and the scope of the journal.

883 Prager, Leonard. *Yiddish Literary and Linguistic Periodicals and Miscellanies: A Selective Annotated Bibliography.* Darby, PA: Published for the Association for the Study of Jewish Languages by Norwood Ed., 1982. 271p.

This bibliography lists close to 400 Yiddish periodicals which were "wholly or partly literary." Dailies are not excluded. The annotations provide the reader with a full bibliographic description of the journal. The author, in the annotation, frequently gives sample contents of a journal. He also cites references where additional information about the journal can be found, and notes the libraries in the United and Israel that have holdings. The author makes it easier for the reader to find information by providing title, contributor, and place of publication indexes.

884 Selavan, Ida C. "Jews." In *The Immigrant Labor Press in North America, 1840s-1970s: An Annotated Bibliography,* Volume 2, 542-725. New York: Greenwood Press, 1988.

This is an annotated bibliography of the Yiddish and Hebrew newspapers published in the United States. The author provides full bibliographic information regarding each publication, lists sources for further reading, and notes some libraries that house the publication. A bibliography of secondary sources with particular emphasis on the Jewish press in the United States accompanies the bibliography. It is indexed.

885 Singerman, Robert. *Jewish Serials of the World: A Research Bibliography of Secondary Sources.* Westport, CT: Greenwood Press, 1986. 377p.

This bibliography of primary and secondary source materials enables the user to study the Jewish press from 1674 to the present. The more than 3,000 citations list and describe books, pamphlets, theses, and articles, as well as jubilee issues of Jewish newspapers and magazines irrespective of language and geographic limitations. Excluded, however, are citations from the daily and weekly journalistic press. The material is arranged geographically and further subdivided by language, as appropriate. In addition, the author devotes chapters to such topics as the history of the Jewish press, and the multi-national Hebrew, Judezmo, and Yiddish serials. The work is cross referenced internally and contains subject and author indexes.

886 Szajn, Israel. *Bibliografie fun di Oysgabes Aroysgegeben durch di Arbeter-Parteyen in Poyln in die Yorn 1918-1938.* Warsaw: Yiddish-bukh, 1963. 182p.

Szajn lists dailies, periodicals, as well as reports, leaflets, and propaganda booklets issued by social, cultural and youth organizations affiliated with Jewish labour organizations in Poland. The bibliography covers the years 1918-1938. It is arranged by issuing organization. Titles are listed alphabetically under each issuing body. The lack of an index makes it difficult to find titles. A supplementary article by I. Szajn was published posthumously under the title "Materialn tsu a bibliografie fun yiddisher periodike in Poyln, 1918-1939." In *Studies on Polish Jewry, 1919-1939*, edited by Joshua A. Fishman, 422-483. New York, Yivo, 1974. This list includes publications published by organizations of all persuasions, as well as private persons. The publications are listed alphabetically by title. A key to places of publications and to the organizations that issued the publications facilitates its use.

887 Szeintuch, Yechiel. *Reshimat ha-Yomanim ve-Kitve ha-'Et be-Yidish she-Pursemu be-Polin ben shte Milhamot ha-'Olam.* Jerusalem: Center for Research on the History and Culture of Polish Jews, Hebrew University, 1986. 190p.
Szeintuch lists 1,500 Yiddish-language dailies, periodicals, literary collections, research symposia, etc. that appeared in nearly 90 localities scattered throughout independent Poland. Bilingual publications are also included. The bibliography is arranged alphabetically by title. The following information is provided for each entry: A. Title, and subtitle B. Frequency of publication and variations, if any C. Place of publication and changes, if any D. Date and number of the first and last issue, including the dates of the cessation of publication and its renewal when known E. Publisher(s). The work is accompanied by an index of places of publication in Yiddish and a city list in Polish and Yiddish.

888 Zeichner, Dvora. *Reshimah Bibliyografit shel ha-Pirsumim be-'Ivrit uve-Yidish she-Yats'u La-or be-Polin le-min Shenat 1944.* Jerusalem: Center for Research on the History and Culture of Polish Jews, Hebrew University, 1987. 82, 102p.
Zeichner lists 566 Hebrew and Yiddish periodicals, newspapers, pamphlets and books that were published in Poland from 1944-1975. The materials are listed alphabetically by author within the following three sections: A. Bibliographies B. Books and newspapers in Yiddish C. Hebrew publications and textbooks for the study of Hebrew language. In the introductory essay, the author discusses Jewish publishing in Poland during this period. The bibliography includes author and title indexes.

AUTHOR INDEX

Abramowicz, Dina 803
Abramowitz, Molly 23
Abramson, Glenda 105
Abramson, Samuel H 152
Achtemeier, Paul J 572
Adelsberg, Sandra 859
Adler, E 767
Aharoni, Yohanan 545
Ahituv, Shmuel 594
Albright, William 538
Alcalay, Reuben 142, 738
Alexander, Miriam 454
Alexander, Yonah 454
Alfasi, Yitshak 730-31
Alsberg, P. A 435, 437
American Jewish Archives
 285-87
American Jewish Comm 293
American Jewish Periodical
 Center 288
Amrami, Yaakov 453
Ancel, Jean 431
Anckaert, Luc 24
Aproot, Marion393
Arad, Yitshak 534
Ariel, Israel 440
Arkhiv Seratim be-Nosim
 Yehudiyim 128
Arnon, Yohanan 25
Arnsberg, Paul 385
Ashkenazi, Shmuel 754
Assaf, David 676
Attal, Robert 26, 247-49, 357,
 390
Avery, Evelyn 858
Avi-Yonah, Michael 545
Avraham, Avraham677-78

Bacon, Gershon C 414-15
Bader, Gershom 10
Bahat, Dan 444
Baker, Zachary 225, 364, 787
Baltsan, Hayim 739
Bamberger, Bernard J 602
Band, Arnold 762
Barkali, Saul 758-59
Baron, Joseph 146
Baron, Salo Wittmayer 232
Bauer, Hans 580
Bauer, Yehuda 505
Bavier, Richard 688
Be'er, Haim 448
Beck, Mordechai 482

Beider, Alexander 847
Beinart, Haim 227
Ben Yehuda, Eliezer 741
Ben-Amos, Dan 827
Ben-Amotz, Dan 740
Ben-Asher, Naomi 121
Ben-Dor, Shoshanah 252
Ben-Dov, Me'ir 445
Ben-Jacob, Isaac 206
Ben-Sasson, H. H 233
Ben-Yehudah, Netivah 740
Ben-Yosef, Aryeh 139
Berent, Irwin M 844
Berger, Alan L 345
Berlin, Charles 130, 133, 258
Berman, Lawrence V 711
Besso, Harry V 776
Bet ha-Sefarim ha-Leumi
 194, 213, 779
Bezalel, Itzhak 781
Bialik, Hayyim Nahman 831
Bible. O. T. Apocrypha and
 Apocryphal Books. 607-
 10
Bible. O. T. English. Aramaic
 586
Bible. O. T. English. JPS 590
Bible. O. T. Hebrew. 587-88
Bilgray, Albert 134
Bin-Gorion, Micha 832
Birnbaum, Philip 691
Blackman, Philip 654
Blank, Debra Reed 456
Bloch, Abraham P 240
Bloomberg, Marty 509
Bloomfield, Brynna C 163
Blum, Ya'akov 680
Blumenkranz, Bernhard368,
 370
Bondoni, Simonetta M 406
Bourquin, David Ray 457
Braham, Randolph L 402
Bratkowsky, Joan G 788
Breslauer, S. Daniel 821-22
Brewer, Joan Scherer 858
Brickman, William W 296
Bridger, David 123
Briggs, C. A 558
Bright, John 540
Brisman, Shimeon 46, 103
Brock, Sebastian P 549
Brown, Francis 558

Brunkow, Robert de V 342
Bry, Dan 483
Bubis, Gerald B 823
Bulka, Reuven P 692
Bunis, David M 777
Busi, Giulio 406
Buttrick, G. A 573

Cahn-Lipman, David 693
Cambridge University Li-
 brary 195-200
Cantor, Aviva 861
Carges, Harry James 510
Carmell, Aryeh 655
Carpi, Judith 458
Casper, Bernhard 24
Catane, Moche 27, 640
Cavignac, Jean 374
Chajes, Saul 755
Charles, R. H 607
Charlesworth, James 605,
 608, 612
Charny, Israel 517
Chazan, Robert 236, 366
Chernofsky, Ellen 163
Chertoff, Mordecai 454
Clasper, James 289
Cleveland Jewish Archives
 290
Cline, Scott 320
Clurman, Judith 876
Cogan, Sarah 328-30
Cohen, Abraham 601
Cohen, Arthur 694
Cohen, Boaz 670
Cohen, Chester 429
Cohen, Hayyim 251
Cohen, Menachem 600
Cohen, Shaye J. 97
Cohen, Susan Sarah 813
Cohn, John 317
Cohn-Sherbok, Dan 106, 695
Comay, Aryeh 742
Comay, Joan 1, 8
Coppenhagen, Jacob 28, 410
Copperman, Hillel 649
Corbeil, Jean Claude 743
Crim, Keith 574
Cronin, Gloria 347
Cukier, Golda 265
Cutter, Charles, 47

Dacy, Marianne 362
Dallenbach, M. Carolyn 289
Davidman, Lynn 858
Davidson, Israel 770
Davies, Raymond Arthur 266
Davis, Enid 65
Davis, Lenwood 321
Davis, Malcolm 195
Davis, Moshe 439
Davis, Nancy 161
de Geus, C. H. J 737
De Lange, Nicholas 228
De Vinney, Timoty 154
Delling, G 606
Diamond, Eliezer 627
Dimant, Devorah 455
Dion, L 867
Dobkowski, Michael 301, 518
Drew, Margaret 515
Drijvers, H. J. W 774
Driver, S. R 558
Dykers, P 605

Ecole   Biblique   et
    Archeologique 585
Edelheit, Abraham 237, 241,
    511-13
Edelheit, Hershel 237, 241,
    511-13
Edelman, Marsha Bryan 868
Edelstein, Meir 505
Eichstädt, Volkmar 377
Eidensohn, Daniel 671
Einspahr, Bruce 559
Eisenbach, Moshe 679
Eisenstadt, Samuel 666
Eissfeldt, Otto 542
Eitinger, Leo 514
Elazar, Daniel 92, 297, 856
Elbogen, Ismar 378
Elkin, Judith 351, 353
Elon, Menahem 661, 663, 672
Elwell, Sue Ellen Levi 93
Endelman, Todd M 391
Engman, Susy 67
Epstein, Baruch ha-Levi 650
Eshel, Ben Zion 624
Eskenasy, Victor 431
Even-Shoshan, Avraham
    564, 744-45

Faber, Salamon 48
Faierstein, Morris 727-28
Feingold, Henry 284
Feldman, Louis 29
Fenton, Paul 201

Fichier Central des Thèses
    82
Fiedler, Jiri 149
Finkel, Avraham 12-13
Fischel, Jack 341
Fischer, Rita Berman 66
Fisher, Eugene 865
Fitzmyer, Joseph 551, 611,
    775
Fohrer, Georg 544
Fortunoff Video Archive 516
Fox, Chaim Leib 271
Fox, Stuart 132
Frank, Daniel 709
Frank, Ruth 49
Frank, Yitshak 641
Frankel, Ellen 114, 833
Frazier, Nancy 262
Freedman, David Noel 569
Freedman, Harry 653
Freimann, Aron 168, 378
Freund, Salomon 60
Fried, Lewis 348
Friedberg, Bernhard 207
Friedman, Nathan Zvi 14
Friedman, Philip 412
Friesel, Evyatar 229
Fritsch, Charles 549
Fuks, Lajb 170, 177
Fuks, Marian 879
Fuks-Mansfeld, R. G 170, 177

Galron-Goldschläger, Joseph
    204
Galvin, Herman 789
Gaon, Moshe David 778
Gelis, Yaakov 447
Gellert, Charles 536
Gershon, Aliza 451
Gesenius, Friedrich 575
Gilat, Geula 483
Gilbert, Martin 230-31, 446,
    506
Gilbo'a, Menuha 878
Ginzberg, Louis 834
Glanz, Rudolf 298
Glikson, Paul 880
Glinert, Lewis 760
Glustrom, Simon 697
Goel, Yohai 459, 764-65
Golan, Zivah 30
Gold, Leonard Singer 192
Goldberg, Isaac 766
Goldberg, Lana 256
Goldberg, Lee 256
Goldberg-Mulkiewicz, Olga

413
Goldschmidt, Lazarus 651
Goldschmidt-Lehmann,
    Ruth 31, 396, 398
Goldstein, David 183, 722
Goldstein, Irene 837
Goldstein, Yaakov 448
Goldwurm, Hersh 11, 17
Golinkin, David 673
Goren, A 869
Gorr, Shmuel 848
Goshen-Gottstein, Moshe
    Henry 761
Green, David 544
Greenberg, Martin 2
Greenberg, Moshe 576, 594
Greenstein, Edward 242
Gribetz, Judah 242
Gries, Zeev 729
Griffiths, David 50
Grintsvaig, Mikhael 477
Gross, Heinrich 371
Gross, Moshe David 658
Grossfeld, Bernard 552
Grossman, Cheryl 67
Gruber, Ruth Ellen 150
Grundman, Moshe 460
Guggenheimer, Eva 849
Guggenheimer, Heinrich 849
Gukovitzki, Israel 642
Gurock, Jeffry 299
Gutman, Israel 533
Guttman, David 705, 812
Guzik, Estelle 836

Haboucha, Reginetta 828
Halamish, Moshe 174
Hall, Blaine 347
Halper, Benzion 202
Halperin, Raphael 3
Halpern, Meir 756
Hamelsdorf, Ora 859, 861
Haraszti, György 403
Harkavy, Alexander 791
Harvard University Library
    215-19
Hasidah, Yisrael 9, 659
Hayes, John 541
Hebrew Union College 219-
    21
Heilman, Samuel 300
Heller, Marvin 178
Herbert, Miranda 18-19, 22
Heschel, Susannah 860
Heskes, Irene 870
Hessell, Carolyn 84-86

Heuer, Renata 386
Hiat, Philip 193
Hill, Brad Sabin 189
Holladay, William Lee 560
Holtz, Barry 44, 55, 311
Hoogewood, F. J 212
Hopkins, Simon 197
Horak, Stephen 416
Hughes, John Jay 72
Hundert, Gershon David 414-15
Hurvitz, Elazar 174
Hyman, Aaron 15, 652

Iakerson, Semen 184-85
Ilsar Mednitzky, Nira 83
Inbal, Shimshon 489, 746
Israelowitz, O 151, 159-60

Jacobs, Joseph 392
Jaffe, Eliezer 488
Jarden, Dov754
Jellicoe, Sidney 549
Jerushalmi, Joseph 32
Jewish Theological Seminary 171-72
Joffe, Judah 790
Jolles, Jacob Zebi 723
Jones, Philip 438
Joüon, Paul 577

Kagan, Berl 179, 430, 807
Kaganoff, Benzion 850
Kaganoff, Nathan 436
Kahana, Abraham 609
Kahana, Barukh 680
Kalimi, Isaac 553
Kantor, Mattis 243
Kaplan, Aryeh 597
Kaplan, Jonathan 238
Kaplan, Steven 252
Karkhanis, Sharad 305
Kasher, Menahem 598, 629
Kasowski, Chaim Josua 566, 633-35
Katsav, Shlomo 180
Katz, Dovid 796
Katz, Eliezer 565
Katz, Nathan 360
Katz, Steven 706
Kaufman, Deborah 129
Kaufman, Stephen 775
Kaufmann, Shoshana 462
Kautzsch, E 575
Kayserling, Meyer 780
Kestenbaum, Ray 261

Khan, Geoffrey 196
Kirshenblatt-Gimblett, Barbara 819
Kirzhnitz, A 881
Klatzkin, Jacob 717
Klausner, Israel 500
Klein, Dennis 520
Klein, Ernest 747
Klein, Michael 199
Klein, Zanvil 33
Kna'ani, Ya'akov 748-49
Knoller, Rivka 521
Knopf, H 195
Kohen, Gershon 186
Kohen, Yitshak Yosef 432
Köhler, Ludwig 561-63
Kohn, Gary 291
Kohn, Phinehas Jacob 628
Kohn, Roger 369
Kolatch, Alfred 701-02, 851
Koppman, Lionel 162
Korros, Alexandra 306
Korsch, Boris419
Kosmin, Barry 419
Kosovsky, Binyamin 636-38
Kosovsky, Moshe 639
Kranzler, David 838
Krell, Robert 514
Kressel, Getzel 34-35, 771
Kuperstein, Isaiah 531
Kurzweil, Arthur 835, 839

Lachower, Fischel 722
Lahad, Ezra 768
Lamb, Connie 347
Lambdin, Thomas 578
Landau, Julian 464
Landau, Ron 4
Laredo, Abraham Isaac 852
Larinson, Zevi 143
Laska, Vera 522
Latner, Helen 703
Lazar, Yisrael 750
Lehmann, Ruth 394-96
Leo Baeck Institute. Library 375, 389
Lerman, Antony 235
Lerski, Halina 418
Lerski, Jerzy 418
Levenston, Edward 753
Leventhal, Dennis 358
Levi, Leo 61
Levitt, Joy 161
Levtow, Patricia 322
Lewin, Isaac 882
Liberman, Serge 363

Libowitz, Richard 523
Liebman, Charles 857
Lifschutz, Ezekiel 307
Lightman, Sidney 147
Linzer, Norman 302
Lipsitz, Edmond 77, 270
Lipstadt, Deborah 323
Liptzin, Sol 800
Liss, Janet 310-12
Lissak, Moshe 442
Loewenthal, Rudolf 359
Lubetski, Edith 211
Lubetski, Meir 211
Luckert, Yelena 420
Lustick, Ian 478
Luzzatto, Aldo 404-05
Lyman, Darryl 877

McCarthy, Justin 481
McNeil, Barbara 18-22
Madison, Charles 801
Magnus, Shulamit 380
Magocsi, Paul Robert 417
Mahler, Eduard 62
Mahler, Gregory 465
Maimonides, Moses
Makhon le-Tatslume Kitve ha-Yad 166-67
Mandelbaum, Jacob 629
Mandelkern, Salomon 567
Marcus, Audrey 87
Marcus, Ivan 94
Marcus, Jacob Rader 134, 319, 332, 344, 367
Marcus, Ralph 466
Mark, Yudel 790
Martsiano, Eliyahu 181
Marwick, Lawrence 757
Massil, Stephen 395
Mayer, Leo 817
Meizlish, Penina 505
Melamed, Ezra Zion 644
Melrod, George 157
Mendelsohn, Ezra 421
Mendes-Flohr, Paul 234, 694
Merowitz, Morton 422
Mersky, Roy 41
Meshorer, Rachel 467
Metz, Helen Chapin 461
Mielziner, Moses 621
Milano, Attilio 407-08
Miller, David Neal 36-37
Miller, James Maxwell 541
Miller, Philip 52
Mokotoff, Gary 507
Moldavi, Moshe 404

Monson, Rela Geffen 308
Moonan, Willard 38
Moonman, Jane 401
Mor, Menahem 455
Morag, Shelomo 200
Moria, M 208-09
Muffs, Judith 520
Mulder, Martin Jan 543
Munitz, Sarah 632

Nadel, Ira Bruce 349
Nadell, Pamela 334
Naor, Mordechai 492
Negev, Avraham 615
Netzer, Amnon 173
Neuberg, Assia 468
Neusner, Jacob 623
New York Public Library 222-24
Norich, Anita 805
Novak, David 713
Noy, Zvi Porat 78
Nulman, Macy 875

O'Connor, M 579
Ofek, Uriel 68
Offenberg, A. 187-88
Olitzky, Kerry 335
Oppenheim, Micha 689
Oppenheimer, Aharon 625
Orbach, Alexander 423
Orenstein, Rena 129
Orenstein, Sylvia 427
Ormann, G 376

Paley, Michael 710
Patai, Raphael 502
Pearson, J. D 164
Pick, Shlomo 632
Piekarz, Mendel 525
Pilarczyk, Krysztof 424
Pinkus, Binyamim 425
Pinsker, Sanford 341
Platnick, Abraham 682
Plaut, W. Gunther 602
Plotkin, Janis 129
Pollak, Michael 359
Polner, Murray 333
Porter, Jack Nusan 316
Posner, Marcia 69-70, 864
Posner, Raphael 176, 571
Postal, Bernard 152, 162
Powell, Mark Allan 554
Prager, Leonard 399, 883
Pritchard, James 547, 617-18
Pruter, Karl 324

Purvis, James 469
Ra'anan, Eliyah 680
Radice, Roberto 40
Rafael, Ruth Kelson 292
Rakover, Nahum 239, 656, 660, 668-69
Raphael, Marc Lee 236, 295
Raphael, Yitzhak 732
Rappaport, Uriel 455
Ratzaby, Yehuda 253
Ravnitzky, Joshua 831
Reed, Stephen 613
Reeg, Gottfried 626
Reich, Bernard 493
Reif, Stefan 198
Reinharz, Jehuda 234
Reisen, Zalman 809
Rheins, Carl 75
Richler, Binyamin 165
Ringelheim, Joan 535
Rischin, Moses 263, 309
Ritterband, Paul 325
Rivlin, Gershon 451
Robinson, Jacob 504, 526
Robinson, Kerry 276
Rockland, Mae Schafter 277
Rockowitz, Anna 797
Rolef, Susan Hattis 491
Romano, Giorgio 409
Rome, David 268, 272
Rosen, Oded 259
Rosenbach, Abraham 326
Rosenberg, S 273
Rosenbloom, Joseph 336
Rosenfeld, Moshe 182, 190
Rosenstein, Neil 845
Rosenthal, Franz 581
Rosenthal, Yemima 479
Rosovsky, Nitza 490
Rosten, Leo 144
Roth, Cecil 397
Róth, Ernst 169
Rothenberg, Joshua 54
Rothschild, Fritz 712
Rottenberg, Dan 840
Rovner, Jay 171
Rozman, Yael 450
Ruben, Bruce 876
Rudd, Inger Marie 862
Runia, David 40

Sable, Martin 354, 527
Sacerdoti, Annie 153
Sack, Sallyann 507, 841-42
Safrai, Shmuel 620
Sala, Marius 782

Salinger, Peter Shmuel 395
Samuelson, Norbert 707
Sanders, Moshe 393
Sarna, Jonathan 306, 310-12
Sater, Ana Lya 351
Saul Lieberman Institute of Talmudic Research 686
Schaechter, Mordkhe 798
Schäfer, Peter 724
Schembs, Hans Otto 382, 385
Schiller, Ely 489
Schlesinger, Benjamin 824-25
Schneider, Susan 863
Schoenburg, Nancy 426
Schoenburg, Stuart 426
Scholem, Gershom 718
Schonberg, David 667
Schreckenberg, Heinz 29
Schultz, Hadassah 100
Schürer, Emil 604
Schwartz, B 337
Schwartz, Bertie 43
Scott, William 589
Seeskin, Kenneth 714
Segal, Chaim 645
Segal, Hyman 63
Segall, Aryeh 226
Seidel, Jefferey 148
Selavan, Ida 884
Sellin, Ernst 544
Seltzer, Robert 698
Sendrey, Alfred 871
Seror, Simon 853
Sever, Moshe 145
Shaked, Shaul 203
Shanks, Hershel 539
Shermis, Michael 866
Shimoni, Gideon 90-91
Shmeruk, Chone 802
Shmueli, Eliezer 449
Shoham, Joseph 101
Shosteck, Patti 820
Shulman, William 530
Shunami, Shlomo 56-57
Shur, Simon 463
Siegel, Richard 75, 111
Siegel, Seymour 712
Siegel, Steven 364
Simon, Maurice 653
Singer, David 826
Singerman, Robert 327, 433-34, 815, 854, 885
Sirat, Colette 708
Sirof, Harriet 494
Sivan, Reuben 753
Skirball, Sheba 537

Slatkine, Menahem 210
Sloan, Irving 340
Slotki, Judah 648
Slotky, Eliahu 683, 725-26
Smooha, Sammy 470-72
Snyder, Esther Mann 473
Sokoloff, Michael 646
Sokolow, Nahum 772
Solis-Cohen, Elfrida 282
Sparks, Hedley Frederick 610
Spector, Sheila 720
Sperber, David 647
Spier, Arthur 64
Starkey, Edward 690
Staub, Jacob 710
Staub, Sh 872
Stavroulakis, Nicolas 154
Stein, Regina 242
Stein, Tzipora 92
Steinberg, Avraham 665
Steinsaltz, Adin 657
Stemberger, G 622
Stern, Eliyahu 480
Stern, Malcolm 313, 335, 843, 846
Stern, Norton 331
Stillman, Norman 245-46, 250
Stone, Michael 603
Strack, Herman 622
Strangelove, Michael 58
Strassfeld, Michael 111-13
Strassfeld, Sharon 111-13
Strauss, Herbert 214, 303, 387, 814
Striedel, Hans 169
Strom, Margot Stern 528
Studemund, Michael 783
Stuhlman, Daniel 205
Stutchkoff, Nahum 792
Sussman, Lance 335
Szajkowski, Zosa 372, 508
Szajn, Israel 886
Szeintuch, Y 887

Ta-Shema, Israel 176
Tabory, Mala 857
Tamarkin, Stan 789
Tapper, Lawrence 264
Teich, Shmuel 17
Teitelbaum, Gene 41
Teller, A 411
Telushkin, Joseph 699
Teutsch, Betsy Platkin 114
Thompson, Henry 555
Tidhar, David 452
Tilem, Ivan 76, 260

Tischler, Alice 873
Tishby, Isaiah 722
Toledano, Joseph 855
Tovi, Yosef 175, 254
Townsend, John 630-31
Trepp, Leo 704
Trionyo, Valia 191
Tsabag, Shemuel 474
Tsanin, Mordekhai 793-94
Tulchinsky, Gerald 274
Tumin, Melvin 315
Tykocinski, H 378

Ungerleider-Mayerson, Joy 490
Universitah ha-'Ivrit bi-Yerushalayim 244
Unterman, Alan 700
Urbach, Ephraim 662

Vajda, Georges 715-16
Verbit, Mervin 80, 98
Vernon, Elizabeth 258
Vilnay, Zev 158
Vinograd, Yeshayahu 191
Vogel, Eleanor 616

Wachsman, Hayyim 568
Wal, Adri van der 556-57
Walden, Daniel 350
Walk, Joseph 388
Wallace, Michael 400
Wallach, Jehuda 442, 475
Walliman, Isidor 518
Waltke, Bruce 579
Waxman, Meyer 734
Weinberg, Bella Hass 225
Weinberg, David 373
Weiner, Miriam 835
Weinreich, Beatrice 829
Weinreich, Max 785
Weinreich, Uriel 795, 799, 829
Weinstein, Jay 818
Weisbach, Lee Shai 314
Weisbard, Phyllis 667
Weiser, R 42
Weisser, Albert 874
Wertheimer, Jack 96
Wexler, Paul 784
Wiener Library 383
Wiesemann, Falk 384
Wigoder, Geoffrey 5, 110, 119, 294, 696
Wijnhoven, Jochanan 721
Wolf, Lucien 392
Wolff, Egon 356

Wolff, Frieda 356
Wolffsohn, Michael 476
Wolheim, William 49
Wolk, Samuel 123
Wunder, Meir 140, 428
Wynne, Suzan Fishl 842

Yaari, Abraham 769
Yad Vashem Martyr's and Heroes 529
Yassif, Eli 830
Yehuda, Zvi 251
Yitzhak, Raphael 503
YIVO Institute for Jewish Research 225
Yonai, Havivah 30
Yudkin, Leon 89, 95

Zeichner, Dvora 888
Zeitlin, William 773
Zfatman, Sarah 806
Zimer, Orah 39
Zinberg, Israel 735
Zlotowitz, Meir 596
Zubatsky, David 7, 844
Zylbercwaig, Zalmen 811

TITLE INDEX

Aderet Eliyahu 726
Agnon: Texts & Contexts 89
Aiding Talmud Study 655
Algemeyne Entsiklopedye: Yidn 104
America and the Holocaust 323
American Immigrants in Israel 462
American Jewish Biographies 333
American Jewish Experience 311
American Jewish Fiction 345
American Jewish History 299, 312
American Jewish Landmarks 162
American Jewish Organizations Directory 279
American Jewish Organizations with Offices in Israel 280
American Jewish Studies 295
American Jewish Women 332
American Jewish Yearbook 281-82
American Reform Judaism 313
American Synagogue History 306
American-Jewish Media Directory 261
Amos 'Oz: Bibliyografyah 32
Amos: A Classified Bibliography 556
An American Jewish Bibliography 326
An Annotated Bibliography About Indian Jews 360
Analytical Franco-Jewish Gazetteer, 508
Anchor Bible 591
Anchor Bible Dictionary 569
Ancient Israel 539
Ancient Near East 617
Ancient Near Eastern Texts 618
Anglo-Jewish Bibliography 394-95
Annotated Bibliography of

the Peshitta 550
Annotated Catalogue of A-V Materials 101
Antique and Rare Books 190
Antisemitic Propaganda: An Annotated Bibliography 815
Antisemitism: An Annotated Bibliography 813
Antisemitism World Report 816
Apocrypha and Pseudepigrapha 607
Apocryphal Old Testament 610
Aramaic Bible: The Targums 586
Archaeological Encyclopedia of the Holy Land 615
Archival ... Study of Canadian Jewry 264
Archive of Australian Judaica 361
Art Scroll Tanach Series 596
Association of Holocaust Organizations: Directory 530
Atid Bibliography 43
Atikim u-Nedirim 190
Atlas 'Ets Hayim 3
Atlas Erets Yisrael li-Gevuloteha 'al pi ha-Mekorot 440
Atlas Karta le-Toldot Erets-Yisrael 441
Atlas Karta le-Toldot Medinat Yisrael 442
Atlas of Israel 443, 546
Atlas of Medieval Jewish History 227
Atlas of Modern Jewish History 229
Atlas of the Holocaust 506
Atlas of the Jewish World 228
Author Biographies Master Index 18

Babylonia Judaica in the Talmudic Period 625
Babylonian Talmud: Index Volume 648

Back to the Sources 44
Basic Bibliography for the Study of Semitic Languages 737
Basic Encyclopedia of Jewish Proverbs 142
Bazak Guide to Israel 155
Bene Melakhim 181
Bet Eked Sefarim 207
Bet Eked Sefarim he-Hadash 208
Bi-Netivot ha-Midrash 649
Bible and Modern Literary Criticism 554
Biblia Hebraica 588
Biblia Hebraica Stuttgartensia 587
Biblical and Judaic Acronyms 757
Bibliografia Italo-Ebraica 409
Bibliografia Tematica Sobre Judaismo Argentino 355
Bibliografie fun di Oysgabes 886
Bibliografye fun Amerikaner un Kanader Yidisher Zikhroynes 307
Bibliographia Judaica 386
Bibliographical ... Medieval Jewish Studies 45
Bibliographie des Juifs en France 370
Bibliographie zum Antisemitismus 214
Bibliographie zum Judenspanischen 783
Bibliographie zur Geschichte de Juden in Bayern 384
Bibliographie zur Geschichte der Frankfurter 382
Bibliographie zur Geschichte der Judenfrage 377
Bibliographie zur Jüdisch Hellenistischen 606
Bibliographisches Handbuch der Neuhebräischen Literatur 773
Bibliography of Anglo Jewish Medical Biog. 398
Bibliography of Australian Judaica 363

Bibliography of Eastern European Memorial (Yizkor) Books 364
Bibliography of Festschriften 52
Bibliography of Hebrew and Yiddish Publications 376
Bibliography of Holy Land Sites 616
Bibliography of Isaac Bashevis Singer 36-37
Bibliography of Israel 454
Bibliography of Israeli Politics 465
Bibliography of Jewish Art 817
Bibliography of Jewish Bibliographies 56-57
Bibliography of Jewish Genealogy 844
Bibliography of Jewish Music 868, 871
Bibliography of Modern Hebrew Literature 763-65
Bibliography of Publications on Jewish Music 874
Bibliography of Targum Literature 552
Bibliography of the Jews of Romania 431
Bibliography on Antisemitism 214
Bibliography on Holocaust Literature 511-13
Biblioteca Española Portugez -Judaica 780
Bibliotheca Anglo-Judaica: A Bibliographic Guide 392
Bibliotheca Historica Italo-Judaica 407-08
Bibliotheca Italo-Ebraica 404-05
Bibliyografyah le-Toldot Yisrael 455
Bibliyografyah shel 'Avodot Doktor 83
Bibliyografyah shel Hevrat ha'-Ovdim 458
Bibliyografyah Shel Kitve Gershom Sholem 27
Bibliyografyah shel Kitve S D Goitain 26
Bibliyografyah Shimushit: Nili, Berit ha-Biryonim 453
Biographical Dictionary of

Early American Jews 336
Biographisches Handbuch der Deutschsprachigen Emigration 387
Biographisches Lexikon der Juden 385
Biography and Genealogy Master Index 19-21
Bithon Yisrael, 1967-1991 460
Bits, Bytes & Biblical 72
Black-Jewish Relations in the U.S. 322
Black-Jewish Relations in the United States 321
Blackwell Companion to Jewish Culture 105
Blackwell Dictionary of Judaica 106
Book List 548
Book of Daniel 555
Book of Jewish Books 49
Book of Jewish Knowledge 693
Book of Jewish Lists 4
Book of Modern Jewish Etiquette 703
Books on Israel 478
Britain and Palestine, 1914-1948 438
Building a Judaica Library Collection 211

California Jewish History 331
Canadian Jewish Periodicals 265
Canadian Jewish Women of Today 269
Canadian Jewry Today 270
Catalog of the Archival Collections 375
Catalogue de la Bibliothèque de l'Ecole Biblique 585
Catalogue des Doctorats Hebraica-Judaica 82
Catalogue of Audio and Visual Collections of Holocaust Testimony 535
Catalogue of Hebrew Books 215-16
Catalogue of Memoirs 293
Catalogue Series 383
CD-ROM Judaic Classics Library 684
Choice of Corals 188
Church, State and the Jews in the Middle Ages 366

Classic Tales 833
Classified Bibliography of the Septuagint 549
Classified Concordance to the Bible 565
Collective Catalogue of Hebrew Manuscripts 166-67
Collector's Guide to Judaica 818
College Yiddish 799
Complete Book of Jewish Observance 704
Complete Dictionary of English and Hebrew First Names 851
Complete United States Jewish Travel Guide 159
Comprehensive Etymological Dictionary of the Hebrew Language 747
Comprehensive Guide to Children's Literature 65
Comprehensive Hebrew Calendar 64
Computer Programs and Databanks 686
Concise Encyclopedia of Jewish Music 875
Concise Hebrew and Aramaic Lexicon 560
Conservative Judaism in America 334
Contemporary Jewish Civilization 90
Contemporary Jewish Ethics 821
Contemporary Jewish Philanthropy in America 325
Contemporary Jewish Religious Thought 694
Corresponding Date Calendar 60
Critical Bibliography of Writings on Judaism 50
Cultura Ebraica in Emilia-Romagna 406

Day by Day in Jewish History 240
Dead Sea Scroll Inventory Project 613
Dead Sea Scrolls: Major Publications 611
Defus ha-'Ivri me-Reshito 182

Indexes | 217

Demographic Studies of Jewish Communities 317
Denial of the Holocaust 521
Descriptive Bibliography of Art Music 873
Descriptive Catalogue of Genizah Fragments 202
Diccionário Biográfico 356
Dictionary Catalog of the Jewish Collection 222-23
Dictionary Catalog of the Klau Library 219-21
Dictionary of Greek and Latin Terms 647
Dictionary of Jewish Biography 5
Dictionary of Jewish Lore and Legend 700
Dictionary of Jewish Names and Their History 850
Dictionary of Jewish Palestinian Aramaic 646
Dictionary of Jewish Surnames from the Russian Empire 847
Dictionary of Judaism and Christianity 695
Dictionary of the Targumim 643
Dictionnaire du Judaisme Bordelais 374
Dikduk ha-'Ivri ha-Shimushi 761
Directory of Day Schools 255
Directory of Holocaust Institutions 531
Directory of Jewish Federations 278
Directory of Research Institutes in Israel 483
Directory of World Jewish Press 81
Documents Modernes sur les Juifs XVIe-XXe Siècles 368
Doing Business in Israel 484

Early Acharonim 11
Eastern European National Minorities 416
Electric Mystic's Guide to the Internet 58
Elenchus Bibliographicus Biblicus 582
Elie Wiesel: A Bibliography 23

'En Mishpat 666
Encyclopaedia Judaica 107-08
Encyclopaedia Judaica Year Book 109
Encyclopedia of Jewish Concepts 691
Encyclopedia of Jewish Genealogy 835
Encyclopedia of Jewish Institutions 259
Encyclopedia of Jewish Symbols 114
Encyclopedia of Judaism 696
Encyclopedia of Library and Information Science, 48
Encyclopedia of Talmudic Sages 10
Encyclopedia of the Holocaust 533
Encyclopedia of Zionism and Israel 502
Encyclopedic Dictionary of Judaica 110
English Jewish History 391
Entsiklopedyah ha-'Ivrit 124-27
Entsiklopedyah Hilkhatit Hasdey David 683
Entsiklopedyah Hilkhatit Refuit 665
Entsiklopedyah la-Hasidut 732
Entsiklopedyah le-Halutse ha-Yishuv u-Vonav 452
Entsiklopedyah le-Toldot Hakhme Erets Yisrael 447
Entsiklopedyah Mikra'it 570
Entsiklopedyah shel ha-TaNaKH 571
Entsiklopedyah shel ha-Tsiyonut ha-Datit 503
Entsiklopedyah Talmudit le-'Inyane Halakhah 664
Eretz Israel Reference Topics 459
Ethnic Dance in Israel with Selected Filmography 869
Ethnographic Topics Relating to Jews in Polish Studies 413
Evreiskie Inkunabuly 184

Facing History and Our-

selves 515
Filmography 128
Films of the Holocaust 537
Filmstrip and Slide Catalog 99
Finding Our Fathers 840
First American Jewish Families 846
First Century Palestinian Judaism 457
First Jewish Catalog 111
Focus on the American Jewish Family 826
Fodor's Israel 156
Foundation Guide for Religious Grant Seekers 276
Franco-Judaica 372
Franz Rosenzweig 24
French Jewish History 373
From Generation to Generation 839
From Stone Age to Christianity 538

Galicia 417
Gallia Judaica 371
Genealogical Resources in the New York Metropolitan Area 836
Genocide In Our Time 518
Genocide: A Critical Bibliographic Review 517
German Jewish History 380
German Jews in America 298
Germania Judaica 378
Gershom Sholem and Hasidism 727
Gesenius' Hebrew Grammar 575
Geshikhte fun der Yidisher Shprakh 785
Giving Wisely 488
Global Jewish Database 685
Grammar of Biblical Aramaic 581
Grammar of Biblical Hebrew 577
Grammar of Modern Hebrew 760
Grammar of the Yiddish Language 796
Grammatik des Biblisch-Aramäischen 580
Graphic Concordance to the Dead Sea Scrolls 612

Great Chasidic Masters 12
Great Jews in Music 877
Great Torah Commentators 13
Groyser Verterbukh der Yidisher Shprakh 790
Guide Book: Jewish Sights 149
Guide to America-Holy Land Studies 436
Guide to Bibliographies of Polish Judaica 424
Guide to Everything Jewish in New York 161
Guide to Films 129
Guide to Israel 158
Guide to Jewish Archives 226
Guide to Jewish Europe 151
Guide to Jewish Genealogical Research in Israel 841
Guide to Jewish History Sources 290
Guide to Jewish Italy 153
Guide to Jewish New York 160
Guide to Jewish Themes in American Fiction 346
Guide to Judaica Videotapes 130
Guide to Libraries of Judaica and Hebraica in Europe 212
Guide to the Archives in Israel 437
Guide to the Hebrew Manuscript Collection 171
Guide to the Holdings of the American Jewish Archives 289
Guide to the Sources for the History of the Jews in Poland 411
Guide to Unpublished Materials of the Holocaust 504
Guide to Yale University Library Holocaust Video Testimonies 516

Hakhme Transilvanyah 432
Halachic Times for Home and Travel 61
Halakhah: Its Sources and Development 662
Handbook of American-Jewish Litera-

ture 348
Handbuch der Jüdischer Chronologie 62
Harper Atlas of the Bible 547
Harper's Bible Dictionary 572
Hasidism: The Present State of Research 729
Hasidism—The Last Decade in Research 728
Hasidut 730
Hebraica (Saec. X ad saec. XVI) 189
Hebräische Handschriften 169
Hebräisches und Aramäisches Lexikon 561
Hebrew 737
Hebrew and Judaic Manuscripts 170
Hebrew Bible Manuscripts 195
Hebrew Book: An Historical Survey 176
Hebrew English Corresponding Calendar 63
Hebrew Incunables in the British Isles 183
Hebrew Incunabula in Public Collections 187
Hebrew Manuscript Catalogs 172
Hebrew Manuscripts: A Treasured Legacy 165
Hebrew Typography in the Northern Netherlands 177
Hebrew-Character Title Catalog 224
Heker ha-Shirah veha-Piyut 767
Heker Yahadut Teman 253
Hermeneia 592
Highlights of the CJF 1990 Population Survey 318
Hillel Guide to Jewish Life on Campus 275
Historical Biographical Dictionaries Master Index 22
Historical Dictionary of Israel 493
History and Guide to Judaic Bibliography 46
History and Guide to Judaic Encyclopedias 103

History of Israel 540
History of Jewish Literature 734-35
History of Jewish Philosophy …Middle Ages 708
History of the Jewish People 233
History of the Jewish People …Age of Jesus Christ 604
History of Yiddish Literature 800
Holocaust in Books and Films 520
Holocaust in University Teaching 91
Holocaust Studies 523, 528
Holocaust Studies: A Directory 527
Holocaust, Israel, and the Jews 536
Holocaust: An Annotated Bibliography 510
Holocaust: An Annotated Bibliography and Resource Guide 519
Holocaust: The Nuremberg Evidence 526
Hundert Yor Yidishe un Hebraishe Literatur in Kanade 271
Hungarian Jewish Catastrophe 402

Igron le-Milim Nirdafot u-Kerovot Mashma'ut 742
Illustrated Atlas of Jerusalem 444
Illustrated Atlas of Jewish Civilization 230
Immigrant Labor Press in North America 884
Index of Articles in Jewish Studies 141
Index of Conservative Responsa and Halakhic Studies 673
Index of Outreach Programs in Israel 485
Index to Brown, Driver and Briggs' Hebrew Lexicon 559
Index to Festschriften 133
Index to Jewish Festschriften 134
Index to Jewish Periodicals

135
Index to Scientific Articles of American Jewish History 344
International Bibliography of Jewish History and Thought 238
International Biographical Dictionary of Central European 387
Internationale Zeitschriftenschau 583
Interpreter's Dictionary of the Bible 573-74
Introduction to Biblical Hebrew 578
Introduction to Biblical Hebrew Syntax 579
Introduction to Hebrew 576
Introduction to Modern Jewish Philosophy 707
Introduction to the Old Testament 544
Introduction to the Talmud 621
Introduction to the Talmud and Midrash 622
Introductory Bibliography for the Study of Scripture 551
Inventory and Appraisal of Research on American Anti-Semitism 315
Inventory of American Jewish History 309
Inventory to the French Jewish Communities 369
Israel, Including the West Bank 157
Israel Business Directory 486
Israel State Archives 435
Israel Yearbook 496
Israel, Polity, Society, Economy 476
Israel: A Country Study 461
Israel: A Selected Bibliography 464
Israeli Education System 487
Israeli Military History 475
Israelitische 'Kerk'en der ... Nederlanden 410
Itonut be-Ladino 778

Jerusalem History Atlas 446
Jerusalem, The Holy City: A Bibliography 469

Jew in the Medieval World 367
Jew in the Modern World 234
Jewish Almanac 75
Jewish American Voluntary Organizations 301
Jewish and Hebrew Onomastics 854
Jewish Autobiograhies and Biographies 7
Jewish Book Annual 52, 283
Jewish Books in Whitechapel 393
Jewish Charity Cookbooks 819
Jewish Children's Books 69
Jewish Christians in the United States 324
Jewish Cities, Towns and Villages 430
Jewish Communal Services in the United States 302
Jewish Communities of the United States 314
Jewish Communities of the World 235
Jewish Community in America 296
Jewish Community in Canada 273
Jewish Community Studies 297
Jewish Dance—Current Bibliography 872
Jewish Education Directory 257
Jewish Elderly in the English-Speaking Countries 812
Jewish Encyclopedia 115
Jewish Ethnic Interaction 320
Jewish Experience 291
Jewish Experience in America 343
Jewish Family 825
Jewish Family Issues 824
Jewish Family Names 849
Jewish Film Directory 131
Jewish Films in the US 132
Jewish Folklore 830
Jewish Folklore Studies 827
Jewish Genealogy: Beginner's Guide 837
Jewish Heritage in America 305

Jewish Heritage Travel 150
Jewish History Atlas 231
Jewish Holocaust 509
Jewish Home Advisor 701
Jewish Immigrants of the Nazi Period 303
Jewish International Activity 857
Jewish Law: Bibliography of Sources 667
Jewish Law-Index to Code 682
Jewish Lists 2
Jewish Literacy 699
Jewish Literature for Children 67
Jewish Materials Resource Guide 84
Jewish Museums of North America 262
Jewish Mysticism: An Annotated Bibliography 720
Jewish Newspapers ... Microfilm 288
Jewish People in America 284
Jewish People: Past and Present 116
Jewish Personal Names 848
Jewish Philosophers 706
Jewish Philosophy 710
Jewish Philosophy in the 1980's 714
Jewish Political Studies 92, 856
Jewish Serials of the World 885
Jewish Sites and Synagogues of Greece 154
Jewish Student's Guide to American Colleges 256
Jewish Studies Courses ... Universities 258
Jewish Teachers Handbook 87
Jewish Theology 713
Jewish Time Line Encyclopedia 243
Jewish Travel Guide 147
Jewish Travelers' Resource Guide 148
Jewish Woman 1900-1985 861
Jewish Woman's Networking Directory 863
Jewish Women and Jewish Law 859
Jewish Women's Studies

Guide 93
Jewish World in Modern Times 237
Jewish Writers of North America 349
Jewish Writings of the Second Temple Period 603
Jewish Yearbook 400
Jewish-American Fiction Writers 347
Jewish-American History and Culture 341
Jewish-Christian Relations 866
Jewish-Polish Coexistence 418
Jews 416
Jews and the Cults 316
Jews in America, 1621-1970 340
Jews in Canadian Literature 272
Jews in Poland and Russia 414
Jews in Spain and Portugal 433
Jews of Arab Lands 245
Jews of Arab Lands in Modern Times 246
Jews of Los Angeles 328
Jews of North America 263
Jews of San Francisco 329
Jews of the Islamic World 250
Jews of Weimar 379
Joint Documentary Projects Bibliographical Series 529
Joseph B. Soloveitchik: A Bibliography 33
Josephus: A Supplementary Bibliography 29
JPS Torah Commentary 593
Judaica 217
Judaica Americana 304, 327
Judaica Collection Card Catalogue 213
Judaica in the Houghton Library 218
Judaica Libraries and Literature 48
Judaica Reference Materials 54
Judaism and Christianity 690
Judaism in New Testament Times 688

Judaism: A People and its History 698
Judeo-Español 782
Judeo-Romance Linguistics: A Bibliography 784
Jüdische Philosophie 715
Jüdisches Lexikon 117
Juifs du Québec 267
Junior Encyclopedia of Israel 494
Junior Jewish Encyclopedia 121
Junior Judaica 122
Justice Louis D. Brandeis 41
Juvenile Judaica 70

Kabbalah 718
Karaite Bible Manuscripts 196
Katalog 389
Katalog Ivkunabulov 185
Katalog shel Osef Z'ak Motseri 194
Kibbutz: A Bibliography 463
Kiryat Sefer 51
Kitve Dov Sadan: Bibliyografyah 34
Kitve G. Kressel: Bibliyografyah 35
Kitve ha-Yad ha-Temaniyim 175
Kitve Sofrim Yehudim Sefaradiyim 781
Klezmer Music in America 867
Konkordantsyah ha -Shelemah veha -Peshutah la-TaNaKH 568
Konkordantsyah le-Sifrut ha-Hekhalot 724
Konkordanz zur Hekhalot Literatur 724
Konkorkdantsyah Hadashah le-Torah, Nevi'im u-Khetuvim 564
Kratkaia Evreiskaia Entsiklopediia 118
Kronologyah le-Toldot ha-Yishuv ha-Yehudi be-Erets Yisrael 479
Kronologyah le-Toldot ha-Yishuv ha-Yehudi ha-Hadash be-Erets 480
Kuntres ha-Teshuvot 670
Kurzbiographien zur

Geschchichte der Juden 388

Ladino Books in the Library of Congress 776
Language and Culture Atlas of Ashkenaz Jewry 786
Language of Judaism 697
La 'ruts Orah 677
Latin America Jewish Studies 351
Latin American Jewry 354
Learning to Learn 482
Legends of the Jews 834
Leket Divrey Bikoret 136
Leksikon fun der Yudisher Literatur un Prese 810
Leksikon fun der nayer Yidisher Literatur 808
Leksikon fun der Yidisher Literatur 809
Leksikon fun Yidish Shraybers 807
Leksikon fun Yidishn Teater 811
Leksikon ha-'Itonut ha-'Ivrit 878
Leksikon ha-Ishim shel Erets Yisrael 448
Leksikon ha-Sifrut ha-'Ivrit 771
Leksikon Koah ha-Magen ha-"Haganah 492
Leksikon Lo'azi-'Ivri Shimushi 752
Leksikon Ofek 68
Leksikon Shel Sofrey Yisrael 772
Leo Rosten's Treasury of Jewish Quotations 144
Les Études de Philosophie Juive du Moyen Âge 716
Lexicon in Veteris Testamenti Libros 562
Library of Congress Subject Headings 204-05
Literary Criticism in Israel 762
Literature of the Sages 620
Lithuanian Jewish Communities 426
Living Torah 597
Luah ha-Pe'alim ha-Shalem 758
Luah ha-Shemot ha-Shalem 759

MacMillan Bible Atlas 545
Mafteah ha-Sheelot veha-Teshuvot shel Hakhme 672
Mafteah ha-Shulhan ha-Shalem 679
Mafteah le-'Itonut Yomit 'Ivrit 137
Mafteah le-Khitve-'Et be-'Ivrit 138
Mafteah le-Maamarim 139
Magna Bibliotheca Anglo-Judaica 397
Magyar Zsidó Levéltári Repertórium 403
Mahazeh ha-'Ivri be-Makor uve-Tirgum 768
Mahazeh ha-'Ivri ha-Mekori veha-Meturgam 769
Manuscript Catalog of the American Jewish Archives 285-87
Martin Buber and His Critics 38
Materials Resource Guide for Jewish Education 88
Medieval Jewish Civilization 94
Medieval Jewish Mysticism 721
Medieval Jewish Religious Philosophy 711
Medinat Yisrael: Bibliyografyah Mu'eret 468
Mediniyut ha-Huts shel Erets Yisrael 474
Menasseh ben Israel 28
Meore Galitsiyah 428
Mi va-Mi bi-Yerushalayim 449
Midrash Rabbah 653
Mikhlol ha-Maamarim veha-Pitgamim 145
Mikra 543
Mikra le-Yisrael 594
Mikra'ot Gedolot 599
Mikra'ot Gedolot ha-Keter 600
Milon 'Olami le-'Ivrit Meduberet 740
Milon / 'Ivri / Amerikani/ Angli / 'Ivri li-Shenot ha-Alpayim 746
Milon Angli-'Ivri Shalem 738
Milon Arami-'Ivri le-Talmud

Bavli 644
Milon Bet-ha-Sefer 745
Milon ha-Lashon ha-'Ivrit 741
Milon Hazuti 'Ivri-Angli 743
Milon he-Hadash 750
Milon Hidushe Shlonski 748
Milon Yidish-'Ivri Shalem 793
Mimekor Yisrael 832
Minor Midrashim 631
Miscellany of Literary Pieces 197
Mishnayot 654
Mishneh Torah 681
Mishpat ha-'Ivri 661
Modern English-Yiddish, Yiddish-English Dictionary 795
Modern Hebrew Literature 95
Modern Jewish Experience 96
Modern Jewish History 236
Modern Jewish Morality 822
Modern Jewish Thought 712
Moreh Derekh bi-Mekorot ha-Mishpat ha-'Ivri 656
Moshav: Bibliyografyah 467
Moshe Montefyori, 1784-1885 31
Multi-language Bibliography of Jewish Law 668
Munahe Rashi 645
Museums of Israel 490
Muze'onim be-Yisra'el 489
My Jewish Roots 838

Nahum, Habakkuk: A Classified Bibliography 557
Nashim be-Yisrael 450
National Registry of Jewish Holocaust Survivors 532
Nazism, Resistance and Holocaust 522
NER Catalog 85
New Bantam-Megiddo Hebrew and English Dictionary 753
New Brown -Driver Briggs -Gesenius Hebrew and English Lexicon 558
New Encyclopedia of Archaeological Excavations 614
New Jewish Encyclopedia

123
New Jewish Yellow Pages 277
New Maturity in Christian-Jewish Dialogue 865
New Standard Jewish Encyclopedia 119
1987-88 Jewish Almanac 260
Nive Talmud 660
Noms des Juifs de France au Moyen âge 853
Noms des Juifs du Maroc 852
Non-Print Catalog 100
Notrikon, ha-Simanim, veha-Kinuyim 756
Nova Bibliotheca Anglo-Judaica 396

Ohel Hayim 174
Old Testament Abstracts 584
Old Testament Library 595
Old Testament Pseudepigrapha 608
Old Testament: An Introduction 542
Once a Jew, Always a German 422
Oral Documents from Latin America 352
Oral History of Contemporary Jewry 244
Organizing a Jewish Women's Library 864
Oriental Manuscripts 164
Ortsnamen Israels nach der Rabbinischen 626
Otsar Beduye ha-Shem 755
Otsar ha-Agadah 658
Otsar ha-Beurim veha-Perushim 628
Otsar ha-Lashon ha-'Ivrit 749
Otsar ha-Lo'azim 640
Otsar ha-Mehabrim 209
Otsar ha-Mishpat 669
Otsar ha-Munahim ha-Pilosofyim 717
Otsar ha-Poskim 'al Shulhan Arukh Even ha-'Ezer 674
Otsar ha-Poskim: Mafteah ha-Sh"uT Hoshen Mishapat 675
Otsar ha-Rabanim 14
Otsar ha-Sefarim 206
Otsar ha-Sefarim Helek Sheni 210

Otsar ha-Shirah veha-Piyut 770
Otsar Imre Avot 143
Otsar Kitve 'Et Toraniyim 882
Otsar Kitve ha-Yad shel Yehude 173
Otsar Leshon ha-Mishnah 633
Otsar Leshon ha-Rambam 676
Otsar Leshon ha-Talmud 634
Otsar Leshon ha-Tanaim 636-38
Otsar Leshon ha-Tosefta 635
Otsar Leshon Talmud Yerushalmi 639
Otsar Leshon Targum Onkelos 566
Otsar Rashe Tevot 754
Our Time 865
Oytser fun der Yidisher Shprakh 792
Oznayim la-Torah 651

Palestine and Zionism 495
Periodical Publications from the Australian Jewish Community 362
Persecution and Resistance under the Nazis 524
Philo of Alexandria 40
Philosophies of Judaism 705
Pictorial History of the Holocaust 534
Pinkas ha-Kehilot 365
Pioneer Jews of the California Mother Lode 330
Pirsume Moshe Devis 39
Plays of Jewish Interest 736
Polish Jewish Historiography Between the Two Wars 412
Polish Jewish History 415
Political Dictionary of the State of Israel 491
Population of Palestine 481
Post War Publications on German Jewry 381
Practical Talmud Dictionary 641
Praza Zydowska w Warszaie 879
Preliminary Inventory of the Jewish Daily and Periodical Press 880

Principles of Jewish Law 663
Printed Jewish Canadiana 266
Printing the Talmud 178
Przewodnik Po Bibliografiach Polskich Judaikow 424
Pseudepigrapha and Modern Research 605
Pseudonymen-Lexicon der Hebräischen und Jiddischen 755
Psychological and Medical Effects of Concentration Camps 514
Published Material from the Cambridge Genizah 196

Rabbinic Sources 630
RAMBI 141
Rashe Tevot ve-Kitsurim 733
Reader's Adviser 53
Recent Scholarship on Maimonides 709
Recueil des Glosses 640
Reference Guide 657
Reform Judaism in America 335
Religion and Society in North America 342
Reshimah Bibliyografit shel ha-Pirsumim be-'Ivrit 888
Reshimat ha-Yomanim ve-Kitve ha-'Et be-Yidish 887
Reshimat Kitve Yad be'Aravit-Yehudit 201
Reshimat Maamarim be-Mada'e ha-Yahadut 141
Reshimat Sifre Ladino 779
Resource Book of Jewish Music 870
Resources for Latin American Jewish Studies 353
Rishonim: Biographical Sketches 17
Russian Jewish History 423
Russian Records Index and Catalog 842

Saga des Familles 855
Sare ha-Elef 629
Saving the Jewish Family 823
Schocken Guide to Jewish

Books 55
Seasons of Our Lives 876
Second Jewish Book of Why 702
Second Jewish Catalog 112
Sefarim 'Ivriyim 'Atikim 191
Sefarim ha-Hitsonim 609
Sefer ha-Admorim 731
Sefer ha-Agadah 831
Sefer ha-Hatumim 180
Sefer ha-Prenumerantn 179
Sefer ha-Shanah li-Kehilot ve-Irgunim Yehudiyim 78
Sefer Otsar ha-Gedolim 16
Sefer Targum ha-La'az 642
Selected Bibliography of Jewish Canadiana 268
Selected Bibliography of the Jews in the Hellenistic-Roman 466
Selected Books on Israel 456
Selected Children's Judaica Collection 71
Selected Hebrew Literature in Translation 766
Sephardic Studies: A Research Bibliography 777
Sex and the Modern Jewish Woman 858
Sha'ul Tshernihovski: Bibliyografyah 30
Shenaton ha-Memshalah 497
Sho'ah u-Sefiheha ba-Aspaklaryat Kitve 'Et 'Ivriyim 525
Shtetl Finder 429
Sifre ha-Defus ha-Rishonim 186
Sifrut Yiddish: Perakim le-Toldoteha 802
Sign and a Witness 192
Simplified Guide to BHS 589
Sino-Judaic Bibliographies 359
Sino-Judaic Studies 358
Siporet be-Yidish 806
Social and Religious History of the Jews 232
Social Research on Arabs in Israel 470-71
Social Research on Jewish Ethnicity in Israel 472
Sociology of American Jewry 300
Sociology of the American

Jewish Community 308
Software Bible 73
Soncino Books of the Bible 601
Source Book on Soviet Jewry 427
Soviet Jewish History 420
Soviet Publications on Judaism ... Israel 419
Spanish and Portuguese Jewry 434
Springwells Jewish Computing Catalog 74
State of Jewish Studies 97
Statistical Abstract of Israel 498
Study and Practice of Judaism 689
Study of Ancient Judaism 623
Study of Judaism 59
Survey of Jewish Affairs 79
Syllabus and Bibliography 47
Syriac and Aramaic 774

Taking Root 274
Talmud Scholar with Dictionary 687
Tanakh 590
Targumic Manuscripts 199
Tentative Bibliography of Geniza Documents 203
Tentative Catalogue of Manuscripts of the Rashi 632
Third Jewish Catalog 113
Timetables of Jewish History 242
To Count A People 319
Toldot ha-Tsiyonut 500
Toldot Tana'im ve-Amoraim 15
Torah ha-Ketuvah veha-Mesurah 652
Torah Scholar 619
Torah: A Modern Commentary 602
Torah Shelemah 598
Torah Temimah 650
Torah: A Modern Commentary 602
Traveler's Guide to Jewish Landmarks 152
Traveling Jewish in America 163
Treasury of Jewish Quotations 146

Twentieth-Century American-Jewish Fiction Writers 350
201 Yiddish Verbs 797
Types and Motifs of the Judeo-Spanish Folktales 828

Unbroken Chain 845
Union Catalog of Hebrew Manuscripts 168
Uri Tsevi Grinberg 25

Video Catalog 102
Visual Testimony 193
Vocalized Talmudic Manuscripts 200

Webster's New World Hebrew Dictionary 739
Western Jewish History Center: Guide 292
What You ... Knew About Judaism 692
Where Once We Walked 507
Who's Who in American Jewry 338-39
Who's Who in Israel and Jewish Personalities 499
Who's Who in Jewish History 1
Who's Who in the Old Testament 8
Who's Who in World Jewry 6
Whole Sephardic Catalog 86
Wisdom of the Zohar 722
With Eyes Toward Zion 439
Women's Studies 860
Word Weavers 66
World in Turmoil 241
World Jewish Directory 77
World of the Talmud 627
World Register of University Studies 80

Yad Eliyahu 725
Yad Moshe 671
Yadahut Tsefon Afrikah 247
Yahadut Amerikah 310
Yahadut Berit ha-Mo'atsot 425
Yahadut ha-Datit ba-Sho'ah 505
Yahadut Teman 254
Yahadut Yavan 390

Yaruts Devaro 678
Yehude Asyah ve-Afrikah 251
Yehude Etyopiyah 252
Yehude ha-Mizrah u-Tsefon Afrikah 248-49
Yehude Mizrah Merkaz Eyropah 421
Yerushalayim be-Rei ha-Dorot 445
Yerushalayim le-Doroteha 477
Yiddish Catalog and Authority File 225
Yiddish Culture in Britain 399
Yiddish Dictionary Source-Book 789
Yiddish Language and Folklore 829
Yiddish Linguistics 788
Yiddish Literary and Linguistic Periodicals 883
Yiddish Literary Studies 805
Yiddish Literature 801
Yiddish Literature in English Translation 803-04
Yiddish Studies Pathfinder 787
Yiddishe Prese ... Gevezener Rushisher 881
Yidish Tsvey 798
Yidish-English-Hebreisher Verterbukh 791
Yidishe Shtet, Shtetlekh 430
Yishuve ha-Yehudim be-Bavel bi-Tekufat ha-Talmud 624

Zar Lo Yavin 451
Zionism: A Bibliography 501
Zionist Yearbook 401